The
Pocket
Players'
Guide

for *Magic: The Gathering —*
Fourth Edition™

with contributions by
Rich Redman,
Eric Doohan,
Richard Garfield,
John Tynes,
Beth Moursund,
Tom Wylie,
Paul Peterson,
Mark Rosewater,
Dave Pettey,
Jim Lin,
Charlie Catino,
Joel Mick,
Steve Conard,
Allen Varney,

D1153733

Dedication

We are grateful to the people in cyberspace who asked the questions, thus revealing what needed to be changed. We'd also like to thank our distributors, our retailers, our customers, and the players of **Magic**, who continue to amaze us with their enthusiasm and support. Thank you all for sharing this adventure with us.

Credits

Art Direction
Christopher Rush

Design and Typesetting
Jonathan Hart Eddy

Additional Production
Betsy Bell

Cover Art
Quinton Hoover

Editing
Michael G. Ryan

Additional Editing
Kathryn Haines, Darla Willis, Paul Hughes

Proofing
Britt L. Miller and Michael G. Ryan

Indexing
Steve Heller

Contributors
Rich Redman, Eric Doohan,
Richard Garfield, John Tynes, Beth Moursund,
Tom Wylie, Paul Peterson, Mark Rosewater,
Dave Pettey, Jim Lin, Charlie Catino,
Joel Mick, Steve Conard, Allen Varney,
The Duelists' Convocation,
T. Brian Wagner, Victor K. Wertz,
Tom Des Brisay, Mark Sundlie

PPG Design Team
Eric M. Doohan, Kathryn Haines,
Rhias K. Hall, Dave Howell, Beth Moursund,
Rich Redman, Christopher Rush,
Michael G. Ryan, Beverly Marshall Saling

Illustrations

Table of Contents

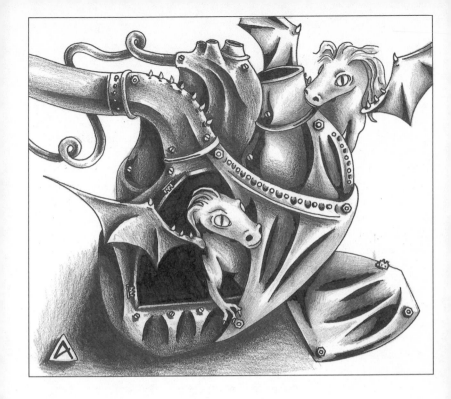

introduction

Rich Redman and Eric Doohan

Welcome to *The Pocket Players' Guide* for **Magic: The Gathering**—*Fourth Edition.*™

In **Magic**, you represent a powerful wizard battling for control of a plane of Dominia. The object of the game is to drive your opponent from the plane, leaving you with sole control. By pitting your deck against your opponent's deck in an arcane duel, you determine who remains in Dominia, and the winner is awarded one random card from the loser's deck. The cards in your deck represent the lands, creatures, spells, and artifacts at your disposal; over time, your deck will develop strengths and weaknesses as it grows and shrinks with each new duel. Meanwhile, you will frequently encounter new mysteries as the multiverse of Dominia grows.

This book serves as your guide to the game itself, as well as serving as an introduction to **Magic**'s intriguing world.

The mission of nearly every **Magic** player, since first acquiring a starter deck, has been to defeat each and every opponent ever encountered. As of the printing of this book, there are over 1,100 **Magic** cards in existence, some still in print and some now out of print—a challenge for collectors and a source of intrigue and mystery for players. Given the odds against the likes of Shivan Dragons and Nightmares emerging from any individual player's deck, many battles have been won without this kind of power. Overcoming these same odds, however, many duels have been lost while such power was in play. Although many players feel that killer combos and a suitcase full of cards are the only tools available to use in becoming the mightiest wizard in Dominia, there is one tool which is far more accessible to every player and which is just as deadly…. Knowledge.

Within this mighty tome, we have collected valuable information that could take you to the next level of play. *The Pocket Players' Guide* was designed to be a companion for the Player—whether you've just picked up your first starter deck or you've joined the ranks of the infamous "Mr. Suitcase," you'll find something here to help you achieve your goal of becoming a better duelist. Inside, you'll find topics ranging from how to build a better deck to what you can do when you feel you've mastered the game and want to find the next challenge.

Additionally, you'll find a complete and expanded rules section placed for easy access early in the rulebook. And for improved convenience, we have also provided a Glossary of Game Terms with a colored page border immediately following the rules section.

We hope that you will find *The Pocket Players' Guide* both useful and intuitive, and we hope that it will prove a worthy companion on the battlefields of Dominia!

notes from the designer
Richard Garfield

The Ancestry of Magic

Games evolve. New ones take the most beloved features of earlier games and add original characteristics. The creation of **Magic: The Gathering** is a case in point.

Though there are about a dozen games that have directly influenced **Magic** in one way or another, the game's most influential ancestor is a game for which I have no end of respect: *Cosmic Encounter,* originally published by Eon Products and rereleased by Mayfair Games. In this game, participants play alien races striving to conquer a piece of the universe. Players can attempt their conquest alone or can forge alliances with other aliens. There are nearly 50 alien races which can be played, each of which has a unique ability: the Amoeba, for example, has the power to Ooze, giving it unlimited token movement; the Sniveler has the power to Whine, allowing it to automatically catch up when behind. The best thing about *Cosmic Encounter* is precisely this limitless variety. I have played hundreds of times and still can be surprised by the interactions different combinations of aliens produce. *Cosmic Encounter* remains enjoyable because it is constantly new.

Cosmic Encounter proved to be an interesting complement to my own design ideas. I had been mulling over a longtime idea of mine: a game which used a deck of cards, the composition of which changed between rounds. During the course of the game, the players would add cards to and remove cards from the deck, so that each new game would have an entirely different card mix. I remembered playing marbles in elementary school, where each player had his or her own collection from which to trade and compete. I was also curious about *Strat-o-matic Baseball*™, in which participants draft, field, and compete with their own teams of baseball players, whose abilities are based on real players' previous year's statistics. Intrigued by the structure of the game, I was irritated that the subject was one for which I had no patience.

These thoughts were the essence of what eventually became **Magic**. My experiences with *Cosmic Encounter* and other games inspired me to create a card game in 1982 called *Five Magics*. *Five Magics* was an attempt to distill the modularity of *Cosmic Encounter* down to just a card game. The nature of *Cosmic Encounter* seemed entirely appropriate for a magical card game—wild and not entirely predictable, but not completely unknown, like a set of forces you almost, but don't quite, understand. Over the next few years, *Five Magics* went on to inspire entirely new magical card games among my friends.

Ten years later, I was still designing games, and Mike Davis and I had come up with a board game called *RoboRally*. Mike was acting as our agent, and among the companies he approached was a brand-new gaming company called Wizards of the Coast. Things seemed to be going well; so that August, Mike and I made our way to Portland, Oregon, to meet over a pizza with Peter Adkison and James Hays of Wizards of the Coast.

Both Peter and James were very receptive to *RoboRally*, but they informed me that they weren't really in a position to come out with a board game right away. This wasn't what I had come out to hear, of course, but I didn't want the trip to be a total waste. I asked Peter what he *would* be interested in. Peter replied that he really saw a need for a game that could be played quickly with minimal equipment, a game that would go over well at conventions. Could I do it?

Within a few days, the initial concept for a trading card game was born, based on another card game I had developed in 1985 called *Safecracker*. It hadn't been one of my best games—but then I remembered *Five Magics*.

The First Designs

I went back to graduate school at the University of Pennsylvania and worked on the card game in whatever spare time I had. It wasn't easy: there were three months of false starts on the project. There are so many aspects of card game design that have to be reconsidered when designing trading card games. First of all, you can't have any bad cards—people won't play with them. In fact, you want to prevent too much range in the utility of cards because players will only play with the best—why make cards people won't play with? Besides, homogeneity of card power is the only way to combat the "rich-kid syndrome" that threatened the game concept from the start. What was to keep someone from going out, getting ten decks, and becoming unbeatable?

This was a major design concern. I had numerous theories as to how to prevent purchasing power from unbalancing the game, none of which were entirely valid but all of which had a grain of truth. The most compelling counter to this "buy-out-the-store" strategy was the ante. If we were playing for ante (the argument ran) and your deck was the distilled fruit of ten decks, then when I did win, I would win a more valuable card. Also, if the game required enough skill, then the players purchasing their power would surely be easy prey for the players dueling and trading their way to good decks. And, of course, there was the sentiment that buying a lot of poker chips doesn't make you a winner. In the end, however, the "rich-kid syndrome" became less of a concern—**Magic** is a fun game, and it doesn't really matter how you get your deck. Playtesting showed that a deck that is too powerful defeats itself. On the one hand, people stopped playing against it for ante unless a handicap was invoked; on the other, it inspired competitors to assemble more effective decks in response.

The first **Magic** release was affectionately named Alpha. It consisted of 120 cards split randomly between two players. The two players would ante a card, fight a duel over the ante, and repeat until they got bored. They often took a long time to get bored; even then, **Magic** was a surprisingly addictive game. About ten o'clock one evening, Barry "Bit" Reich and I started a game in the University of Pennsylvania Astronomy lounge, a windowless, air-conditioned room. We played continuously until about three a.m.—at least that's what we thought until we left the building and found that the sun had risen.

I knew then that I had a game structure that could support the concept of individually owned and tailored decks. The game was quick, and while it had bluffing and strategy, it didn't seem to get bogged down with too much calculation. The various combinations that came up were enjoyable and often surprising. At the same time, the variety of card combinations didn't unbalance the game: when a person began to win, the victory didn't turn into a landslide.

From Alpha to Gamma

Except for the card mix, little has changed about **Magic** since Alpha. In Alpha, walls could attack and losing all your lands of a particular color destroyed the associated spells in play, but otherwise the rules are much the same now as they were in the early stages of playtesting.

Moving from Alpha to the Beta version was like releasing a wild animal. The enjoyable game that was Alpha now burst the confines of the duel to invade the lives of the participants. Players were free to trade cards between games and to hunt down weaker players and challenge them to duels, all the while gamely facing or cravenly avoiding those who were more powerful. Reputations were forged—reputations built on anything from consistently strong play to a few lucky wins to good bluffing. The players didn't know the card mix, so they learned to stay on their toes during duels. Even the most alert players would occasionally meet with nasty surprises. This constant discovery of unknown realms in an uncharted world gave the game a feeling of infinite size and possibility.

For the Gamma version, new cards were added and many of the creature costs were increased. We also doubled the pool of playtesters, adding in a group with *Strat-o-matic Baseball* experience. We were particularly anxious to find out if **Magic** could be adapted to league play. Gamma was also the first version which was fully illustrated. Skaff Elias was my art director; he and others spent days poring over old graphic magazines, comic books, and game books, searching for art for the cards. These playtest decks were fairly attractive for crummy black-and-white cardstock photocopies. For the most part, the cards were illustrated with serious pictures, but there were a lot of humorous ones as well. Heal was illustrated by Skaff's foot. Power Sink showed Calvin (of *Calvin and Hobbes*) in a toilet; after all, what is a toilet but a power sink? Berserk was John Travolta dancing in *Saturday Night Fever*. Righteousness pictured Captain Kirk, and Blessing showed Spock doing his "live long and prosper" gesture. An old comic book provided a Charles Atlas picture for Holy Strength, and a ninety-eight-pound weakling getting sand kicked in his face for Weakness. Instill Energy was Richard Simmons. The infamous Glasses of Urza were some X-ray glasses we found in a catalog. Ruthy Kantorovitz constructed a darling flame-belching baby for Firebreathing. I myself had the honor of being the Goblins. The pictures and additional players greatly added to the game atmosphere. It became clear that while the duels were for two players, the more players playing, the better the game was. In some sense, the individual duels were a part of a single, larger game.

Striking the Balance

Each playtest set saw the expulsion of certain cards. One type of card was common in Alpha and Beta, rare in Gamma, and is now nonexistent: the type that made one of your rival's cards yours. Yes, Control Magic used to permanently steal a creature from your opponent. Similarly, Steal Artifact really *took* an artifact. Copper Tablet no longer even remotely resembles its original purpose, which was to swap two creatures in play. ("Yes, I'll swap my Merfolk for your Dragon. On second thought, make that my Goblins—they're uglier.") There was a spell, Planeshift, which stole a land, and another, Ecoshift, which collected all the lands, shuffled them, and redealt them—really nice for the user of four or five colors of magic. Pixies used to be a real pain—if they hit you, you swapped a random card from your hand with your opponent. These cards added something to the game, often in the form of players trying to destroy their own creatures before their opponents took them for good or even trying to take their own lives to preserve the last shreds of their decks. In the end, however, it was pretty clear that the nastiness this added to the game environment wasn't worth the trouble, and no card should ever be at risk unless players choose to play for ante.

It was around this time that I began to realize that almost any decision made about the game would be opposed, often vehemently, by some players. The huge amount of dissent about what should and what should not be part of the card mix led players to make their own versions for playtesting—a significant task that involved designing, constructing, shuffling, and distributing about 4,000 cards. Each of these games had its merits, and the playtesters enjoyed discovering the quirks and secrets of each new environment. The results of these efforts will form the basis for future **Deckmaster** games that use the structure of **Magic: The Gathering** while containing mostly new cards.

To Build a Better Deck

Playtesting a **Deckmaster** game is difficult. Probably the only games harder to playtest are elaborate, multiplayer computer games. After developing a basic framework for **Magic** that seemed fairly robust, we had to decide which of the huge selection of cards to include and with what relative frequencies. Common cards had to be simpler, but not necessarily less powerful, than rare cards—if only rare cards were powerful, players would either have to be rich or lucky to construct a decent deck. Sometimes a card was made rare because it was too powerful or imbalancing in large quantities, but, more often, rare cards were cards that were intricate or specialized—spells you wouldn't want many of anyway. But these design guidelines only got us so far. The whole game's flavor could change if a handful of seemingly innocent cards were eliminated or even made less or more common. When it came down to actually deciding what to include and what to do without, I began to feel like a chef obliged to cook a dish for 10,000 people while using 300 ingredients.

One thing I knew I wanted to see in the game was players using multicolor decks. It was clear that a player could avoid a lot of problems by stripping down to a single color. For this reason, many spells were included that paralyzed entire colors, such as Karma, Elemental Blast, and the Circles of Protection. The original plan was to include cards that thwarted every obvious simple strategy and, in time, to add new cards which would defeat the most current ploys and keep the strategic environment dynamic. For example, it was obvious that relying on too many big creatures made a player particularly vulnerable to the Meekstone, and a deck laden with Fireballs and requiring lots of mana could be brought down with Manabarbs. Unfortunately, this strategy and counterstrategy design led to players developing narrow decks and refusing to play people who used cards that could defeat them flat out. If players weren't compelled to play a variety of players and could choose their opponent every time, a narrow deck was pretty powerful.

Therefore, another, less heavy-handed way to encourage variety was developed. We made it more difficult to get all the features a player needs in a deck when playing a single color. Gamma, for example, suffered from the fact that blue magic could stand alone. It was easily the most powerful magic, having two extremely insidious common spells (Ancestral Recall and Time Walk), both of which were made rare but are now out of print. It had awesome counterspell capabilities. And it had amazing creatures, two of the best of which are now uncommon.

Blue magic now retains its counterspell capability but is very creature poor and lacks a good way to deal direct damage. Red magic has little defense, particularly in the air, but has amazing direct-damage and destruction capabilities. Green magic has an abundance of creatures and mana but not much more. Black is the master of anticreature magic and has some flexibility but is poorly suited to stopping noncreature threats. White magic is the magic of protection and the only magic with common banding, but it has little damage-dealing capability.

Sometimes seemingly innocuous cards would combine into something truly frightening. A good part of playtest effort was devoted to routing out the

cards that contributed to so-called "degenerate" decks—those narrow, powerful decks that are difficult to beat and often boring to play with or against. Without a doubt, the most striking was Tom Fontaine's "Deck of Sooner-Than-Instant Death," which was renowned for being able to field upwards of eight large creatures on the second or third turn. In the first **Magic** tournament, Dave "Hurricane" Pettey walked to victory with his "Land-Destruction Deck." (Dave also designed a deck of Hypnotic Specters, Mind Twists, and Disrupting Scepters that was so gruesome I don't think anyone was ever really willing to play it.) Skaff's deck, "The Great White Death," could outlive just about anything put up against it. Charlie Catino's "Weenie Madness" was fairly effective at swamping the opponent with little creatures. Though this deck was probably not in the high-win bracket of the previous decks, it was recognized that, playing for ante, Charlie could hardly lose. Even winning only one in four of his games—and he could usually do better than that—the card he won could be traded back for the island and the two Merfolk he lost, with something extra thrown in.

In the end, I decided that the degenerate decks were actually part of the fun. People would assemble them, play with them until they got bored or their regular opponents refused to play against them, and then retire the deck or trade off its components for something new—a **Magic** version of putting the champion out to stud. Most players ended up treating their degenerate decks much like roleplayers treat their most successful characters: they were relegated to the background to be occasionally dusted off for a new encounter.

After the pursuit of sheer power died down, another type of deck developed: the Weird Theme deck. These decks were usually made to be as formidable as possible within the constraints of their themes. When Bit grew bored of his "Serpent Deck" (he had a predilection for flopping a rubber snake on the playing surface and going "SsssSssSs" whenever he summoned a serpent), he developed his "Artifact Deck," which consisted of artifacts only—no land. It was fun to see the "Artifact Deck" go up against someone who used Nevinyrral's Disk. But the king of weird decks was, without a doubt, Charlie Catino's. In one league, Charlie put together a deck that I call "The Infinite Recursion Deck." The idea was to set up a situation where his opponent couldn't attack him until Charlie could play Swords to Plowshares on a creature. Then he would play Timetwister, causing the cards in play to be shuffled with the graveyard, hand, and library to form a fresh library (Timetwister is now out of print). Swords to Plowshares actually *removes* a creature from the game, so his rival had one less creature. Repeat. After enough iterations, Charlie's rival was bloated with life given by the Swords to Plowshares, having maybe 60 life points, but there were no creatures left in his deck. So Charlie's Elves started in—59 life, 58 life, 57 life—and the curtain closes on this sad game. I still can't think about this deck without moist emotional snorts. The *coup de grace* is that this league required players to compete their decks ten times. And, since his games often lasted over an hour and a half, Charlie received at least one concession.

Words, Words, Words

It was not just determining the right card mix that players and designers found challenging; this has become increasingly clear to me as I participate in the never-ending process of editing the rules and the cards. As my earliest playtesters have pointed out (in their more malicious moods), the original concept for **Magic** was the simplest game in the world because you had all the rules on the cards. That notion is long gone.

To those who didn't have to endure it, our struggle for precision was actually rather amusing. My own rules discussions about card wordings were mostly with Jim Lin, who is the closest thing you will ever encounter to a combination rules lawyer and firehose. A typical rule-problem session would go:

Jim: Hmm—there seems to be a problem with this card. Here is my seven-page rules addition to solve the problem.

Richard: I would sooner recall all the cards than use that. Let's try this solution instead.

Jim: Hmm—we have another problem.

[Repeat until . . .]

Richard: This is silly—only incredibly stupid and terminally anal people could *possibly* misinterpret this card.

Jim: Yes, maybe we *have* been thinking about this too long. If you're playing with that kind of person, you should find some new friends.

A specific example of something we actually worried about is whether Consecrate Land would really protect your land from Stone Rain. After all, the first, which is no longer in print, says "All enchantments on target land are destroyed. Land cannot be destroyed or further enchanted until Consecrate Land has been destroyed." The second says it destroys the land. Isn't that a contradiction? It still hurts my head getting into a frame of mind where that is confusing. It is perhaps a little like wondering why anyone would give you anything for money, which is, after all, just paper.

But, then again, I could never tell what was going to confuse people. One of the playtesters, Mikhail Chkhenkeli, approached me and said, "I like my deck. I have the most powerful card in the game. When I play it, I win on the next turn." I tried to figure out what this could be; I couldn't think of anything that would win the game with any assurance the turn after casting. I asked him about it and he showed me a card that would make his opponent skip a turn.

I was confused until I read exactly what was written: "Opponent loses next turn." It was my first real lesson in how difficult it was going to be to word the cards so that no two people would interpret the same card in a different way.

The Magic Marketplace

Another thing I realized in the second year of playtesting really surprised me: **Magic** turned out to be one of the best economic simulations I had ever seen. We had a free-market economy and all of the ingredients for interesting dynamics. People valued different cards in different ways—sometimes because players simply weren't evaluating accurately but much more often because the cards really had different value to different players. For example, the value of a powerful green spell was lower for a person who specialized in black and red magic than for one who was building a deck that was primarily green. This gives a lot of opportunity for arbitrage. I would frequently find cards that one group of players weren't using but that another group were treating like chunks of gold. If I was fast enough, I could altruistically benefit both parties and only have to suffer a little profit in the process.

Sometimes the value of a card would fluctuate based on a new use (or even a suspected new use). For example, when Charlie was collecting all the available spells that produced black mana, we began to get concerned—those cards were demanding higher and higher prices, and people began to fear what he could need all that black mana for. And, prior to Dave's "Land-Destruction Deck," land destruction spells like Stone Rain and Ice Storm (now out of print but reading, "Destroys any one land") were not high-demand spells. This, of course, allowed him to assemble the deck cheaply, and, after winning the first **Magic** tournament, to sell off the pieces for a mint.

Trade embargoes appeared. At one point, a powerful faction of players would not trade with Skaff or anyone who traded with Skaff. I actually heard conversations such as:

Player 1 to Player 2:	I'll trade you card A for card B.
Skaff, watching:	That's a moronic trade. I'll give you card B and cards C, D, E, and F for card A.
Players 1 and 2 together:	We are *not* trading with *you*, Skaff.

Needless to say, Skaff was perhaps a bit *too* successful in his early duels and trades.

Another interesting economic event would occur when people would snatch up cards they had no intention of using. They would take them to remove them from the card pool, either because the card annoyed them (Chaos Orb, now out of print, for example) or because it was too deadly against their particular decks. Consider the wording of the Chaos Orb: " 1 : Flip Chaos Orb onto the playing area from a height of at least one foot. Chaos Orb must turn completely over at least once or it is discarded with no effect. When Chaos Orb lands, any cards in play that it touches are destroyed, as is Chaos Orb." This required opponents to spread their cards in play as far apart as possible, and that was just *too* annoying.

I think my favorite profit was turned during an encounter with Ethan Lewis and Bit. Ethan had just received a pack of cards, and Bit was interested in trading with Ethan. Bit noticed that Ethan had the Jayemdae Tome, began to drool, and made an offer for it. I looked at the offer and thought it was far too low, so I put the same thing on the table.

Bit looked at me and said, "You can't offer that! If you want the Tome you have to bid higher than my bid."

I said, "This isn't an offer for the Tome. This is a gift for Ethan deigning to even discuss trading the Tome with me."

Bit looked at me in disbelief and then took me aside. He whispered, "Look, I'll give you this wad of cards if you just leave the room for ten minutes." I took his bribe, and he bought the Tome. It was just as well—he had a lot more buying power than I did. In retrospect, it was probably a dangerous ploy to use against Bit—after all, he was the person who was responsible for once gluing poor Charlie's deck together, for washing a different deck of Charlie's in soap and water, and for putting yet more of Charlie's cards in the blender and hitting frappé.

Probably the most constant card-evaluation difference of opinion I had with anyone was over Lord of the Pit. I received it in just about every playtest release we had, and it was certainly hard to use. I didn't agree with Skaff, though, that the only value of the card was that you might get your opponent to play with it. He maintained that *blank* cards would be better to play with because blank cards probably wouldn't hurt you. I argued that if you knew what you were doing, you could profit from it.

Skaff asked me to cite a single case where it had saved me. I thought a bit and recalled the most flamboyant victory I had ever experienced using the Lord of the Pit. My opponent knew he had me where he wanted me—he had something doing damage to me and a Clone in hand, so even if I cast something to turn the tide, he would be able to match me. Clone, now out of print, reads "Upon summoning, Clone acquires all characteristics, including color, of any one creature in play on either side; any creature enchantments on original creature are not copied. Clone retains these characteristics even after original creature is destroyed. Clone cannot be summoned if there are no creatures in play." Well, of course, the next cast spell was my Lord of the Pit; he could Clone it or die from it, so he Cloned it. Then each time he attacked, I would heal both of the Lords, or cast Fog and nullify the assault, and refuse to attack. Eventually, he ran out of creatures to keep his Lord of the Pit sated and died a horrible death.

Skaff was highly amused by this story. He said, "So, when asked about a time the Lord of the Pit saved you, you can only think of a case where you were playing somebody stupid enough to Clone it!"

Dominia and the Role of Roleplaying

Selecting a card mix that accommodated different evaluations of the cards wasn't enough; we also had to develop an environment in which the cards could reasonably interact. Establishing the right setting for **Magic** proved to be a central design challenge. In fact, many of our design problems stemmed from an attempt to define the physics of a magical world in which duels take place and from building the cards around that definition, rather than letting the game itself define the physics. I was worried about the cards' relationship to one another—I wanted them to seem part of a unified setting, but I didn't want to restrict the creativity of the designers or to create all of the cards myself. Everyone trying to jointly build a single fantasy world seemed difficult, because it would inevitably lack cohesion. I preferred the idea of a multiverse, a system of worlds that was incredibly large and that permitted strange interactions between the universes in it. In this way, we could capture the otherworldly aspects of fantasy that add such flavor to the game while we preserved a coherent, playable game structure. Almost any card or concept would fit into a multiverse. It would also not be difficult to accommodate an ever-growing and diverse card pool—expansion sets with very different flavors could be used in the same game, for they could be seen as a creative mingling of elements from different universes. So I developed the idea of Dominia, an infinite system of planes through which wizards travel in search of resources to fuel their magic.

In its structured flexibility, this game environment is much like a roleplaying world. I don't mean to suggest that this setting makes **Magic** a roleplaying game—far from it—but **Magic** is closer to roleplaying than any other card or board game I know of. I have always been singularly unimpressed by games that presumed to call themselves a cross between the two because roleplaying has too many characteristics that can't be captured in a different format. In fact, in its restricted forms—as a tournament game or league game, for example—**Magic** has little in common with roleplaying. In those cases, it is a game in the traditional sense, with each player striving to achieve victory according to some finite set of rules. The more free-form game, however—dueling with friends using decks constructed at whim—embodies some interesting elements of roleplaying.

Each player's deck is like a character. It has its own personality and quirks. These decks often even get their own names: "The Bruise," "The Reanimator," "Weenie Madness," "Sooner-Than-Instant Death," "Walk Into This Deck," "The Great White Leftovers," "Backyard Barbeque," and "Gilligan's Island," to name a few. In one deck I maintained, each of the creatures had a name—one small advantage to crummy photocopied cardstock is the ease of writing on cards. The deck was called "Snow White and the Seven Dwarfs," containing a Wurm named Snow White and seven Mammoths: Doc, Grumpy, Sneezy, Dopey, Happy, Bashful, and Sleepy. After a while, I got a few additional Mammoths, which I named Cheesy and Hungry. There was even a Prince Charming: my Veteran Bodyguard. (The trusty Veteran Bodyguard is out of print, but it reads "Unless Bodyguard is tapped, any damage done to you by unblocked creatures is done instead to Bodyguard. You may not take this damage yourself, though you can prevent it if possible. No more than one Bodyguard of your choice can take damage for you in this manner each turn.")

As in roleplaying, the object of the game in the unstructured mode of play is determined largely by the players. The object of the duel is usually to win, but the means to that end can vary tremendously. Most players find that the duel itself quickly becomes a fairly minor part of the game compared to trading and assembling decks.

Another characteristic of **Magic** which is reminiscent of roleplaying is the way players are *exploring* a world rather than knowing all its details from the start. I view **Magic** as a vast game played among all the people who buy decks rather than as just a series of little duels. It is a game for tens of thousands in which the designer acts as a gamemaster. The gamemaster decides what the environment will be, and the players explore that environment. This is why there were no marketed lists of cards when the cards were first sold: discovering the cards and what they do is an integral part of the game. Now there are so many cards, and so many cards that are no longer in print, that although Wizards of the Coast supplies card lists, no one can remember them all.

And as in a roleplaying game, the players contribute as much to an exciting adventure as the gamemaster. To all the supporters of **Magic**, and especially to my playtesters, I am extraordinarily grateful. Without them, this product would certainly be inferior, if it existed at all. Every one of them left a mark, if not on the game itself, then in the game's lore. Any players today who have even a tenth of the fun I had playing the test versions with those people will be amply pleased with **Magic**.

ɲature of Dominia

John Tynes

Dominia is a multiverse of constant change and unorthodox challenges. Worlds spin, planes shift, and realities collide more often than you or I blink. In an infinite multiverse of unguessable possibilities and unending change, what is the most precious commodity to those who understand the nature of Dominia?

Stability.

Dominia has gods, though it was not created by gods. These gods roam from world to world, plane to plane, reaping the powers of each in the form of mana—magical energy. They know one another by the common name of planeswalkers. They are neither omnipotent nor omniscient, but they are worlds beyond the vast majority of Dominia's inhabitants in both power and intellect. Planeswalkers alone know what mana is and which forms it takes.

Of course, there are many wizards in Dominia who are not planeswalkers and who therefore know nothing of the five forms of mana. Nor do they know the secrets of planar travel or the secrets of summoning creatures to one's side in battle—these secrets, like all the spells seen in the game, are the exclusive provenance of the planeswalkers. Yet even these mighty beings, who can call to their service creatures from across space and time, fear change... and seek stability.

Planeswalkers cannot travel with complete freedom—like all of nature, they are subject to the shifting planes. A sudden (albeit natural) wrench in the fabric of one plane's reality can leave a planeswalker cut off from the routes of travel he or she knows best. To a planeswalker, the multiverse is a labyrinth of roads, gates, and mystical passages that is, at best, only partially understood. Most planeswalkers can navigate fairly well so long as they remain on planes well known to them. But if they should find themselves on an uncharted plane, they must find a new way, a new passage, back to the planes with which they are familiar. Some planes, however, move so fast and so far that it could be years before a passage is again discovered. Planeswalkers do not routinely fear death, but they *do* fear loss of freedom and mobility. Many planeswalkers have been lost on strange planes so long that by the time they are finally able to return, they were not only long-forgotten, but their knowledge of the paths between planes and of the power sources they used to tap was hopelessly out of date.

To counter this fear, planeswalkers seek stability. They seek planes that have reliable, well-worn passages among them. They also seek diversity in both magical energy and natural life: energy to power their magics and life to bend to their will. All of these things have been found surrounding and enveloping a world known to the planeswalkers as Dominaria (DAH-min-ARR-ee-uh)— "the song of Dominia." It is on Dominaria and the planes it routinely touches that many planeswalkers have come to reside.

Dominaria is a massive world, supporting a staggering variety of beings and cultures. The surface of Dominaria is divided into dozens of small continents, each of which developed more or less independently until extended ocean travel and trade became common. The result of this prolonged isolation was and is a nexus of small civilizations with very different beliefs, customs, and life forms.

But the influence of Dominaria extends beyond the surface of the world. For reasons even the planeswalkers do not comprehend, Dominaria has become the focal point for a variety of other planes that maintain either constant or frequent connections to it. These other planes are other *universes,* which touch Dominaria in various locations and by varied means. Some planes are always "in phase" with Dominaria, and many inhabitants don't even realize that they have passed from one plane to another—the journey is both routine and seamless. Other planes come and go, sometimes touching at the same point, sometimes not. Many of these plane-gates are understood by those who live in the area, and the times at which the planes touch are celebrated with festivals and excitement. Still other planes are drawn to Dominaria's stable presence, caress it briefly, and move on.

The stability of Dominaria and its sister planes has drawn many planeswalkers there. Dominaria is vast, and its sources of mana are large and easily tapped. The exceptional diversity of creatures present means that the planeswalkers have many, many beings to call upon in their great magical duels. Furthermore, the ease with which planeswalkers can slip between Dominaria and any of its sister planes is very attractive to them. Given that the loser of a magical duel must leave the current plane, the variety and stability of these intersecting planes is even more attractive. On other worlds, having to flee to the nearest plane means not always knowing where one will end up. In the realms of Dominaria, however, the degree of safety in interplanar travel is a known quantity and a comforting one.

Imagine a large globe, hanging in space, covered in gossamer webs. As it spins, single strands of fine silk unspool and extend forth from the globe like slender arms. Another, smaller globe is drawn to the larger one, and as it grows near it is caressed by a single thread. This thread melds with the smaller globe, forming a connection, and the two globes spin together. Other globes approach, and each in turn is caressed and caught by a thread until there are several globes firmly attached. Still others approach, are caressed and kissed, but then move on. Among those that stay, the threads joining them occasionally break, but momentum keeps the freed globe in place until another thread can lay claim to it once more.

The large globe is the plane on which Dominaria resides; the smaller globes are not other worlds but other planes. Those that are caught and held are the planes with which Dominaria has either constant or very frequent connections; those that are touched but move on are those planes which form a connection only briefly and which might well never return again.

The stability provided by Dominaria is the reason why so many planeswalkers call it home. There are other planes, to be sure—Shandalar, where mana flows like water; Rabiah, where desert kingdoms battle powerful djinns; and countless others—but for planeswalkers, Dominaria is the place to be.

The sages of Minorad have a saying: "To know a thing, change that thing." Dominia may, to some degree, be understood from the perspective of an ordinary human or even from that of a planeswalker. Its constant shifts and shimmies may, to some degree, be understood and anticipated. But, ultimately, none may truly know Dominia, for none may truly change it—Dominia changes itself and knows itself. And that is the nature of Dominia.

A Timeline of Dominaria

Dominaria, the world on which dozens of planes intersect, has a long and exciting history. From the long-lived perspective of planeswalkers, however, there are several major defining events that stand out.

Because Dominaria is a world with many cultures, there is no single calendar or way of telling the year. Different lands have their own ways of marking the passage of time. As a result, the timeline below is uncertain at best, but has been assembled with the aid of the planeswalker Taysir.

About four thousand years ago, the Brothers' War occurred on the continent of Terisiare. This terrible conflict between the artificer twins Urza and Mishra resulted in great advances in the creation and usage of magical artifacts, but the massive magical devastation of their conflict resulted in climatic shifts and changes in weather patterns. The tale of this conflict is seen in the *Antiquities* expansion, and in some cards in *Fourth Edition.*

A few decades later, on the southern continent of Sarpadia, the changes in weather (which heralded the onset of the Ice Age) made resources scarce, and eventually the empires of Sarpadia went to war. The outcome was disaster for nearly everyone. This tale is told in the *Fallen Empires* expansion. Also, the events of *The Dark* expansion occur elsewhere in Dominaria.

As the decades passed by, the magical disaster of the Brothers' War continued to have a massive effect on Dominaria and a terrible time known as The Dark began. Knowledge of this period is sketchy at best, but it is remembered as a time of treachery and intrigue when the rich and powerful grappled to seize control of as much magic as possible at the cost of the peoples they ruled. Massive destruction and despair enshrouded Dominaria for several hundred years.

The Dark time came to a close as the Ice Age began, and glaciers began creeping outwards from the poles. Weather grew colder worldwide, and many civilizations fell. The struggles of The Dark were a distant memory; at this time, the struggle for simple survival was supreme.

Two thousand years into this terrible Ice Age, events became interesting. On the continent of Terisiare, civilizations had risen and fallen as the glaciers had advanced. Ultimately, the lone civilized land of Kjeldor was menaced by the forces of a necromancer, Lim-Dûl, as seen in the *Ice Age* expansion. Late in the fighting, the forest goddess Freyalise (actually a planeswalker) magically reversed the course of the Ice Age, and the glaciers began to recede far ahead of the natural schedule.

It is now the present day on Dominaria. The Ice Age is a distant memory, and the people and places of ***Magic: The Gathering***—*Fourth Edition* are present on a large continent commonly known as the Domains. The people and places of the *Arabian Nights* expansion are also present during this time period, as is the action of the novels. On the continent of Stonehaven, the action of the comic books transpires as well.

Dominaria's past is long and full of conflict. In the cards of the game, you will find bits and pieces of this history and of others, but these bits are not a complete history. Such a history does not, in fact, exist: it resides instead in the minds and hearts of the multitudes—planeswalkers and mere mortals alike—who have called Dominaria home.

©DK95

the Magic: The Gathering— Fourth Edition annotated rules
The WotC Rules Team, with annotations by Beth Moursund

Learning the Rules

Like most games, **Magic: The Gathering** is easier to learn from another playerer than from a stuffy old rulebook. That's not always possible, though, so we've tried to make this book as straightforward and easily understood as possible. Don't let the size of the rulebook throw you; a lot of the stuff in here can wait until you've played a few games.

Selene says: As if the rules aren't already long enough, my friend Mathias and I will be popping in to add more comments and examples. Everything printed in normal type (like the first paragraph here) is part of the actual rules; when you buy a starter deck of **Magic** *cards, that material is what's in the rulebook. Everything printed in italics (like this) is additional explanation, examples of how the rule affects play, or answers to questions that a lot of players have asked before this book was written. We'll also point out some of the subtle ways that rules can combine or affect each other, especially in the places that tend to surprise new players. Finally, the* **Magic** *designers found a few ambiguities that managed to sneak into the rules; they hope to correct them in future editions. To make this annotated version match precisely the current rules, we've left the original text intact but marked these problem areas in red (just like this).*

To start, read through this book until you get to the end of the first sample game. This should give you enough information to play a little bit and get used to the game. Words in **bold** type have special technical explanations and definitions associated with them. These are outlined in the glossary in the back of the rulebook, but you really don't need to worry about them until after you've tried the game a few times.

Occasionally, you may run across a **card** that contradicts the rules. In such a situation, the card always takes precedence.

> *Mathias says: That's one of the things that makes* **Magic** *so exciting and so different from most games. You may think you're winning, but then your opponent may play a card that you've never seen before or may use a common card you've seen many times in a way that you never thought of.*

Overview

Magic: The Gathering is a collectible trading card game created by Richard Garfield and produced by Wizards of the Coast, Inc. There are more than three hundred different cards in the core set of **Magic: The Gathering**, and new cards are being designed every day.

As a wizard seeking the knowledge of this book, you already know that the cards in your deck represent the various creatures, spells, and artifacts with which you will face another wizard and battle for control of a plane in Dominia. So where do you begin?

Players begin with 20 **life** each. If you're lucky, you may be able to get more than that during the game; some spells can boost your life point total to more than 20. You **win** if your opponent's life total drops to 0 or less or if your opponent can no longer **draw** a card. You can **damage** your opponent by casting spells, attacking with your creatures, or using the effects of other cards in **play**. When your opponent tries to damage *you,* you can defend yourself with other spells, block or destroy your opponent's creatures, or even turn her own cards against her.

> *Selene says: Actually, it's possible to go below zero life points and then recover without losing, if you get those points back quickly enough, because you only check for losing at certain specific times. Look under "Winning" in the glossary for the details. If both players end up with zero or less at one of these times, the game is a* **draw**.

Getting Started

To play, each player needs a deck of at least forty cards. You can build your deck from a selection of all of the cards you own; you don't have to confine yourself to cards from a particular starter deck. You'll also need some way of keeping score. Some players use pencil and paper, while others prefer counters or some other method. It's best to have a large, flat playing area for laying out your cards; expect a game in progress to take up most of a standard card table.

*Mathias says: Depending on which cards you play with, you may also need some **tokens** or **counters** to represent certain things in the game. Pocket change works fine for this, or you can use any small objects you happen to have around. We've used jelly beans, dice, and bits of torn paper, among other things.*

To begin the game, both players shuffle their decks. You must also give your opponent the opportunity to shuffle or cut your deck. Once both decks have been shuffled, they're put face down on the table. If you're playing for **ante**, then each player turns over the top card and lays it face up. This card is the ante; whoever wins the game will get to keep both cards. Set the ante cards aside, because you're going to need plenty of room!

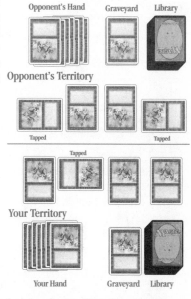

Opponent's Hand   Graveyard   Library

Opponent's Territory

Tapped   Tapped

Tapped

Your Territory

Your Hand   Graveyard   Library

Selene says: Playing for ante is always optional. If you're not comfortable putting your cards on the line, check with your opponents to see if they're willing to play just for fun instead. Some players almost always play for ante; others almost never do. You probably won't want to play for ante during your first few games, when you are still getting used to the rules and your cards.

Mathias says: Ante, though, is a balancing factor. If you're not risking any of your cards, then you're likely to fill your deck with all of the best cards you own. This gives an advantage to whichever player has the bigger collection. But if you're playing for ante, then you are willing to risk the loss of any card in your deck, which makes the duel fairer for a player who has fewer cards. After all, even the strongest deck can be beaten by an unlucky shuffle!

Each player then draws an opening **hand** of seven cards from his or her deck. After you draw your initial hand, the rest of your deck becomes your draw pile, or **library**. Near your library, leave some space for a **graveyard**, or discard pile. Most of the cards you bring into play will go into your **territory**, or your half of the playing surface. A few of your cards may go into your opponent's territory instead. If you play cards in enemy territory, be sure to retrieve them when the game is over. As some experienced players have discovered many times, this is an easy way to lose a great card!

> *Selene says: I usually keep a pad of stick-it notes handy while playing. If one player's card goes into another player's territory, I just tear off a strip of a stick-it note and stick it onto the card. If we're playing a multiplayer game (see page D-1), we all write our initials on the strips to make it easier to keep track of who owns what.*

> *Mathias says: Sometimes I play with people who use plastic card sleeves to protect their cards while playing. This makes it easy for both of us to see when one of their cards is in my area, and this keeps me from accidentally shuffling their cards into my deck… though some of mine still get shuffled into theirs occasionally.*

You are now ready to start a game, or **duel**. Determine randomly who goes first. If you and your opponent duel again afterward, whoever loses this duel will get to go first next time.

The Cards

There are two basic types of cards, **spells** and **lands**. Lands are easy to spot: they say "land" in between the picture and the text box. Lands are the most common kind of card in **Magic**, since they usually provide the **mana**, or magical energy, for all your spells. You can lay out one land per **turn**, and you may use the land for mana as soon as it is in play.

When you get mana from a land, you have to **tap** that land. Tapping a card means turning it sideways. This indicates to you and to your opponent that the card's effects have been temporarily used up. Don't worry; your cards will **untap** at the beginning of your next turn. The symbol ⊕ (tap) on a card indicates that if you use that card to generate a particular effect, then you have to tap it (turn it sideways). The particular effect that card generates is listed right after the ⊕ symbol.

When you tap a land, you get a point of mana to add to your **mana pool**. You can then use this mana to cast spells.

> *Selene says: Actually, there are a few special types of land that don't give you mana. For example, Oasis is a land which can tap to prevent a point of damage to a creature, but it doesn't give you any mana. Always read the card if you're not sure; if a card can be tapped*

for mana, it will say so. If it doesn't say so, then it can't. Remember the very first rule: if a card contradicts the rules, then the card always takes precedence.

Mathias says: You only get mana from a land when you tap the land for mana. If some spell happens to tap one of your lands, the land doesn't generate any mana. Also, the land can only produce mana at the time you tap it; if something forces the land to stay tapped, then the land can't generate any more mana. Tapping a land for mana is always done at interrupt speed; we'll explain what that means later.

There are five different types of **basic lands**, each of which produces mana of a different color. Correspondingly, there are five different **colors** of spells, each of which has a particular character (see "Color Chart" below). There are also colorless and multicolored spells. We'll discuss spell color in greater detail a little later.

Color Chart

☠ **Black Magic:** Black magic's power comes from the swamps and bogs; it thrives on death and decay. Many wizards shun black magic's self-destructive nature even as they long for its ruthlessness. Black's traditional foils are green and white.

💧 **Blue Magic:** Blue magic flows from the islands and thrives on mental energy. Other wizards fear the blue magicians' ability with artifice and illusion, as well as their mastery of the elemental forces of air and water. Blue's traditional foils are red and green.

🌳 **Green Magic:** Green magic gets its life from the lush fecundity of the forest. Like nature itself, green magic can bring both soothing serenity and thunderous destruction. Green's traditional foils are blue and black.

🔥 **Red Magic:** Red magic feeds on the vast energy boiling deep in the heart of the mountains. Masters of earth and fire, red magicians specialize in the violence of chaos and combat. Red's traditional foils are blue and white.

✴ **White Magic:** White magic draws its vitality from the untouched, open plains. Though white magicians focus on spells of healing and protection, they also devote plenty of time to the chivalrous arts of war. White's traditional foils are black and red.

Selene says: Note that mana and land are not the same thing. Mana can come from other places besides land, such as from Llanowar Elves, which taps for one point of green mana, or from Apprentice Wizard, which taps to convert one blue mana into three colorless mana. This is why the rules refer to "green mana," "blue mana," and so on, instead of "forest mana," "island mana," and such.

The Cards, Continued

Now that you've identified the land cards, the other ones must be spells. Notice that none of them actually say "spell" on them; that's because there are six different types of spells and it's important to know which type you're casting. So spells are labeled as instants, interrupts, sorceries, enchantments, artifacts, and summons. The differences between these various types of spells will be discussed in detail later on. The main differences are as follows:

- **Instants** and **interrupts** (both of which are considered **fast effects**) are one-time effects that go to the graveyard as soon as they are cast. You can cast fast effects during your opponent's turn.

- **Sorceries** are also one-time effects that go to the graveyard as soon as they are cast. You can cast sorceries only during your own turn.

- **Enchantments** (including **enchant worlds**), **artifacts**, and **summons** (**creatures**) are permanent spells that remain in play when cast. Once a **permanent** is in play, you don't have to pay the casting cost again. The permanent will remain in play until it is **destroyed**. You can cast permanents only during your turn.

Mathias says: There's a lot to say about each of these types of spells, but we'll wait until the more detailed discussion.

Let's take a look at a sample spell card, the Hurloon Minotaur. We'll look briefly at each of the labeled sections, then come back and look more closely at some of the concepts involved.

Card Name: In this case, the card's name is Hurloon Minotaur. Don't count on the "summon" line to give you the complete name of a creature.

Selene says: Don't confuse the name of the creature with the "type" of creature, which will appear under the picture.

Casting Cost: This is the **cost**, in mana, to cast the spell that the card represents. The cost to bring the Hurloon Minotaur into play is ❶❷❷. This stands for two red mana and one "extra" mana. The "extra" mana in a **casting cost** can be paid for with mana of any color or with **colorless mana**. For a more detailed explanation of casting cost, see "Basic Spellcasting" on p. B-8.

Border: The border serves as an easy visual reminder of the color of the card. A spell's color is technically defined as the color of the mana required to cast it, not counting the "extra" mana. The Hurloon Minotaur requires red mana, so it is a red spell when cast and a red creature while in play. The border helps you remember its color.

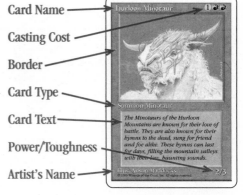

Card Name

Casting Cost

Border

Card Type

Card Text

Power/Toughness

Artist's Name

Mathias says: Notice that the "color" of the card is defined by the color of the mana in the casting cost, not the border.

Cards with no colored mana in their casting cost (or no casting cost at all) are defined as "colorless," not "brown" or "gray"; that's why artifacts and lands are colorless.

Card Type: This card is a summon spell ("Summon Minotaur"), so it is a permanent. Once cast, summon spells remain in play as creatures.

Selene says: For Summon spells, everything after the word "summon" is the "creature type." Other types of spells don't have that extra sub-type. Furthermore, some cards will affect all creatures of a particular type; for example, the Goblin King gives all Goblins a bonus. The type is the only thing that matters for these effects. The Goblin Rock Sled looks like a goblin, and even has "goblin" in its name, but the card type is "Summon Rock Sled" and not "Summon Goblin." This means that it isn't really a goblin and that it isn't affected by the Goblin King. Similarly, the Goblin King itself is "Summon Lord," so it doesn't affect itself.

Card Text: This text box will contain extra information about the card, describing any special abilities it may have. The Hurloon Minotaur doesn't have any special abilities, so the text box is filled in with flavor text. Flavor text is written in italics and has nothing to do with actual game play. We just put it in there to let you know more about the history and multiverse of Dominia.

Artist's Name: In this case, the artist is Anson Maddocks.

Power and Toughness: Only creatures will have power and toughness ratings, so any card with numbers in the lower right corner is a creature. The numbers indicate the creature's **power**, or attack strength, and **toughness**, or defense strength. The Hurloon Minotaur has a power of 2 and a toughness of 3. Power and toughness are explained in detail under "The Care and Feeding of Creatures" on p. **B-14**.

Mathias says: It's important to remember that only certain parts of a card have any bearing on its gameplay. The card's name, art, flavor text, artist's name, and border don't influence what a card actually does. For example, if you look at the picture on a Frozen Shade card, it looks as if the creature is floating. This may fool you into thinking that a Frozen Shade can fly, but since the card text doesn't say "Flying," the Shade isn't considered to be flying for game purposes. And even though the flavor text on the Gray Ogre says something about refusing to eat vegetarians, it can still damage other creatures and your opponent, no matter what their eating habits are.

Selene says: Also, cards don't interact in strange ways based solely on their names. Ironroot Treefolk doesn't take extra damage from a Fireball and Water Elemental isn't immune to it, even though trees burn well and water doesn't. You can play Terror against a Wall of Stone, although it might seem odd for a block of stone to die of fright. An Air Elemental can benefit normally from Firebreathing, a creature can have both Holy Strength and Unholy Strength at the same time, and so on. Just keep in mind that it's "magic," so it doesn't have to make sense… or rather, the rules have to make sense, but the story told by the cards doesn't have to.

Basic Spellcasting

Let's take a closer look at the casting cost of a spell. The casting cost is always written in **mana symbols**. For each of the five colors of mana, there is a separate, distinct symbol; each time that symbol appears, it represents one mana of the appropriate color. Numbers in gray circles represent "extra" mana, which can be any color, any combination of colors, or colorless. To cast a spell, you must pay its entire casting cost. A spell with a casting cost of 💧 would require one blue mana to cast. A spell with a casting cost of 1 💧 would require one blue mana plus one other mana. This other mana could also be blue, or it could be black, green, colorless, or whatever.

Mathias says: The "extra" mana doesn't have to be all of the same type, by the way. You could cast a spell with a cost of 4 🌲 by paying 🔵✳️⚫️💀🌲.

Okay, a quiz: what's the difference between a spell with a casting cost of 2 🌲 and one with a casting cost of 1 🌲🌲? If the only lands you have in play are one forest, which provides green mana, and five mountains, which provide red mana, the distinction is important. You could cast the first spell using two mountains and your forest. You couldn't cast the second spell, because it requires two green mana and you only have one forest.

Selene says: On the other hand, if you've built a deck that contains only green spells and forests, so that all of your mana is green, then there's no difference for you between those two costs… and in general, a creature that costs 1 🌲🌲 tends to be a little better than one that costs 2 🌲. So a deck that's built with just one color seems to have an advantage. Then why doesn't everyone play single-color decks? Well, each color is good at certain things and not so good at other things, so if you limit yourself to a single color, your deck will have no defense against some strategies.

Mathias says: Not to mention those spells which affect a particular type of land or which stop all damage from one color. If you choose to play a solid black deck, then don't complain when your opponent pulls out a Circle of Protection: Black (an enchantment which stops damage to a player from black sources) or a Karma (which does damage each turn based on the number of Swamps you have in play) and you have no way to get rid of it.

Any card whose casting cost includes more than one color of mana is considered multicolored; it is all the colors in its casting cost. For example, a card with 💀 and ❤️ in its casting cost is considered both black and red. Thus, a spell that affects only black cards would affect it, and a spell that says it does not affect red cards would not affect it. Either Circle of Protection: Black or Circle of Protection: Red would prevent damage dealt by this card.

Selene says: Remember that artifacts and lands are "colorless," not "gray" or "brown," and remember that "artifact" is not a color. If I use Thoughtlace to turn an artifact blue, it's now a blue artifact, and either Circle of Protection: Blue or Circle of Protection: Artifacts could stop damage from it. "Colorless" isn't a color, either.

Occasionally you will see ⓧ in the casting cost of a spell. This represents a variable amount of mana, which can be any color or colorless. For such X **spells**, X can be any number, even 0. The text of an X spell will explain what the X represents. For example, the casting cost of the Disintegrate spell is ⓧ ➋. The card text reads, in part, "deals X damage to target creature or player." So if you cast Disintegrate using four mana of any color plus one red mana (the ➋), the spell will deal 4 damage to the target of your choice.

Mathias says: Why would you ever want to play a spell with an X of 0? Well, if your opponent has a Black Vise (an artifact which deals damage to you if you have more than four cards in your hand) in play, you may just want to get cards out of your hand, even if they don't do anything. Besides that, some spells can do useful things even when X is zero. For example, the spell Disintegrate mentioned above does X damage to a target, but it also prevents the target from regenerating for the rest of the turn. During one game, Selene had a Mahamoti Djinn (a blue creature) with a Regeneration enchantment (which allowed the Djinn to regenerate) on it, which was hurting me a lot. I had a Red Elemental Blast in my hand, which I could have used to destroy the Djinn, but Selene would just have regenerated it, and I didn't have quite enough mana to kill the Djinn with my Disintegrate. So I hit the Djinn with a 0-point Disintegrate first, which made it unable to regenerate when I Red Elemental Blasted it a moment later.

Selene says: Remember that, to cast a spell, you must pay its entire casting cost. So when you cast a spell with an X in the casting cost, you have to announce what the X is and then pay the appropriate amount of mana. You can't wait to see what your opponent's response is before deciding what you want X to be. Once you've given X a value, you can't change it later. For example, if I cast Stream of Life (which costs ⓧ ♠ and gives a player X life), I have to say how many life points I'm trying to get and then pay that much mana. I can't wait to see if Mathias is going to cast a Counterspell (which would counter my Stream of Life) before I decide how much mana to spend. The same rule applies to using the abilities of cards in play that have an X in their activation costs; it also applies to other costs paid for a spell that aren't part of the casting cost, including splitting a Fireball between targets or pumping extra black mana into a Drain Life to deal damage.

That brings us to another element of spellcasting: targeting. Some spells must have a valid **target** or you can't cast them. For example, you can't cast an "Enchant Creature" spell without a suitable creature on which to cast it.

Likewise, you can't cast a spell that "destroys target red permanent" unless it's aimed at a red permanent.

That's enough to cover basic spellcasting for now. We'll revisit some of the more complex issues of spellcasting later on.

The Phases of a Turn

In **Magic**, each player's turn is divided into seven smaller parts called **phases**. You may not always have something to do during a given phase, but that phase still happens. The phases take place in the following order:

Untap   Upkeep   Draw   Main   Discard   End   Heal

In Any Order

Play one land
and/or
Make one **attack**
and /or
Cast spells

Heal creatures and clear temporary effects

*Selene says: This section is a quick overview of the phases. There are more detailed explanations about what can and can't happen in each phase and in what order things happen within the phases coming up later, starting on p. **B-42**; look there if you're looking for a specific rule.*

Your turn starts with your **untap** phase. Any of your cards that were **tapped** become untapped.

After untap comes **upkeep**. Some cards require you to perform a particular action during this phase. Such cards will say what this action is and what the consequences are if you don't do it. If you don't have such a card in play, then you don't have to do anything during this phase.

Next, draw one card from the top of your library. If you don't have any cards left to draw, you lose.

 Mathias says: A clarification—you don't lose as soon as your library empties. You lose if you are required to draw a card from your library and have no card in your library left to draw.

During your **main phase**, you may do any or all of the following, in any order:

- Put one land into play
- Make one attack (more on this later)
- Cast spells

 Selene says: Remember that land is not a spell, so putting a land into play is not casting a spell.

You may cast sorceries, enchantments, artifacts, and creature summons before and after the attack, but not during it. As long as you have enough mana to pay for them, you can cast all the spells in your hand if you want to.

If your hand has more than seven cards in it at the end of your main phase, you must discard back down to seven during the **discard phase**. You can't discard if you have seven or fewer cards. Your graveyard, or discard pile, must always remain face up.

 Mathias says: By the way, you can look through any player's grave-yard, including your own, at any time you wish. That's why your graveyard is required to be face up. Some spells even let you pull cards out of the graveyard.

Why do we call "**end**" a phase? Well, it isn't always obvious when you're done, so you must tell your opponent you're ready to end your turn.

At the end of your turn, all surviving creatures **heal** from any damage they have taken, and all "until end of turn" effects wear off. Notice that creatures on both sides, not just yours, heal back to full capacity at the end of your turn.

A Sample Game

So, are you confused yet? Relax—you know more than you think you do. To prove it, let's start a sample game and see if you can keep up. For now, we'll use simplified examples; as you learn more about the rules, you'll see how things can get a little more complex.

Brett and Keisha each have a deck of about sixty **Magic** cards. Brett has a stack of twenty stones to use as life, plus a few extra stones to mark any of his cards that get played in Keisha's territory. Keisha prefers to keep her score with pencil and paper. She also has a few sticky notes to put on any of her cards that get played in Brett's territory.

First Keisha and Brett shuffle their own decks and cut each other's deck. They set aside the top card of each deck as the ante and draw their first seven cards. They flip a coin; Brett gets to go first. Whoever loses this duel will go first next time.

Since this is Brett's very first turn, he won't have anything to do during his untap and upkeep phases. He draws a card (**draw phase**) and lays down a mountain (main phase). He has more land in his hand, but he can only lay out one land per turn, so the mountain will have to do for now. He does have a spell he can cast, though, so he taps the mountain and casts a Lightning Bolt. Lightning Bolt is an instant that costs ⚡, which Brett can get from the mountain. It deals 3 damage to any target. There aren't any creatures in play yet, but he still has a valid target: Keisha! Any "target" includes players, too. So Keisha's life total drops from 20 to 17, and she hasn't even had a turn yet. Brett can't cast any more spells because his mountain is tapped, so he tells Keisha he's done (end phase).

This is Keisha's first turn, so she doesn't have anything to do during untap or upkeep. She draws a card (draw phase) and discovers that she doesn't have any land in her hand. With no land she doesn't have any mana to cast a spell, so she can't do anything during her main phase either. She still has eight cards in her hand, so she has to discard one of them. She does so (discard phase), then tells Brett she's done (end phase).

Brett untaps his mountain (untap phase) and still has nothing to do during his upkeep phase. He draws a card (draw phase) and lays down a forest (main phase). He then taps the forest to cast Wild Growth, an "Enchant Land" card (also main phase). Wild Growth must be cast on a particular land; whenever Brett gets mana from that land, it will yield 🌲 in addition to its normal mana. Brett puts the Wild Growth on his mountain. Now every time he gets mana from that particular mountain, he will get ⚡ *and* 🌲. He tells Keisha he's done (end phase).

Keisha doesn't have any untapping or upkeeping to do, so she draws and gets a land this time. She lays out the swamp, taps it, and uses the mana to cast a Dark Ritual. Dark Ritual is an interrupt that costs 💀 to cast and puts 💀💀💀 in Keisha's mana pool. She uses this mana to cast Scathe Zombies, a summon spell with a casting cost of 2 💀. Once successfully cast, the Zombies card becomes a 2/2 creature. Keisha would really like for her Zombies to run over and stomp on Brett—she's still annoyed about the Lightning Bolt thing—but they can't. Why not? That'll be covered in the next section, "The Care and Feeding of Creatures." So Keisha tells Brett she's done.

We'll get back to our sample game in a moment. But since we now have a creature on the table, it's time to look a little more closely at creatures in general.

The Care and Feeding of Creatures

In **Magic**, creatures will usually be your main line of attack and defense. Creatures come into play whenever a summon spell is successfully cast. Remember that summon spells are **permanents**, so creature cards remain in play and you don't have to pay their casting costs again. Creatures can participate in combat—attacking, defending, and dealing damage to the players and to each other.

All creatures have two numbers separated by a slash in the lower right corner of the card. The first of these numbers indicates the creature's **power**, the amount of damage this creature deals in combat. The second number represents the creature's **toughness**, or the amount of damage the creature can absorb before it dies. When something changes a creature's power and toughness to specific numbers, such as 0/2, play as if these numbers appear on the card. Other cards may legally change these numbers.

 Selene says: If a creature's power is less than zero, it still deals zero damage in combat. See "Power" in the Glossary following these rules for the specifics about negative-power creatures.

Remember the Hurloon Minotaur on page B-7? It has a power of 2 and a toughness of 3. If the Minotaur engages in combat with another creature or damages your opponent, it deals 2 damage. If it receives 3 damage, either in combat or from some other **source**, it has taken **lethal damage**.

Mathias says: Some enchantments or other effects give a creature bonuses or penalties to its power and/or toughness. Anything that refers to a creature's power or toughness means the current power or toughness, not the numbers printed on the card. For example, the Dwarven Warriors have the ability to make a creature with power no greater than 2 unblockable. Suppose I have a Hurloon Minotaur (normally 2/3) enchanted with Giant Strength, which gives a creature +2/+2. The enchanted Minotaur is a 4/5 creature, and the Dwarven Warriors can't make it unblockable, even though the power actually printed on the card is 2. (If a spell really wants to alter the power printed on the card rather than alter the creature's current power, it will say so. Remember, if a card contradicts the rules, the card wins.)

Selene says: So what was that bit about altering a creature's power and toughness to specific numbers? You won't run into this very often, but a few cards will say to actually change the power or toughness of a card to a specific value instead of simply adding to or subtracting from its current value. For example, the Sorceress Queen has the ability "◈*: Target creature other than Sorceress Queen becomes 0/2 until end of turn." If something changes a creature's power or toughness to a specific value, then you treat it as if the card had that number printed on it, and any pluses or minuses are applied on top of that. So if the Sorceress Queen zapped the Hurloon Minotaur with the Giant Strength on it, then the Minotaur would become a 0/2 creature with a +2/+2 enchantment on it, making it 2/4 total.*

When a creature receives lethal damage, it goes to the **graveyard**. Any non-lethal damage a creature receives is erased at the end of every turn. For example, if the Minotaur receives 1 damage during an attack, it will heal back up to full strength as soon as the turn ends.

 Mathias says: Notice that everyone's creatures heal at the end of every turn, not just at the end of their own turns. This is true even in a multiplayer game.

Many spells in **Magic** can prevent damage to your creatures. Damage prevention spells help your creatures stay alive to fight more battles for you.

So, why couldn't Keisha attack with her Zombies in the sample game? A creature can't attack during the turn it was summoned. **Magic** players have a couple of nicknames for this: **summoning sickness** and "jet lag" are two of the most popular. Anything that brings a creature into play on your side causes it to have summoning sickness. Note that while you can't attack with a newly summoned creature, you *can* use it to defend during your opponent's next turn.

 *Selene says: The full rules about summoning sickness appear in the "Creatures" section, on p. **B-28**.*

Creature Combat

During your turn, you may make one attack, sending your creatures out to do battle with your opponent. This attack, which is one of the optional actions you can take during your main phase, can include any number of your creatures. Either player may use fast effects during the attack, but no one can cast sorceries or lay out permanents during the attack.

Selene says: "Any number" of your creatures includes zero. Sometimes it can be useful to declare an attack with no creatures just to limit your opponent's choices. For example, the spell Siren's Call—which forces all of your opponent's creatures that can to attack—can only be cast before the attack begins. If I suspect that Mathias has a Siren's Call, I may declare an attack early in my turn so that he has to either use the spell right away or not use it at all. Then I can attack with zero creatures if he chooses not to use it. But if you do this, it uses up your attack for that turn; you can't declare an attack with zero creatures and then declare another attack later in the turn.

Keep in mind that when you attack, you *always* attack your opponent. You can't attack your opponent's creatures, and you can't attack yourself or your own creatures.

*Mathias says: Remember, though, that casting a spell or using an ability of a creature is not an attack. You can cast spells that damage and destroy your own creatures, or you can use a card's special ability against yourself. Why would you want to do this? Usually you wouldn't… but no matter how bizarre an action seems, someone can probably come up with some obscure circumstances under which it becomes good strategy. These escapades make great stories and are often told and retold at **Magic** gatherings.*

The basic steps in the attack are as follows:

- Declare attackers
- Declare defenders
- Resolve damage

Selene says: A more detailed breakdown of the attack sequence follows these rules; this breakdown also provides a few rules for special cases that aren't covered here. If you need to know exactly when you can cast spells in this sequence, what will keep a creature from dealing damage, or any other tricky questions, see the detailed version.

To begin the attack, you must announce that you are attacking. Next, tell your opponent which of your creatures are attacking, and tap them. You must declare and tap all of your attackers now; you can't add or subtract creatures later on. Creatures that are already tapped can't attack.

Mathias says: Any or all of your untapped creatures, except those with summoning sickness, can attack, including those whose power is zero or less. (The exception to this rule is walls, which will be discussed a bit later.)

Now your opponent declares which of her creatures are blocking yours. Only her untapped creatures may **block**; tapped creatures are unavailable. Keep in mind that your opponent gets to choose which creatures block which; you can't launch an attack directly at any of your opponent's creatures. Each of your opponent's **defending creatures** can be assigned to block one of your **attacking creatures**. Multiple defenders can block one attacker, but one defender can't be assigned to block multiple attackers. Defending doesn't tap a creature.

Selene says: Once an attacking creature is blocked, it stays blocked, no matter what happens to the blocker. Killing or removing the blocker doesn't "unblock" the attacker—neither does casting a spell which, if cast earlier, would have made the block illegal, nor does otherwise changing the attacker's evasion abilities.

Mathias says: We're going to jump the gun a bit here and mention a couple of rules about the attack which aren't given anywhere except in the Glossary and Attack Summary but which deserve some additional explanation. Once a creature has been declared as an attacker or blocker, the only ways to get it out of the combat are to remove it from play, change its controller, or use a card that specifically says that it removes the creature from combat. Untapping an attacking creature doesn't stop it from being an attacker or prevent it from dealing damage; it just lets it tap again later or block on the following turn. Tapping a blocking creature doesn't stop it from being a blocker, either, but it does prevent it from dealing damage.

Selene says: A combatant which is destroyed, or which takes lethal damage from a fast effect, before the damage-dealing step goes to the graveyard; this takes the creature out of play, so it won't deal damage during the attack. Similarly, a creature that is returned to your hand or is removed from the game entirely before the damage-dealing stage doesn't deal damage. And since your creatures can't attack you or block each other, an attacking creature that is then controlled by the defending player (or vice versa) will be taken out of the attack. One way this could happen, for example, is if you're attacked by a creature with a Control Magic enchantment on it (which allows your opponent to take and use one of your creatures), and you use a spell to destroy the Control Magic right after the creature attacks but before you declare blockers. The creature would return to your side of the table and would no longer be an attacker. Since the creature tapped to attack, however, it will still be tapped when it comes back to your side, so you can't use it to block unless you have some way to untap it.

Once the blockers have been assigned, the creatures deal their damage. During this damage resolution step, neither player may use any fast effects except **damage prevention** effects and interrupts. Attacking creatures deal their damage to the defenders blocking them, while defenders deal their damage to the attackers they block. If more than one defender blocks a single attacking creature, whoever controls the attacking creature gets to split its damage as desired among the defenders blocking it. Attacking creatures that aren't blocked deal their damage to the defending player. Creatures that take lethal damage go to the graveyard.

Another quiz: Do you remember how much damage these creatures deal, or how you can tell whether or not they've taken lethal damage? You can find the answer under "The Care and Feeding of Creatures" on p. **B-14**. Creatures deal damage equal to their power. If they take damage equal to or greater than their toughness, they have taken lethal damage and go to the graveyard.

 Mathias says: See the section on **Regeneration** *that's coming up later for an exception to this.*

Those are the basics of creature combat. There are some other elements that can make it a little trickier, but for now, let's check in with Brett and Keisha and see how that game is going.

Sample Game, Continued

Keisha has just cast Scathe Zombies, a 2/2 creature. It's Brett's turn.

Brett untaps his forest and draws. He lays down a mountain. He taps that mountain and the mountain with Wild Growth on it. The first mountain gives him 🔴, while the second one gives him 🔴🔴; the extra 🔴 comes from the Wild Growth enchantment. He uses this mana to cast a Hurloon Minotaur. The Minotaur, as you may remember, has a casting cost of 1 🔴🔴 and becomes a 2/3 creature when cast. Brett can't attack with his Minotaur because it has summoning sickness, so he tells Keisha he's done.

Keisha untaps her swamp and draws. She lays down a forest and decides against casting any spells for now. Her Zombies could attack if she wanted them to, but she sees the Minotaur on Brett's side. Although the Minotaur can't attack yet, it can still defend, and if it blocked the Zombies it would deal enough damage to kill them. Keisha decides discretion is the better part of valor and tells Brett she's done.

Brett untaps his mountains, draws a card, and then decides to attack. He declares that he is attacking and taps the Minotaur. He'd love to kill Keisha's Zombies, but he can't attack them directly; he has to attack Keisha and leave it up to her to decide whether or not her Zombies will block. She looks at the power and toughness of each of the creatures. Her Zombies are 2/2; the Minotaur is 2/3. If she blocks the Minotaur with her Zombies, each of them will take 2 damage since each creature has a power of 2. The 2 damage would kill her Zombies, which have a toughness of 2. The Minotaur, with a toughness of 3, would survive.

Keisha doesn't think that's a very good deal, so she decides not to block with her Zombies, hoping that she can find some way to take care of the Minotaur before too much longer. She tells Brett she's not blocking and takes 2 damage from the Minotaur. Between that and the Lightning Bolt she took earlier, she is now down to 15 life. His attack over, Brett taps his mountain—the one without the Wild Growth—and summons Mons's Goblin Raiders, a 1/1 creature with a casting cost of . He could have summoned the Goblins before his attack, but he was waiting to see what would happen. Brett has no further spells to cast, so he tells Keisha he's done.

Keisha doesn't have anything to untap, so she draws. She taps her forest and her swamp and summons Grizzly Bears, a 2/2 creature with a casting cost of 1. She then declares she's attacking. Though the Grizzly Bears can't attack due to summoning sickness, Keisha still has her Zombies, which she taps. Brett decides to block them with his Goblins. It would be really great if he could block with his Minotaur, but it's still tapped from last turn's attack, and tapped creatures can't block.

The Zombies and Goblins are now in combat. The Zombies (2/2) deal 2 damage to the Goblins. At the same time, the Goblins (1/1) deal 1 damage to the Zombies. The Zombies live, but the Goblins die and are put into Brett's graveyard. Even though the Zombies did more damage to the Goblins than necessary to kill them, the "extra" 1 damage does *not* go through to damage Brett; unless the card specifically says otherwise, only unblocked creatures get to deal their damage to the defending player. Keisha tells Brett she's done. At the end of her turn, the damage to the Zombies is healed.

Brett untaps his mountain and his Minotaur and draws a card. He taps his mountain again to summon another Mons's Goblin Raiders. Brett then lays out a swamp, taps it, and casts Unholy Strength, an "Enchant Creature" spell that gives a creature +2/+1. It has a casting cost of 🌑. Brett casts the Unholy Strength on his Goblins, making them considerably less wimpy. With the +2/+1 added to the Goblins' original 1/1, the Goblins are now 3/2.

Next, Brett declares his attack and taps his Minotaur as an attacker. The Goblins can't join in the attack (you guessed it—summoning sickness). Keisha's Zombies are tapped from her last attack, so she can't use them to defend. If she wanted, she could defend with the Bears, but they are 2/2 and the Minotaur is 2/3. In combat the Bears would die and the Minotaur would survive. She's still not willing to make that trade, so she chooses not to block. She takes 2 more damage and is now down to 13 life. Brett has no spells to cast after the attack, so he tells Keisha he's done.

Keisha untaps her forest, her swamp, and her Zombies and draws a card. She lays out another forest and taps it. Then she taps her swamp. She uses the mana to summon another Grizzly Bears (a 2/2 creature with a casting cost of 1 🌑). She then declares her attack and taps her Zombies. Her latest Bears, of course, can't attack this turn because they were just summoned. Her first Bears could attack, but she chooses to attack only with the Zombies. Brett decides to block the Zombies with his Goblins. The Zombies are 2/2, and the Goblins with Unholy Strength are 3/2, so Brett expects both creatures will die.

But wait! Keisha has a fast effect to play before the damage resolution step. She taps her last forest and casts Giant Growth, an instant with a casting cost of 🌑. Giant Growth gives a creature +3/+3 until the end of the turn. Keisha casts it on her Zombies, making them suddenly 5/5! They deal 5 damage to the Goblins, who can only absorb 2. The Goblins deal 3 damage, but the Zombies can handle 5. Thus the Goblins go to Brett's graveyard but the Zombies survive. The Unholy Strength enchantment that was on the Goblins has to go to the graveyard too; it was destroyed along with the Goblins. Again, the "extra" damage doesn't carry over to Brett; the Goblins just get extra squashed. Keisha tells Brett she's done. The damage to the Zombies is healed, and the +3/+3 from the Giant Growth wears off.

Brett untaps his mountain and swamp and draws a card. He then taps his forest, the mountain with Wild Growth, and the swamp. He uses this mana to cast a Giant Spider, a 2/4 creature with a casting cost of 3 🌑. He then declares his attack and taps his Minotaur as the attacker. Keisha decides that this time she's going to block the Minotaur with both of her Bears—yes, she can do this. The Bears are each 2/2, so each of them will deal 2 damage to the Minotaur, for a total of 4. The Minotaur is 2/3, so it gets to deal 2 damage before it dies. As the attacking player, Brett gets to decide how this damage is distributed among the Bears. He could deal 1 damage to each of them, but then they would both survive the attack. So he decides to distribute both points of damage to the Bears on the left. The Minotaur and the Bears on the left go to their respective graveyards, while the Bears on the right survive. After a few pithy comments about people ganging up on a guy, Brett tells Keisha he's done.

Keisha untaps her forests and her swamp and draws a card. She lays out a mountain and declares her attack. She taps her remaining Bears and her Zombies as attackers. Brett has only one creature on his side: the Spider. He can only block one of Keisha's attackers with it, since a defender can't block more than one attacker. He chooses to block the Zombies with his Spider. The Zombies (2/2) deal 2 damage to the Spider. The Spider (2/4) deals 2 damage to the Zombies. The 2 damage is enough to send the Zombies to the graveyard, but the Spider survives. Meanwhile, the Bears go through unblocked and deal their 2 damage to Brett. Brett is now down to 18 life.

After her attack, Keisha taps her mountain and casts a Lightning Bolt on the Spider! Lightning Bolt is an instant with a casting cost of ❷; it deals 3 damage to any target. By itself, the Bolt wouldn't have been enough to kill the Spider. But the Spider has already taken 2 damage from the Zombies this turn, and the damage from the Bolt makes a total of 5. Since the Spider has a toughness of 4, it dies and goes to Brett's graveyard.

Keisha really wishes she had a Raise Dead, a sorcery with a casting cost of ☠. Raise Dead would allow Keisha to take her Zombies back out of her graveyard and put it into her hand. Maybe she'll draw one next turn. Keisha tells Brett that she's done, and he replies that he certainly hopes so.

Well, that battle is really starting to heat up. Before we continue it, though, it's time to revisit some of those basic rules in a little more depth.

Advanced Spellcasting

You already know the basics of how to cast a spell. Now let's look a little more closely at spells, starting with properties of certain **permanents**. Permanents, as we said earlier, are spells that stay in play once cast; you don't have to pay the casting cost again to keep them in play. Enchantments, summons (creatures), and artifacts are all permanent spells. Land is also considered a permanent, although it isn't a spell.

Selene says: This terminology can get a little confusing. Once a permanent comes into play, it's not a spell anymore; it's just a permanent. It can't be targeted by things that only target spells. For example, Spell Blast is an interrupt that can counter any spell. You can Spell Blast a Summon spell while it is being cast, but once the crea-

ture has been successfully summoned, it is no longer a spell and you can't
Spell Blast it later on.

Some permanents have **activation costs**, which are costs required to generate special effects those permanents can provide. Activation costs are usually
written in the following format: [cost]: [effect]. Only a permanent's **controller** can pay its activation cost and generate its special effect. The controller
of a permanent is usually the person who cast it, although some spells allow
you to "steal" your opponent's permanents and become their controller. If you
take control of an opponent's card during the course of a game, always return
it to its **owner** at the end of game unless the card you used to gain control
specifically states that you become the owner of the controlled card. If the
controlled card is put into the graveyard during play, **bury** it in its owner's
graveyard.

> Mathias says: Also, if you take control of a permanent, you're just
> getting control over the permanent itself. Any enchantments on
> that permanent don't change controllers. For enchantments with
> a continuous effect, like Holy Strength, this doesn't make a difference;
> they're always working, no matter who controls them. But for enchant-
> ments with an activated effect, like Firebreathing or Regeneration, it
> makes a big difference. Only the controller of the enchantment can acti-
> vate it, no matter who controls the permanent.

Paying the activation cost of a permanent is always optional; you don't have
to use a card's special ability unless you want to. Unless the card specifies otherwise, you can use a special effect anytime you can use an instant, such as
during your opponent's turn. Some special abilities specify that they are
played "as interrupts"; this means you can play them whenever you can play
an interrupt. Don't worry too much about this distinction just yet; the
difference won't be important until later, when we start worrying about timing. Even though these effects are played like instants or interrupts, it's important to remember that they are *not* really instants, interrupts, or any other
kind of spell, so things that affect instants, interrupts, or spells won't work on
them.

> Selene says: For example, the Prodigal Sorcerer has a special ability
> "⊙: Prodigal Sorcerer deals 1 damage to target creature or player."
> You might think, since he's a Sorcerer, that this must be a spell and
> can be countered by a Counterspell. But if you did, you'd be wrong.
> Only playing a non-land card from your hand counts as a spell. None of
> the special abilities that various permanents have count as spells.

Suppose you have a creature card that says "🕱🕱,⟳: Jumps up and down until end of turn." You can pay two black mana and tap the card, and then the creature will jump up and down until the end of the turn.

Okay, another quiz: can you make it jump up and down during your opponent's turn? For your answer, remember that you can use a special effect whenever you can use an instant. Instants can be played during either player's turn.

Selene says: If an effect just costs mana, you can use it as many times as you want in the same turn, so long as you have enough mana to pay for it. For example, a Circle of Protection: Black says "1: Prevent all damage against you from one black source." When Mathias attacks me with a Drudge Skeletons and two Scathe Zombies, I can put three points of mana into the Circle and prevent the damage from all three of those black creatures. But if I only have three untapped lands, I might decide to only use the Circle against the two larger creatures and take the point of damage from the Skeletons, so that I'll have a point of mana available to power the Circle later if I need it for something nasty like a big Drain Life (a black sorcery that deals damage to either a player or a creature).

Mathias says: If an effect has an activation cost which can be paid multiple times, you can choose to pay the cost many times as a single activation. For example, Pestilence says "🕱: Pestilence deals 1 damage to all creatures and players." So you can choose to power it up for one damage at a time, or you can pump two, three, or even more mana into a single activation to deal more than one damage at once. Choosing between these options can be a very important part of your strategy. For example, say I'm playing against Selene. I have a Pestilence and Selene has a Circle of Protection: Black. If I power up the Pestilence for five mana all at once, Selene would only need to spend one mana to stop the damage with the Circle, since all five points of damage would be a single event. But if I power it with one point of mana at a time, Selene has to spend one mana to prevent each point of damage. If I have more Swamps than Selene has untapped lands, then Selene will run out of mana and have to start taking damage. On the other hand, if I happened to have a Drudge Skeletons (a 1/1 creature that can regenerate for 🕱) and I was playing against someone who didn't have a Circle of Protection, I would probably want to pump all the mana into the Pestilence at once. That way, my Skeletons would only need to regenerate one time. If I pumped it one point at a time, the Skeletons would take lethal damage from each one-point activation and I'd need to spend ☠ each time to regenerate it, so I would end up spending half my black mana on regenerations.

Selene says: But remember that you can only do this if you can pay the cost multiple times. With Pestilence this is not a problem, since the cost to activate the effect is only mana. But if the cost includes a ⟳, like the Prodigal Sorcerer, you can only use it once at a time, since it's impossible to tap a card twice without untapping it in between. Additionally, if an effect calls for a sacrifice, the sacrifice is part of the cost (see "sacrifice" in the Glossary). If you had an effect that said "①: Sacrifice a land to deal 5 points of damage" and you wanted to use it to do 15 points of damage all at once, you'd have to pay 3 mana and sacrifice 3 lands. (Don't bother looking—there's no such card. I just made it up for the example!)

These special abilities, along with instants and interrupts, are collectively known as **fast effects**. There are some pretty complex timing issues involved with fast effects, but we'll wait for a discussion of those until after you've played a couple of games.

Mathias says: It's important to remember that if a permanent has an ability with ⟳ in the cost, you only get to use that ability when you specifically tap it to pay for the ability, not when you tap it to attack or it is tapped by some external effect. For example, if I play Paralyze on Selene's Prodigal Sorcerer, the Sorcerer becomes tapped, but this does not let her use its ability to deal one point of damage to a target. We'll talk more about this in the Timing section.

Next, let's take a closer look at the six different types of spells.

Instants, interrupts, and sorceries are temporary spells that go to the graveyard as soon as they are cast. Sometimes their effects last only until the end of the turn, especially for instants. Other times, the effects of such spells may be permanent; these effects last until the end of the game. For example, Thoughtlace is a blue interrupt that permanently changes the color of another card in play to blue. In contrast, the Giant Growth spell that Keisha cast is an instant. It gives a creature +3/+3, but this bonus wears off at the end of the turn.

Selene says: A bit of a clarification here—the effects of interrupt spells are always permanent if they modify another card, even if the spell itself doesn't say so. Thoughtlace fits into this category because it changes the color of its target. But, for example, Blue

Elemental Blast doesn't modify its target—it counters or destroys it. Those are one-time effects, not changes. If I cast Blue Elemental Blast on an Uthden Troll, it destroys the Troll once and that's it. If the Troll regenerates, the Blast doesn't come back to destroy it a second time.

Mathias says: Also remember that when we say an effect is "permanent," we mean that it lasts only for as long as the target remains in play. If Selene casts Thoughtlace to turn my Frozen Shade blue and the Shade gets killed a few turns later, then the Shade card goes to the graveyard and the effect of the Thoughtlace ends. I can cast Animate Dead to bring the Shade back, and it will be a normal black Shade, not a blue one. Similarly, Unsummoning a Thoughtlaced creature returns the creature to its owner's hand, and this, too, ends the effect of the Thoughtlace.

Selene says: One more comment about interrupts modifying things—if you use an interrupt to modify a permanent spell as it is being cast, the change also applies to the permanent created by the spell. Consider the Thoughtlace again as an example: if I cast Thoughtlace on a Summon spell as it is being cast (perhaps to save it from being countered by a Blue Elemental Blast) then the creature created by the Summon will also be blue.

Some interrupts can **counter** a spell as it is being cast. If a spell is countered, it goes to the graveyard with no effect. The **caster** of the countered spell still has to pay the casting cost. Like instants, interrupts can be played during your opponent's turn.

Mathias says: Only an interrupt can counter a spell, and a spell can only be countered as it is being cast. Once both players say they don't want to cast any more interrupts, the spell changes from "being cast" to "successfully cast." Once a spell reaches this point, it can no longer be interrupted or countered, though it can still be responded to, as you'll see later.

Sorceries can only be cast during the main phase of your turn, and even then you can't cast them during an attack. Sorceries are powerful spells that can raise the dead, destroy lands and creatures, and wreak general havoc.

Remember, spells that require a **target** can't be cast if there is no valid target in play. See "Basic Spellcasting" on p. B-8 if you don't remember what a target is.

Creatures, artifacts, and enchantments are brought into play by permanent spells. Permanent spells can only be cast during the main phase of your turn, and even then not during an attack. Once you have successfully cast a permanent spell, the card remains in play to represent whatever the spell brought into being. A permanent in play is no longer considered a spell, but rather an artifact, enchantment, or creature.

Selene says: Sorceries and permanent spells have different rules than instants do about when you can cast them, but once you start casting them, they all use exactly the same rules.

Permanents remain in play until they are killed, destroyed, or disenchanted or until the game ends. You can't just choose to get rid of a permanent once you have created it, even if it starts to do you more harm than good. Remember that land cards are also considered permanents, although they are never spells.

Mathias says: This rule can sometimes be really annoying. For example, Selene casts an enchantment called Power Leak on my Pestilence; because I have my Pestilence in play, Power Leak does 2 points of damage to me every turn unless I pay extra mana. I can't just toss the Pestilence away, even though I want to now.

A word to the wise: be sure to read your permanents carefully before putting them into play! Some permanents have special abilities that affect only your opponent, but some of them will affect you too. Be sure you're not hurting yourself worse than your opponent when you put a permanent into play.

Selene says: A few examples—Winter Orb is an artifact that allows all players, including the person who cast it, to untap only one land during each untap phase. Smoke does the same thing for creatures. Each of these can either help you or hurt you, depending on what cards you and your opponent happen to have in play at the time.

Mathias says: And a few more examples—Bad Moon gives all black creatures +1/+1, and Crusade gives all white creatures +1/+1, no matter who controls them. Tsunami destroys all islands, including islands belonging to its caster. Think carefully before casting these sorts of spells, and make sure you're not going to regret it later.

Now let's look at each of the types of permanents in greater detail.

Creatures

Summon spells bring creatures into play. We've already covered quite a bit about creatures, but we've still got to talk about a few more details.

As you've already learned, summoning sickness prevents a creature from attacking during the turn it is summoned. If a creature has a special ability that includes the ⊙ symbol in its activation cost, that ability can't be used during the turn the creature is summoned, either. In fact, you can't use it until the creature is on your side at the very beginning of your turn—your next upkeep. If an ability's activation cost doesn't have the ⊙ symbol in it, you can use that special ability right away.

 Selene says: Summoning sickness does not tap a creature! This is one of the most common mistakes that new players make. Also, despite the name, notice that summoning sickness applies any time a creature comes into play on your side. It doesn't matter whether the creature got there by means of a Summon spell, or by a spell that brings a creature into play from the graveyard, or by destroying a Control Magic that your opponent had cast on one of your creatures earlier in the game, or whatever. All that matters is whether it was in play under your control continuously since your most recent untap phase.

Mathias says: It doesn't even matter whether the card was a creature at the start of the turn or not. Suppose I have four swamps in play. At the start of my main phase, I lay down another swamp, and then cast Kormus Bell, which turns all swamps into 1/1 creatures. The four swamps which I had at the start of my turn can attack, even though they weren't creatures at the beginning of the turn, but the swamp that I just played can't because it hasn't been in play since my last untap phase.

If a creature has a special ability that doesn't require an activation cost at all, then that ability is always "on," even when the creature is tapped.

 Selene says: For example, my Lord of Atlantis says "All Merfolk gain islandwalk and get +1/+1." Since there is no activation cost, this ability starts working as soon as the Lord comes into play and keeps working all the time, even when the Lord is suffering from summoning sickness or is tapped.

All summon spells say "Summon <creature type>" between the picture and the text box. This is because a few spells affect all creatures of a given type. For example, if you cast a spell that had some effect on all bugs in play, it would affect all cards that said "Summon Bug."

Mathias says: The Lord of Atlantis that Selene just mentioned affects all cards that say "Summon Merfolk." But the Lord of Atlantis card itself says "Summon Lord," so it doesn't give itself islandwalk, even though the picture looks like the Lord should count as one of the Merfolk.

Some creatures say "Summon Wall." **Walls** are special creatures that lack the ability to attack. Many walls have a power of 0, while others can actually deal damage. Even if a wall can deal damage, it can only be used to block an attacking creature. For all other purposes a wall is a normal creature, so it can be enchanted, killed, and so on just like other creatures.

Selene says: Some players think of wall cards as a wall surrounding the wizard. That's not the best image to use, though, because it makes you think that one wall should be able to block a whole army of attacking creatures. Walls block just like any other creature, so each wall can normally only block one attacking creature. If you need an image, think of it as a small wall placed right between one attacking creature and you. Also, even though walls can't attack, they can still be tapped by other cards. And a creature that is tapped can't block, even if it's a wall.

Legends are considered creatures except that there may be only one legend of the same name in play at a time. If a second legend of the same name is brought into play, it's immediately buried. If more than one legend of the same name is brought into play at the same time, all of them are buried.

Mathias says: Legends are one of the few cases where the name of the card actually makes a difference in play. If you're wondering what in the world a legend is, don't worry; the basic Magic: The Gathering set doesn't have any legends in it. This rule is just here in case you add cards from one of the expansion sets, as some of them do, indeed, have legend cards. A legend is any card that says "Summon Legend" or "Summon (something) Legend" on it.

Artifacts

Artifacts are magical devices that have certain effects on the game. Unlike other types of spells, artifacts are colorless; they can be cast with any color of mana or with colorless mana. Some artifacts have a **continuous effect** that is always "on" whenever the artifact is untapped and in play. Other artifacts require you to pay an activation cost to trigger their effects. If an artifact effect doesn't have an activation cost listed, it's continuous. Unlike creatures, artifacts can be used during the same turn they come into play.

> *Selene says: For example, if I have enough mana, I could cast a Rod of Ruin and then immediately pay three more mana to tap the Rod and do a point of damage to a target. I don't have to wait until the Rod has been in play at the beginning of my turn, like I would if it were a creature.*

Some artifacts, however, are also creatures. These say "**artifact creature**" as their spell type. Artifact creatures must follow the same rules as other creatures, so an artifact creature can't attack during the same turn it is brought into play. However, artifact creatures aren't summon spells; they're artifact spells.

Tapping a non-creature artifact always turns it "off," even if the artifact's ability doesn't have a ⊙ in its activation cost. Tapping an artifact creature doesn't necessarily turn it "off," since artifact creatures follow the creature rules. A tapped artifact creature can still use a special ability as long as it doesn't have a ⊙ in its activation cost.

> *Selene says: For example, the Howling Mine lets everyone draw an extra card during their draw phase. But if I cast Twiddle to tap the Mine during Mathias's upkeep phase, it will stop working and Mathias won't get to draw an extra card that turn. However, if a card counts as both an artifact and a creature or an artifact and a land at the same time, then tapping it won't turn it off.*

Enchantments

Magic includes many kinds of enchantments. Some of them target a particular type of permanent already in play, so you can play them on creatures, artifacts, lands, or even other enchantments. It's pretty obvious which of these are which: they say "Enchant Land," "Enchant Creature," and so on. These enchantments are considered **targeted**; you can't cast them if there is no valid target in play.

> *Mathias says: Not only can't you cast a targeted enchantment without a valid target, but a targeted enchantment can't even stay in play without a valid target. When a card leaves play for any reason, any enchantments on it go to their owner's graveyard. Also, if the enchanted card somehow changes so that it's no longer a legal target for the enchantment, then the enchantment goes to the graveyard. For example, Mishra's Factory is a land which can temporarily change into a combination land/artifact creature called an Assembly Worker. You can*

cast an Enchant Creature spell on an Assembly Worker, but when the Assembly Worker stops being a creature at the end of the turn, the Enchant Creature card will be buried and sent to the graveyard. Similarly, if I have a Black Knight (which has Protection from White) with Giant Strength, which is a red enchantment, on it, and Selene casts Sleight of Mind to change my Knight to "Protection from Red" instead of "Protection from White," the enchantment's target will no longer be legal, so the enchantment will be buried. (See Protection from ‹color› on p. **B-40** for a detailed explanation of Protection.)

Other enchantments just say "Enchantment" as their spell type. These are global enchantments. They always go into play in your territory; you can't play them "on" your opponent. Global enchantments don't require a target.

*Selene says: A few global enchantments, such as Lifetap, refer to "target opponent." These are still played in your own territory, but if you are playing in a multiplayer game, you must choose at the time you cast them which opponent they will target. They then apply only to that player for the rest of the game. See p. **D-1** for a discussion of multiplayer rules.*

Unlike many other cards, enchantments never tap. Even if an enchantment is on a tapped creature, it's always "on."

Enchant world cards are treated like enchantments, except that only one enchant world may be in play at a time. If one enchant world is brought into play while another is already in play, the one already in play is buried.

Selene says: Notice that this is opposite to the way legends work. If you bring into play a second legend with the same name as one already in play, the second one is buried. If you bring a second enchant world into play (no matter what the name is), the first one is buried.

Well, now that you know nearly all there is to know about the different types of spells, it's time to revisit creatures one last time.

Creature Special Abilities

Many creatures have one of the following special abilities listed as the first thing in the text box of the creature card. Some creatures will have more than one special ability, although most have only one.

Selene says: If a creature is given the same ability more than once, the additional copies of the ability are useless. For example, a creature enchanted with two Flights doesn't fly extra high; it's treated just the same as a creature which only has flying once.

Mathias says: On the other hand, bonuses such as power/toughness enhancers do add up. So if I put two Giant Strengths on my Hurloon Minotaur, it becomes 6/7—it doesn't just stay at 4/5, as it would if only the first Giant Strength counted.

Regeneration: Some creatures have the ability to regenerate, usually with an activation cost. If such a creature takes enough damage to send it to the graveyard, you can pay the activation cost for its regeneration ability and prevent it from dying. Keep in mind that this ability doesn't allow regenerating creatures to come back from the dead; if you don't pay for the regeneration, the creature goes to the graveyard and stays there like any other creature. (Though you can't use most fast effects during the damage resolution step, you can use **damage prevention** abilities, including regeneration. For more information, see "damage prevention" in the Glossary.)

For example, Drudge Skeletons is a black 1/1 creature with the ability "💀: Regenerate." If your Skeletons take lethal damage, no matter how much, you can save them from going to the graveyard if you pay 💀. If they are killed again the same turn, you may spend another 💀 to regenerate them again. If you don't pay this cost, they go to the graveyard and stay dead.

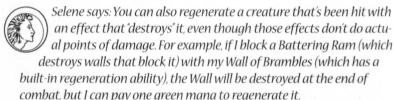

Selene says: You can also regenerate a creature that's been hit with an effect that "destroys" it, even though those effects don't do actual points of damage. For example, if I block a Battering Ram (which destroys walls that block it) with my Wall of Brambles (which has a built-in regeneration ability), the Wall will be destroyed at the end of combat, but I can pay one green mana to regenerate it.

Mathias says: Notice that a regenerated creature doesn't actually go to the graveyard, so it won't trigger any effects—good or bad—that would have been caused by it going to the graveyard.

Examples of these include Creature Bond (an enchantment that deals damage to a player when the enchanted creature goes to the graveyard), Sengir Vampire (a creature which gains a +1/+1 counter whenever something it damaged that turn goes to the graveyard), and Soul Net (an artifact which lets you pay ① to gain a life whenever a creature goes to the graveyard). None of these special effects will happen if the creature regenerates.

When a creature is regenerated, it returns to life tapped and fully healed. All of the creature's enchantments remain. Creatures killed while they are tapped can still be regenerated. But if a creature gets hit with a card that says it **buries** or **sacrifices** the creature, the creature can't regenerate and goes directly to the graveyard. You can't regenerate a creature that is **removed from the game** either; such a creature must be set aside and returned to its owner only when the game is over.

Selene says: Not only do the enchantments on a creature remain when it regenerates, but all special effects that were applied to the creature remain as well. The only thing regeneration does is allow the creature to ignore any damage it has taken so far this turn. This rule can both help you and hurt you. For example, if a fast effect gives your creature +3/+3, and then you have to regenerate it, the creature will still have the +3/+3; that's a help. But if a fast effect reduces your creature to zero toughness, and you try to save it from the graveyard by regenerating it, the creature will still have zero toughness. So it will just keep trying to go to the graveyard until you run out of mana or give up and stop regenerating it.

Mathias says: One more thing to remember—you can't regenerate something "just because." You can only regenerate something which is on its way to the graveyard. I can cast a Regeneration enchantment on one of Selene's creatures and activate it to save the creature from the graveyard if I wanted to keep the creature alive for some reason, but I couldn't activate it when the creature was healthy as a sneaky way to tap the creature.

If a creature regenerates during combat but before the damage resolution step, then it doesn't deal or receive any damage.

*Selene says: This rule makes it so you can always stop a creature from damaging you or another creature during the **damage dealing** part of the attack if you have a way to destroy it. If the creature doesn't regenerate, it goes to the graveyard—so it doesn't deal damage. And if the creature does regenerate, it's prevented from dealing damage by the rule.*

Mathias says: For example, if Selene's Drudge Skeletons (a 1/1 creature with the ability to regenerate for 🕱) is attacking me, then before the damage dealing part of the attack, I have time to use a fast effect to destroy the Skeletons. If I have a Royal Assassin, which can destroy any tapped creature as a fast effect, then I can use my Assassin on the Skeletons now, since it's attacking and thus is tapped.

Since the Skeletons has just been hit by an effect that is trying to destroy it, a damage prevention step occurs (this is not the normal damage prevention step of the attack). During this particular damage prevention step, Selene must decide whether or not to regenerate her Skeletons. If she doesn't, then the Skeletons will be sent to the graveyard at the end of this specific damage prevention step and before the damage dealing part of the combat; thus, the Skeletons will not be able to deal damage in combat. If Selene does regenerate the Skeletons, then, by the previous rule, the Skeletons will be removed from combat and will not be able to deal or receive damage during the damage dealing part of the attack.

Selene says: *If my Skeletons had had a Venom on it, an enchantment which causes all non-wall creatures blocking the enchanted creature to be destroyed at the end of combat, and Mathias had been silly enough to block the Skeletons with his Royal Assassin before destroying it with the Assassin's special ability, then the Assassin would be destroyed at the end of combat even though the Skeletons was destroyed and dealt no damage in combat.*

Mathias says: *That's right; in fact, since the creature is not removed from the attack, any special effects caused by its attacking or blocking will still happen—even if those effects include damaging some target.*

First Strike: During the attack, a creature with first strike deals all its damage before receiving any. If it deals enough damage to destroy the opposing creature, it doesn't take any damage since the other creature dies before getting a chance to strike. For example, if a White Knight (2/2, first strike) blocked a normal 4/1 creature, the 4/1 creature would take 2 damage and die before it was able to deal its 4 damage to the Knight. First strike isn't a guarantee of survival, though; if the Knight tried to block a Giant Spider (2/4), the Knight would still deal its 2 damage first, but that wouldn't be enough to kill the Spider. The Spider would then get to deal its 2 points to the Knight and the Knight would die.

Mathias says: *One way to help out your creatures with first strike is to damage whatever they're fighting, or reduce its toughness, before damage dealing begins. Suppose I block one of Selene's Giant Spiders with my Black Knight (2/2, first strike). Just like the White Knight mentioned above, my Black Knight will die since it can't kill the Spider. Suppose, however, that I soften the Spider up by hitting it with a Lightning Bolt before damage dealing. After my Black Knight deals dam-*

*age to it, the Spider will be 2/4 with 5 points of damage, so it will die
before it can deal damage back to the Knight.*

If two creatures with first strike oppose each other, they deal their damage simultaneously but before anybody else. Giving a creature that already has first strike an extra first strike enchantment doesn't make it any faster.

Trample: In the sample game, we said that any "extra" damage beyond what is needed to kill a blocking creature doesn't carry through to damage the defending player. We also said that only unblocked creatures can ever damage an opponent. Trampling creatures get around both these restrictions.

If an attacking creature has **trample** ability, it can roll right over defending creatures and deliver any unabsorbed damage to the defending player. For example, if your opponent's Scryb Sprites (1/1) blocked your War Mammoth (3/3, trample), the Sprites would die and the "extra" 2 damage would carry through and hit your opponent. This damage is called trample damage.

 *Selene says: Notice that trample only matters when an attacking
creature with trample is blocked. Trample has no effect when the
creature with trample is defending or using a special ability. Also*

notice that if all the blockers of an attacking trampler are removed before damage dealing, the attacker will deal its full damage to the defending player, even though it's still considered blocked, since there is nothing to absorb any damage. So if the Sprites which had blocked the Mammoth had been killed by a Prodigal Sorcerer before damage dealing, the Mammoth would have dealt all 3 damage to the defending player. Even if the Sprites were regenerated from the Prodigal Sorcerer's hit, the Mammoth would still deal all its damage to the player, since a creature that regenerates before damage dealing can't have any damage assigned to it.

Mathias says: The damage from a trampling creature will only spill over if the creature actually takes lethal damage. Reducing or preventing the damage will reduce or prevent spillover. If the blocker has an ability or enchantment that reduces the damage it receives to zero, such as Protection (see "**Protection**") or Uncle Istvan's special ability, then there will be no damage left to spill over and the defending player won't take any damage. Similarly, if a 2/2 Ogre blocks a 3/3 War Mammoth and you use a Samite Healer to prevent one point of damage to the Ogre, then no damage will spill over to the player. Regenerating the blocker doesn't prevent the damage, though; if you regenerate a creature with trample damage on it, the extra damage will still move to the defending player.

When you're resolving damage from multiple creatures, trample damage is always assigned last. This may not make much sense to you now, but it'll be important later.

Flying: Only creatures with flying can block other creatures with flying. If you attack your opponent with a creature that can fly, and none of her creatures can fly, your creature gets through unblocked no matter how many nasty creatures she has. Even better, any untapped flier you have can still block her non-fliers when it's their turn to attack.

Selene says: Flying is called an "**evasion ability**" or "**stealth ability**," since it allows a creature to evade or sneak past blockers. Two important points to remember: a flying creature can block either a flier or a non-flier, and a flying creature can't be blocked by a non-flier, even if its controller would like it to be. You can't "turn off" an evasion ability. Thus, you can't choose to make a flier a non-flier, now blockable by your opponent's non-fliers.

Landwalk: Some creatures have a special stealth ability that is commonly called landwalk, although the cards don't actually say "landwalk." Instead, they say "swampwalk," "forestwalk," "islandwalk," or the like. Creatures with a particular landwalk can't be blocked if the opponent has a land of that type in play.

For example, Shanodin Dryads are 1/1 forestwalking creatures. If you have Dryads in play, your opponent has a forest in play, and you decide to attack with your Dryads, your opponent can't block them. Even if your opponent has Dryads or other forestwalkers in play, they can't block your Dryads either.

> *Mathias says: That last bit confuses some players. If a flier can block another flier, then why can't a forestwalker block another forestwalker? The real answer is "because the rules say so." But if you want a "story" explanation, think of it this way: being able to sneak through the forest or ooze through the muck of a swamp doesn't make it any easier for you to see or catch someone else who is also sneaking through the trees or oozing along.*

Banding: Creatures with the ability "banding" may choose to join forces with other creatures during an attack or defense.

You can form a band of attacking creatures out of any number of creatures that have banding; you can even include one creature that doesn't have banding. You must declare which creatures you want to band when you declare your attack; attacking bands can't form or disband after your opponent declares defense. When your banded group of creatures attacks, your opponent's creatures have to block this band as one or let it through as one. If a defending creature blocks any of the banded creatures, then it blocks them all. Any damage this defending creature deals gets distributed among the creatures in your attacking band as you desire. Banding doesn't allow creatures in a band to "share" other special abilities.

Did you catch all that? Here's a quiz to find out: You have a Benalish Hero (1/1, banding), a Mesa Pegasus (1/1, flying, banding), and a War Mammoth (3/3, trample). You want to attack with these three creatures. Can you band them? For your answer, read the first sentence in the above paragraph. You can form an attacking band out of any number of banders plus up to one non-bander. So the Hero, Pegasus, and Mammoth can band to attack.

Quiz, part two: Can a creature without flying block this band? For your answer, remember that banding doesn't allow creatures to "share" other special abilities. The Pegasus still flies, but the Hero and the Mammoth can't. Also, if one of them is blocked, then the whole band is blocked. So a non-flier could block the Hero or the Mammoth and thereby block this band.

Quiz, part three: Would the band trample? No, since banding creatures don't "share" special abilities. The Mammoth, however, would still trample.

Quiz, part four: If your opponent blocks the band with a 2/2 creature, how much trample damage gets through? Now's the time to dig out that sentence about trampling, the one that didn't make sense earlier. Trample damage is always assigned last. So if the Hero/Pegasus/Mammoth band gets blocked by a 2/2 creature, the damage from the Hero and the Pegasus kills the defending creature and all 3 points of the Mammoth's trample damage carry over to your opponent.

Quiz, part five: If that 2/2 creature blocks your band as described above, how many of your creatures die? The answer is up to you; since you're the band's controller, you get to assign the damage among all the creatures in the band. You probably want to assign both points of damage to the Mammoth; that way, all of your creatures survive.

Quiz, part six: If your opponent blocks the band with a 4/4 creature instead, how many of your creatures die? Again, the answer is up to you. Most likely, you'll want to assign all 4 points to the Hero, keeping the Pegasus and Mammoth alive. Yes, you can do that; when we say you can distribute the damage however you like, we really do mean however you like, so long as all the damage ends up hitting one or more of the creatures in your band.

Selene says: Quiz, part seven: What's the airspeed velocity of an unladen Scryb Sprite? Oops, sorry—got a bit carried away with the quizzes there. But seriously, banding has always been the most misunderstood of all the special creature abilities; that's why they put so many questions and answers here. Remember that all of these apply to ‹attacking› bands. Defending bands follow a different set of rules, described next; don't try to apply any of the above examples to a defending band!

Banding works a little differently when you're defending. In the sample game, Keisha blocked Brett's Minotaur with two Bears. Brett then got to decide how the Minotaur's damage would be distributed between the Bears. If one of the Bears had had banding, however, Keisha would have gotten to distribute the damage.

If even one creature in a defending group has banding, then the controller of the group gets to decide how the attacker's damage gets distributed. For example, you can block one really big attacker with four creatures. If even one of your defenders has banding, you get to decide how the attacking creature's damage gets assigned. Remember, though, that only creatures that could legally block the attacking creature on their own can band together to block the attacker.

Mathias says: Read that last sentence two or three times. Only creatures that can legally block the attacking creature on their own can band together to block the attacker. This is very important. Defensive banding has no bearing on which blocks are or aren't legal; every blocker must block as an individual, just as if none of them had banding. Defensive banding only affects the damage distribution. So, for example, if I attack with a flying creature like a Sengir Vampire, Selene can't block it with a Sea Serpent. It doesn't matter how many flying banding creatures like the Mesa Pegasus Selene may have; banding doesn't let creatures share abilities, so they can't "help" the Sea Serpent, a non-flier, to block the Vampire, a flier. The Pegasi can block the Vampire, but the Sea Serpent can't fly and so can't join them to block it. Selene could block with a whole bunch of non-banding fliers like Scryb Sprites and one Mesa Pegasus, though, and assign all of the damage to one Sprite.

Selene says: Because defensive banding doesn't matter until damage dealing, it's possible to change who is going to assign damage to a group of blockers by giving something banding after defense is chosen, or by killing something with banding before damage dealing. Suppose Mathias attacks with a Sengir Vampire which has already grown to 6/6 from killing things. I block with a Mesa Pegasus and two Serra Angels (4/4, flying), hoping to be able to kill the Vampire and spread the damage safely among my Angels so I don't lose any creatures. Mathias, however—being the sneaky sort—casts Terror on the Pegasus before damage dealing, burying it. The two Angels are no longer a band, so Mathias now gets to assign the damage and will undoubtedly put all six points onto one Angel. If I had a Helm of Chatzuk in play, though, this strategy wouldn't work, since I could use the Helm's special effect to give the banding ability to one of the Angels after the Pegasus died.

This damage-sharing ability only applies to damage taken in combat. Other damage, like that from Lightning Bolts, still hits only the creature it targets.

Mathias says: If I had a Prodigal Sorcerer in play, I could use it instead of the Terror in that example to kill the Pegasus. Selene couldn't assign the damage from the Sorcerer to an Angel, because banding defensively only affects combat damage.

Selene says: One more thing to keep in mind for damage distribution—remember the rule that said if a creature regenerates during combat but before the damage resolution step, then it doesn't deal or receive any damage? This applies to banded creatures as well;

the regenerated creature is still part of the band, but you aren't allowed to assign any damage to it. You have to split the damage among creatures that didn't regenerate. If all of the blockers regenerated, then the damage can't be assigned to any of them and it just goes away—unless, of course, it was from an attacking creature with trample, in which case it spills over to the defending player.

Protection: Creatures with "protection from" a particular color are mostly invisible to cards of that color. For an example, we'll use the color blue, but protection works the same way if the creature has protection from any other color.

A creature with protection from *blue* has the following abilities:

- It can't be blocked by *blue* creatures.
- Any damage it takes from a *blue* **source** is reduced to 0.
- No *blue* spells or effects can specifically target it. Any *blue* spells or effects that don't target that creature in particular can still affect it, but if they deal any damage, that damage is reduced to 0.
- No *blue* enchantments can be played on the creature. Any *blue* enchantments already on the creature are destroyed when it gets protection from *blue*.

Mathias says: If I power up a Pestilence, Selene's White Knights (which have protection from black) will be fine. The effect of Pestilence is non-targeted, so the damage will reach the Knights, but the damage will be reduced to 0 by their protection. On the other hand, if Selene plays Wrath of God (a white spell which buries all creatures in play), my Black Knights (which have protection from white) will be buried along with everything else, since the effect is non-targeted and doesn't deal any damage, and protection doesn't save the creature from being put in the graveyard through means other than damage. Remember that protection is not complete invulnerability, and you should have no problems.

Selene says: If you attack and band a non-protected creature with a creature that has protection from some color, your opponent can block the non-protected creature with something of that protection color, and the blocker will indirectly block the protected creature. That's the only way a Black Knight and White Knight can ever fight each other. If that happens, you can assign all of the the damage to the protected creature, which will reduce the damage to zero.

"Inflatable" Creatures: Some creatures have an activation cost that lets you increase their power and/or toughness. For example, the Frozen Shade (0/1) has the following special ability: "💀: +1/+1 until end of turn." This means that for every 💀 you spend, the Shade gets +1/+1, but this bonus wears off at the end of the turn. You can spend as much black mana as you like to increase the Shade's power and toughness each turn. Some players call these creatures "inflatable" because you can pump them up. This ability can be used even when the creature is tapped.

> *Mathias says: Keep in mind that you can activate a special ability any time that fast effects are legal, including in the middle of an attack. It's usually best to wait until after blocking is declared to pump up creatures, because you can put the mana where it will do the most good. For example, if I have two Frozen Shades, I'll attack with both of them but not inflate them yet. If Selene blocks one of them with a small creature, I can pump just enough mana into it to kill the blocker, and put the rest of my mana into the unblocked one to do as much damage to Selene as I can.*

Rampage: After defense is chosen but before damage is assigned, an attacking creature with "Rampage: *" gets +*/+* until the end of the turn for each creature beyond the first assigned to block it. The * varies but is defined on the rampaging creature's card.

> *Selene says: The rampaging creature gains its bonus as soon as the block is declared, and it keeps the bonus for the rest of the turn, no matter what happens to the blockers. Rampage is another ability that you won't find on any of the cards in the basic **Magic: The Gathering** set; it's included here because some of the cards from expansion sets use it. Rampage is very effective against a player who likes to use a lot of small creatures for blocking. It's impossible to kill a rampaging attacker with 1/1 blockers, no matter how many you have, because the more blockers you assign, the bigger the attacker gets. Like trample, rampage only works when the creature is attacking, not when it's blocking.*

A Final Note: Some enchantments and instants in **Magic** can convey one of these creature special abilities to a creature that doesn't naturally have it. If you've got a creature with that kind of enchantment on it, just pretend like the text for that special ability appears in the text box of the creature card—at least until the enchantment is removed.

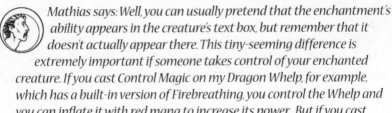

Mathias says: Well, you can usually pretend that the enchantment's ability appears in the creature's text box, but remember that it doesn't actually appear there. This tiny-seeming difference is extremely important if someone takes control of your enchanted creature. If you cast Control Magic on my Dragon Whelp, for example, which has a built-in version of Firebreathing, you control the Whelp and you can inflate it with red mana to increase its power. But if you cast Control Magic on a creature that I've enchanted with a Firebreathing spell, the inflating ability is part of the enchantment, not part of the creature, and I still control the enchantment; you can't pump mana into my enchantment.

You're well on your way to becoming a master wizard now! Let's take a more detailed look at the turn sequence, and then we'll see how Brett and Keisha are getting along.

More on the Turn Sequence

We outlined the phases of a turn earlier; now it's time to examine each of them a little more closely.

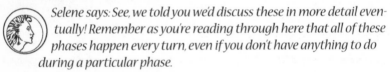

Selene says: See, we told you we'd discuss these in more detail eventually! Remember as you're reading through here that all of these phases happen every turn, even if you don't have anything to do during a particular phase.

Untap: At the beginning of your turn, all of your cards untap simultaneously. You may not "forget" to untap any of your cards. Neither you nor your opponent may use spells or fast effects during untap.

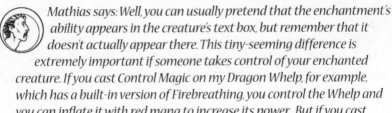

Mathias says: Notice that everything untaps simultaneously, so you don't get to untap any particular card "before" or "after" another card. If any choices have to be made about whether or not to untap something, all such choices are made before anything untaps. Suppose I have a Winter Orb in play, an artifact which would keep me from untapping more than one land during untap, but it's been tapped somehow before my turn begins, so it's deactivated. When I go to decide what will and won't untap, my lands will see that the Orb is tapped, and therefore that it's okay for them to untap. My lands and the Orb (and everything else) will untap all at once, and then my upkeep phase will begin.

Selene says: Some cards say that they don't untap during the untap phase or that they prevent another card from untapping; these cards override the rule about untapping everything. (Remember, if a card contradicts the rules, then the card takes precedence.) Some of these, like the Winter Orb that Mathias just mentioned, only prevent things from untapping; others prevent normal untapping but provide a way that you can untap the card by paying a cost. For example, Paralyze is an enchantment that prevents a target creature from untapping during the untap phase, but it allows the creature's controller to untap it during the upkeep phase by paying 4. In either case, restrictions on untapping in the untap phase do not prevent the card from being untapped later by some other effect, such as by Instill Energy or Twiddle.

Upkeep: Cards that require action during your upkeep phase tell you specifically what you need to do. Any player may use fast effects during upkeep.

*Mathias says: If there are several cards in play that all say to do something during your upkeep phase, you get to choose which order to do them in. If a permanent has an **upkeep cost**, you can't activate any special abilities that it may have until you've paid that cost. If it has abilities that are always on, however, then they continue to work all of the time, even before the upkeep cost is paid.*

Draw: Draw the top card from your library. If you have no more cards left in your library, you lose the duel. Either player may use fast effects during draw.

Selene says: You only lose if you have to draw a card and can't; you don't lose as soon as your library becomes empty. This makes a big difference if the last card in your library is the one you need to defeat your opponent. You can use fast effects both before and after drawing, and as in the upkeep phase, if there are several cards in play that say to do something during your draw phase, you get to choose which order to do them in.

Main: During your main phase, you can, in any order:

- Play one land
- Launch one attack
- Play any number of spells

The main phase is the only time you can cast sorceries or any of the permanent spells: artifacts, creatures, or enchantments. You may not cast any of these spells during your attack. Any player may use fast effects during the main phase.

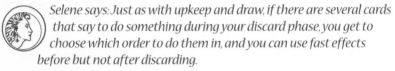 *Mathias says: Note that you can cast spells either before, after, or both before and after the attack; that you can cast spells before and after playing a land; and that you can play a land either before or after the attack (but not both, because you can only play one land per turn). You may find it helpful to always play the land first, though; sometimes when I wait to play a land later, I get so caught up in what I'm doing that I forget to play it at all.*

Discard: If you have more than seven cards in your hand, you must discard down to seven. You may not discard if you have seven or fewer cards in your hand. Any player may use fast effects during discard.

Selene says: Just as with upkeep and draw, if there are several cards that say to do something during your discard phase, you get to choose which order to do them in, and you can use fast effects before but not after discarding.

End: You tell your opponent you're done. Your opponent may respond to this declaration with fast effects, to which you can respond with fast effects of your own. All of these fast effects happen during your turn.

Mathias says: Anything that a card says happens "at end of turn" happens at the very end of the end phase, after both players have said they don't want to use any more fast effects. As with the other phases, if there's more than one such effect happening during your turn, you get to choose the order, but unlike the other phases, you can't use other fast effects in between these automatic effects. If any of the automatic effects cause damage or destruction, you do get the opportunity to use damage prevention/redirection and regeneration as usual, though.

Heal creatures and clear temporary effects: All surviving creatures—both yours and your opponent's—heal back up to full strength. Effects that last "until end of turn" wear off. This phase is instantaneous, so neither player can cast fast effects.

Selene says: All of the "until end of turn" effects wear off simultaneously with each other and with damage, so a creature which is only alive at end of turn due to Giant Growth, for example, won't find its toughness dropping just before the damage goes away. Since they happen in two different phases, this means that "until end of turn" lasts just slightly longer than "at end of turn."

Now let's get back to Brett and Keisha.

Sample Game, Continued

Brett has no creatures left; Keisha has one Grizzly Bears (2/2). It is Brett's turn.

Brett untaps his mountain, his forest, and his swamp and draws a card. He lays down another mountain and taps it. He then taps the swamp and the mountain with the Wild Growth and uses the mana to summon a Dragon Whelp, a 2/3 creature with a casting cost of 2 🔴🔴. The Dragon Whelp has the following special abilities listed: "Flying. 🔴: +1/+1 until end of turn. If you spend more than 🔴🔴🔴 in this way during one turn, destroy Dragon Whelp at end of turn." So Brett has an inflatable flier.

Next, Brett taps his forest to cast Wooden Sphere, an artifact with a casting cost of 1. Using Wooden Sphere, Brett can pay 1 and gain 1 life each time he or Keisha successfully casts a green spell. Brett has no more spells to cast, so he tells Keisha he's done.

Keisha untaps and draws. She lays down another swamp, then taps both swamps and uses the mana to cast Deathgrip. Deathgrip is a global enchantment with a casting cost of 💀💀; its ability reads, in part: "💀💀: Counter target green spell." So as long as Keisha has the black mana to spend, she'll be able to counter Brett's green spells. Keisha's not going to let Brett use his Wooden Sphere if she can possibly avoid it!

First, though, Keisha's going to cast a green spell of her own. She taps both forests and her mountain and casts Wanderlust. Wanderlust is an "Enchant Creature" that costs 2 🌲. It deals 1 damage to the target creature's controller during his or her upkeep phase. This is one of those nasty creature enchantments, so she plays it on Brett's creature, the Dragon Whelp. In response to Keisha's spell, Brett taps his last mountain to activate his Wooden Sphere. He gains 1 life, which puts him back up to 19. Keisha has no more spells to cast. She could attack with her Grizzly Bears, but Brett's Dragon Whelp would make short work of them. So she tells Brett she's done.

Brett untaps. During his upkeep phase, he takes 1 damage from the Wanderlust spell. Ouch! Brett is at 18 life. He draws a card, then looks at Keisha's territory. He wants to cast a green spell, but he's worried about that Deathgrip enchantment. Since Keisha doesn't have any black mana she can use to pay the activation cost, Brett can cast a green spell safely, for now. He taps a forest and summons Shanodin Dryads, a 1/1 creature with a casting cost of 🌲. The Dryads, as we mentioned earlier, have forestwalk. Brett then taps his swamp to activate his Wooden Sphere and gain 1 life. He's back up to 19.

Next, Brett declares his attack and taps his Dragon Whelp. The only creature Keisha has on her side is the Bears, and they couldn't block the Whelp if they wanted to, because the Whelp flies and they don't. So the Whelp will get through and deal its damage. Before it actually deals its damage, though, Brett taps two mountains to "pump up" the Whelp to 4/3. He has one more mountain, but that one has a Wild Growth enchantment on it and would give him an extra green mana that he can't use. This would be bad, since unspent mana damages its controller; see "mana pool" in the Glossary for more on **mana burn**. The Whelp deals 4 damage to Keisha, bringing her down to 9 life. Brett has nothing more to do, so he tells Keisha he's done.

Keisha untaps. She's got a plan for her defense, but that Dragon Whelp is going to be trouble!

Time to Play

Now you know enough to take your cards and play a few trial games of **Magic**. Don't worry if you don't remember every single detail; within a week this stuff will all seem pretty basic. Take your time and consult this rulebook when you get stuck. After you've played a couple of games, come back to this book and read the final sections.

Good luck!

Timing

Usually, figuring out what happens first in **Magic** is pretty easy. Sometimes, though, both players want to use contradictory effects at the same time; you may have seen this happen in your trial games. **Magic** has timing rules that should cover most of these situations. These timing rules are a little difficult to understand if you haven't played at least a couple of games, though, so go ahead and try a few if you haven't done so already.

> Mathias says: Two general comments on what follows—first, all of the fast effect rules apply equally to spells and to non-spell effects. So whenever you see "cast," it applies equally to activating an effect. Second, playing a land is not casting a spell, and doesn't follow the spell rules. You can't "respond to" someone playing a land, and you can't play a land as a response to your opponent's actions or during the casting of a spell.

Generally, if both players want to do something at the same time, the player whose turn it is gets to go first. Every time you take an action, you must give your opponent the opportunity to respond with fast effects. Although we don't specifically mention this "response" step in the examples in this rulebook, don't take that to mean that it's okay to skip it. Most of the time, your opponent won't respond to every single action you take, but you've got to give her the opportunity. If you proceed to your next action without pausing, you have to "back up" if your opponent requests it.

Selene says: It's a good idea to get in the habit of asking, "Any reactions?" after announcing each spell or effect. That way, you won't ever have any disagreement about whether or not you gave your opponent the opportunity to respond. Similarly, make sure that you announce the end of each phase and get a nod or some acknowledgement from your opponent before going on to the next one and that you don't begin tapping creatures for an attack before your opponent has passed on the opportunity to cast pre-attack fast effects. If you play with the same people all the time, you may decide to dispense with this, but when playing an unfamiliar opponent or playing in a tournament setting, you can save yourself a lot of trouble.

To further complicate matters, you can respond to your opponent's response with fast effects of your own. Then she can respond to your response to her response, and so on until you're both done or you both run out of mana. But how do you figure out what happens in the end?

Resolving Existing Effects

Before you get too excited about resolving all kinds of fast responses, you need to resolve existing effects. This includes the continuous effects of permanents in play—the ones that are always "on" and have no activation cost—and the results of previous effects that have already been resolved. That way, you'll know what kind of "initial state" you're starting with when it comes time to resolve the fast stuff. Normally, this isn't a problem—but what happens if you cast an enchantment that changes one of your opponent's lands into an island, and on the next turn your opponent casts an enchantment on the land to turn it into a mountain, and then on the next turn you cast another enchantment on the land to turn it back into an island? None of these enchantments were countered or removed, so they're all sitting there on top of the land. Obviously, the land can't be both an island and a mountain at the same time!

Whenever you have multiple existing effects in play, apply them in the order that they occurred. So your first enchantment would change the land into an island. The next turn, when your opponent casts her enchantment, the land would turn into a mountain. Later, when you cast your second enchantment, it would turn into an island again. Even though the first two enchantments end up being irrelevant, they remain on the land. After all, there are ways to turn your opponent's enchantments against her, and you wouldn't want to miss the opportunity to do this to her, would you?

Mathias says: The order that the spells were cast can sometimes make a difference even for permanents that aren't placed on top of the same card. For example, consider Conversion, which turns all mountains into basic plains, and Phantasmal Terrain, which turns the land it enchants into a basic land of the caster's choice. If you have an island that's been turned into a mountain with Phantasmal Terrain, and someone casts Conversion, then the phantasmal mountain will be turned into a plains. But if the Conversion was cast first, and then the Phantasmal Terrain was cast later, it stays a mountain. But remember that a mountain brought into play after the Conversion is in play becomes a plain immediately; it would require an effect cast after the Phantasmal Terrain to make it a mountain again.

Resolving Fast Effects

Now that we've got existing effects out of the way, here comes the fun part: resolving all those fast effects. First, let's talk about interrupts.

Interrupts always happen "faster-than-instantly" and are the only type of effect that can truly **counter** another effect, though not all of them do. Interrupts are resolved immediately after they are cast, unless they themselves are interrupted. If one interrupt interrupts another interrupt, the second interrupt is resolved first; that way, it can truly interrupt the first one. If both players attempt to interrupt the same spell or effect—yes, you can interrupt your own spells—then any interrupts cast by the controller of the original spell or effect are resolved first.

*Selene says: Even if you read that paragraph carefully, you are probably still confused. The full rules on timing of interrupts can get rather complex when both players are interrupting each other's spells; see the Timing article which begins on p. **B-95**. In brief, interrupts are resolved immediately after they are cast unless they themselves are interrupted OR the caster of the original spell intervenes by interrupting his or her own spell.*

Got that? Now let's look at other fast effects.

You can cast non-interrupt fast effects in response to any action, including other non-interrupt fast effects. The only exception is that you can't cast a non-interrupt fast effect in response to an interrupt; the interrupt is by definition faster. A "**batch**" of non-interrupt fast effects—responses to responses to responses—is resolved last to first. This rule is often stated as "last in, first out," abbreviated LIFO. The single exception to the LIFO rule for non-interrupt fast effects is effects that deal damage; damage is always resolved last.

Mathias says: One question we've seen many times is whether you can ruin your opponent's spell by casting Mana Short (an instant which taps lands and drains the mana pool) at just the right time. The answer is: you can't. Since you can't cast a non-interrupt in response to an interrupt, and tapping a land for mana is always an interrupt, you can't wait for your opponent to tap a bunch of land and then cast Mana Short right before she casts her spell. Also, if your opponent casts a permanent such as an enchantment, you can't respond to that with a fast effect that targets the permanent, since the permanent isn't created until the spell resolves. So if I play Immolation on one of Selene's creatures, Selene can't cast Disenchant on the Immolation until after that whole batch of effects has resolved and creatures are checked for lethal damage. If the Immolation drops the creature's toughness to 0, it will die before Selene ever gets a chance to play the Disenchant—and since Disenchant isn't a damage prevention spell, Selene can't cast it as the creatue is going to the graveyard, either.

Selene says: The player whose turn it is has a real advantage with this sort of thing—if both players want to cast a spell at the same time, the one whose turn it is always gets to go first, even if her spell is an enchantment and the other player's spell is a fast effect. For example, I can summon a creature and then cast a Red Ward on it without ever giving Mathias a chance to kill it with a Lightning Bolt. The Lightning Bolt is an instant which targets a creature, so Mathias can't cast it until after my creature comes into play. Once my creature comes into play, I want to cast my Red Ward at the same time as Mathias wants to cast his Lightning Bolt, and since it's my turn I get to cast my spell first. If Mathias responds by casting the Lightning Bolt anyway, the spells form a "batch" and resolve in last-to-first order, with all damage assignment taking place at the very end of the batch. So the Lightning Bolt resolves first, but doesn't do any damage yet; then the Red Ward resolves, giving my creature Protection from Red; and then finally the damage resolves, but the Ward reduces it to zero.

Keep the following guidelines in mind when resolving fast effects:

- Don't resolve damage or decide whether or not a creature is dead until all fast effects have been resolved. Premature burial is a very messy situation.

Mathias says: Note that "don't check whether it's dead" includes checking a creature whose toughness is lowered due to an effect. Even if a creature's toughness drops to zero or less during a batch, it doesn't die until the end of the batch. It is possible for a creature to survive an effect which lowers its toughness below zero if another effect in the same batch raises its toughness again.

Selene says: If an effect "destroys" or "buries" a creature, however, then the creature heads for the graveyard immediately when the effect resolves, and everything else goes on hold for a moment while you deal with regeneration and/or death effects. Checking for damage and toughness are the only things that wait until the end of the batch. Normally, you can't begin any new spells or effects until the entire batch has finished resolving, but things that happen when a creature goes (or tries to go) to the graveyard are an exception to every can't-cast-spells-now rule.

- Remember that destroying the **source** of an effect doesn't prevent the effect itself from happening. Once a grenade has been lobbed, it does no good to shoot the creature that threw it. The only way to actually counter an effect is with an interrupt.

*Mathias says: Even destroying the source with an interrupt, as the effect is being used, won't stop the effect. If I use my Brothers of Fire's ability to deal a point of damage to a creature, Selene can't stop that by Blue Elemental Blasting the Brothers, since its effect has already been paid for. To stop the effect, Selene would have to use something which counters abilities. (Don't bother looking through your cards for this, though—nothing in the basic **Magic: The Gathering** set can counter a non-spell effect.)*

- Removing or altering the **target** of an effect, on the other hand, can sometimes prevent the effect. If the target of an effect disappears or becomes invalid before the effect is resolved, that effect fizzles; you can't choose a different target once the effect is cast.

Selene says: If I save the targeted creature in Mathias's example by casting an Unsummon (an instant which returns a creature to its owner's hand) in response to Mathias's activating the Brothers of

Fire, the Brothers' effect will fizzle (because the creature it was targeting is already gone). Spells which fizzle are still considered successfully cast, by the way; the grenade still explodes, even if there's nothing there for it to blow up.

An example would probably be pretty welcome about now. Let's say that you have Grizzly Bears (2/2) in play, and you want to attack with them. Your opponent has a lot of creatures to block with, but none of them fly. So you cast Jump, a blue instant that grants flying until end of turn, on the Bears. Your opponent responds to the Jump with a Red Elemental Blast (REB), a red interrupt that destroys any blue spell being cast. You respond to the REB with a Blue Elemental Blast (BEB), a blue interrupt that destroys any red spell being cast. Your opponent responds by casting Terror, a black instant that buries any creature, on the Bears. You respond to the Terror by casting Unsummon, a blue instant that allows you to take a creature back into your hand, on those poor, beleaguered Bears. You'd both love to go on like this forever, but for now you're out of mana. It's time to resolve this stuff.

As interrupts, the REB and BEB resolve first. The REB tries to interrupt and destroy the Jump, but the BEB interrupts and destroys the REB before it can do its job. This means the Jump sticks around and prepares to get those Bears airborne. It has to wait its turn, however, as we resolve the other fast effects under LIFO.

The last in was the Unsummon spell, so it resolves first and returns the Bears to your hand. Next comes the Terror. Since the Bears aren't around anymore, the spell fizzles and goes to the graveyard. Your opponent can't choose a new target for it; the target must be announced at the time the spell is cast. Finally, the Jump is cast at the Bears. Without a target, this spell also fizzles.

Mathias says: Note that in the above example, the Red and Blue Elemental Blasts both resolve before Terror is cast. Also, the Terror was actually cast in response to the Jump, once your opponent determined that the Jump had made it through the interrupts without being countered, since instants can't be cast in response to interrupts. This doesn't make any difference in the end results, and when you're playing, you'll usually just call out spells without worrying about exactly what is responding to what. But on rare occasions, these types of details will be very important. See the Timing article, starting on p. B-95, for more details.

Remember that if any of these fast effects had dealt any damage, those effects would be resolved last in the chain, regardless of when they were cast.

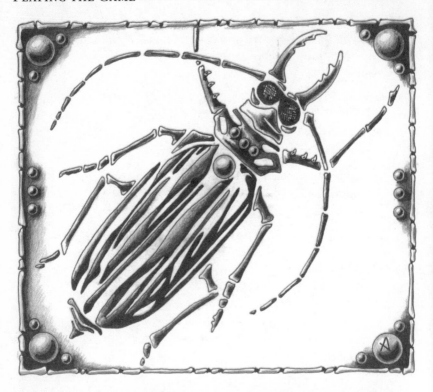

Selene says: Well, that's not exactly true. The effect resolves at its normal time in the chain; it's only the damage from the effect that waits until the end. This usually doesn't make a difference, but a few spells do several things at the same time and have both damage and non-damage parts to their effects.

Mathias says: I had promised that, before leaving the timing section, we'd talk about tapping. As we said before, if you have a permanent with a ability and someone casts a spell to tap that card, they don't get to use the special ability or to force you to use the ability—the ability is only powered when you specifically tap the card to pay for the ability. But if you want to use the ability, you can! Your opponent's spell (if it isn't an interrupt) can't resolve until you have the chance to respond with as many fast effects as you want, so your permanent won't be tapped yet. Using the ability of a permanent is a fast effect, so you can respond to your opponent's spell by activating this ability, tapping the card yourself to pay the cost. When the effects finally resolve in last-to-first order, your opponent's spell will just be trying to tap an *already-tapped card, which doesn't do anything. (No, it won't untap it again, even if the spell was Twiddle; when you cast Twiddle, you announce whether you're tapping or untapping, and you can't change it later even if you want to.) If your opponent's spell was an interrupt, then you wouldn't be able to respond by using a non-interrupt fast effect like the ⟲ effect, but you could still interrupt it.*

Another Sample Game

Our first sample game was pretty simple. Let's try a more complicated one that incorporates all the rules you've learned. We've cut down quite a bit on the explanations, so take this opportunity to quiz yourself and see if you can follow what's going on. If you need to, look through the earlier sections of the rulebook.

Andre and Sara shuffle their decks and cut each other's deck. Each turns over the top card as ante; the ante is set aside. Both draw seven cards, and they play scissors-paper-stone to see who goes first.

Andre gets to go first, so he draws a card and lays out a plains. He taps the plains to cast a Benalish Hero, a 1/1 creature with banding that has a casting cost of ✹. He tells Sara he's done.

Sara draws a card and lays out a forest. She taps the forest to cast Scryb Sprites, a 1/1 creature with flying that has a casting cost of ♣. She tells Andre she's done.

Andre untaps, draws, and lays out another plains. He taps both plains to cast a White Knight, a 2/2 creature with first strike and protection from black. The White Knight has a casting cost of ✹✹. Andre decides not to attack with his Hero, since Sara's Sprites could block and kill it. He tells Sara he's done.

Sara untaps, draws, and lays out a swamp. She taps the swamp and her forest to cast Drudge Skeletons, a 1/1 creature with a casting cost of ① ☠. They have a special ability that reads: "☠: Regenerate." Sara then announces that she's attacking with the Sprites. Andre has no creatures with flying, so he can't block the Sprites. The Sprites deal their 1 damage, bringing Andre down to 19 life. Sara tells Andre she's done.

Andre untaps, draws, and lays out a mountain. He taps the mountain and both plains to cast a Gray Ogre, a 2/2 creature with a casting cost of ② ❂. He then announces that he's attacking with the Benalish Hero and the White Knight. He could band them if he wanted, since the Hero has banding, but he decides not to. Why?

Well, let's see what happens. Since the Knight has protection from black, the Skeletons can't block it. They could block the Hero, but they would take lethal damage. Since Sara has no black mana available to regenerate them, they would be destroyed. Because of this, Sara decides to block neither creature. If Andre had banded the Hero and the Knight, the Skeleton could have blocked the entire band and Andre's creatures wouldn't have dealt any damage to Sara, although her Skeletons would have been killed. As it is, though, Sara takes 3 damage, bringing her down to 17 life. Andre tells Sara he's done.

Sara untaps, draws, and lays out a swamp. She taps the swamp to cast Dark Ritual, a black interrupt that provides three black mana. She uses one black mana to cast another Dark Ritual, bringing her up to five black mana in her mana pool. She then taps her forest to add one green mana and casts a War Mammoth, a 3/3 trampling creature with a casting cost of 3 🌲, bringing her down to two black mana in her mana pool. She uses this last mana to cast Howling Mine, an artifact that requires both players to draw an extra card during their draw phases. Finally, Sara attacks with the Sprites again, and Andre still can't block them. He takes 1 damage and goes down to 18 life. Sara tells Andre she's done.

Andre untaps, draws two cards thanks to the Howling Mine, and lays out another mountain. He taps the mountain to cast Mons's Goblin Raiders, a 1/1 creature with a casting cost of 🔴. He then taps both plains to cast a Samite Healer, a 1/1 creature with a casting cost of 1 ✳. The Healer has the following special ability: "🌀: Prevent 1 damage to any player or creature." Next, Andre declares his attack and taps the Knight and the Hero as his attackers. This time, he announces that they are attacking as a band.

Sara decides to block with her Skeletons, because the band could kill her Mammoth. This block is legal, since the Knight can't "share" its protection from black with the Hero. The Skeletons take 3 damage and deal 1 damage to the band. Andre directs this damage to the Knight, where the Knight's protection from black reduces it to 0. The Skeletons are destroyed, but Sara still has a swamp left untapped. She taps it now to regenerate the Skeletons; the Skeletons return to life tapped and fully healed.

Andre isn't done yet, though. He taps his remaining mountain to cast a Lightning Bolt, an instant with a casting cost of 🔴. The Lightning Bolt deals 3 damage to any target, and Andre aims it at Sara's Skeletons. The unlucky Skeletons are destroyed yet again. Sara could still regenerate them if she had the mana, but all her swamps are tapped, so the Skeletons go to the graveyard. Andre tells Sara he's done, and Sara tells Andre he's going to regret being so mean to her Skeletons.

Sara untaps, draws two cards, and lays out another forest. She taps both forests and both swamps to cast a Giant Spider, a 2/4 creature with a casting cost of ③ ♠. The Spider's special ability is that it can block creatures that fly, although it doesn't fly itself. Sara announces she's attacking with the Sprites and the Mammoth. Andre still can't block the Sprites, but he decides to block the Mammoth with the Goblins.

Since the Mammoth tramples, it will deal just enough damage to the Goblins to destroy them: 1 point. The additional 2 damage carries over to Andre. Added to the point from the Sprites, that makes 3 damage for Andre. In future turns he can use his Healer to prevent a point of this, but the Healer wasn't on Andre's side at the beginning of his last turn, so it still has summoning sickness. The Goblins go to the graveyard and Andre takes 3 damage, bringing him down to 15 life. Sara smiles as she tells Andre she's done. Andre begins to think he does indeed regret wasting that Lightning Bolt on her Skeletons last turn.

Andre untaps, draws two cards, and lays out an island. He then taps both of his mountains and one of his plains, bringing out the Hurloon Minotaur, a 2/3 creature with a casting cost of ① ② ②. Next he casts an Ornithopter, a 0/2 artifact creature with flying that has a casting cost of ⓪ .

Andre takes a look at all the cards in play. Right now, his Ogre, Knight, Hero, and Healer are eligible to attack. There's no point in attacking with the Healer, though; its special ability is far more valuable than the 1 damage it can deal, and if he attacks with the Healer now he won't be able to tap it again later to use its ability. Sara's Spider would be all too happy to take on any one of his other creatures, since it could kill any of them and none of them could kill it. Even if he bands the Hero with one of the 2/2 creatures, the result would be the same; the Spider would live, and one of his creatures would have to die. He could use his Healer to prevent a point of the Spider's damage, but he'd rather save the Healer for Sara's attack. So Andre decides not to attack and tells Sara he's done.

Selene says: While there's no point to Andre attacking with his Samite Healer, it will make a great blocker if Sara has any 1/1 attackers that the Healer can block. The Healer would block the attacker, and the two would deal each other 1 point of damage normally. After damage dealing, the Healer would tap to prevent the point of damage it just took, and even though it would then be tapped, this wouldn't undo the damage it had just dealt to the attacker. So the attacker would die, while the Healer would be fine. This doesn't work when he's attacking, since the Healer has to tap to attack and thus can't make use of his special ability. Also, remember that this sort of thing only works because the Healer's ability is a damage prevention ability that is used after damage is dealt. Most creatures couldn't use special abilities during combat that required tapping and still deal damage, like the Prodigal

Sorcerer, for instance. The Sorcerer's special ability allows you to tap it to deal 1 damage to any creature or player. Since this is not an interrupt or a damage prevention ability, it cannot be used during damage prevention and, thus, if you wanted to use this ability after declaring the Sorcerer as a blocker, it would have to be used before damage dealing occurs. In this case, the Sorcerer would be tapped during damage dealing and would not deal damage equal to his power during this step. Since the Sorcerer is a 1/1 creature and only deals 1 damage during damage dealing (unless it has been affected by other spells or effects), it is rarely used to block or attack; it can just as easily deal 1 damage using its special ability and avoid the perils of creature combat.

Sara untaps and draws two cards. She lays out a mountain and decides not to cast any spells for now. Instead, she announces she's attacking with the Sprites, the Spider, and the Mammoth. Andre looks at his choices for defense. If the Hero, the Knight, and the Ogre all block the Spider, they can kill it. Since the Hero has banding, Andre can split the Spider's damage between the Ogre and the Knight so all three will survive. If the Minotaur blocks the Mammoth, the Minotaur will die, but he can use his Healer to prevent 1 damage to the Minotaur and keep it alive. Finally, the Ornithopter can block the Sprites without any trouble. Andre declares this blocking scheme, hoping to kill the Spider and take no damage, all without losing any of his own creatures.

Sara has ideas of her own, however. She taps a forest and casts Giant Growth on her Spider, giving it +3/+3 for a total of 5/7; Giant Growth is an instant with a casting cost of 🌳. Next, she taps her mountain to cast a Lightning Bolt (an instant with a casting cost of 🔴) on the Ornithopter, dealing 3 damage to it. Andre responds to Sara's fast effects by tapping his island and casting Unsummon (an instant with a casting cost of 🔵) to return his Ornithopter to his hand.

Neither player wants to use any more fast effects, so the fast effects are resolved using the "last in, first out" (LIFO) rule—except for the Lightning Bolt, which deals damage and therefore gets resolved last. First, the Unsummon brings the Ornithopter back into Andre's hand. Then, the Giant Growth temporarily turns the Giant Spider into a Giant Giant Spider, so it will deal 5 damage and can absorb 7. Finally, the Lightning Bolt goes off, but since the Ornithopter isn't there anymore, the Lightning Bolt fizzles and goes into Sara's graveyard.

 Mathias says: Remember that the Lightning Bolt actually went off in its normal place in the batch (ahead of the Giant Growth); it's just that the damage isn't applied until the end of the batch.

Now that the fast effects are resolved, it's time for the damage resolution step. Andre distributes all 5 points of the Spider's damage onto the Ogre, which is destroyed and goes to his graveyard. The Mammoth deals 3 damage to the Minotaur, but Andre taps the Healer and prevents 1 damage. (The Healer's special ability is one of those **damage prevention** effects, the only non-interrupt fast effects you can use during the damage resolution step. See the Glossary for details.) The Sprites deal no damage. Although Andre took the Ornithopter back into his hand, it left combat after it had been declared as a blocker. In such a situation, the attacking creature is still blocked. The Sprites can't deal their damage to Andre, and they don't have a defending creature to battle anymore, so they don't deal any damage at all. Andre takes no damage, and Sara announces she's done.

Andre untaps and draws. He'd better get together a decent defense pretty soon, or he'll really be in danger!

House Rules

If you don't like one of the rules of the game, or if you find yourself in a situation that the rules don't seem to cover, you're welcome to come up with a "house rule." We don't mind; in fact, we encourage it. You should, however, know what the official rules are just in case you end up playing in somebody else's house. Some common house rules are:

- You don't have to play for ante if you don't want to.
- In an ante game, the winner must offer to trade the loser's card back to him or her.
- "No-Land Mulligan": If you get no land in your initial seven-card draw, you can reshuffle and draw again.
- "All-Land Mulligan": Same as the above, only with no spells.
- Everyone must follow certain rules of deck construction. These are too varied to mention any specific rules, but the general idea is to give newbies a chance against "card lords" with five of every card.
- The winner of each duel must contribute $1 to the pizza fund—great for a big group on a Friday night!

Mathias says: One of the oldest (and best) arguments for using deck construction rules is the "Lightning Strikes More Than Twice" deck, which is nothing but mountains and Lightning Bolts. While effective against many other decks, the deck is pretty boring to play, doesn't exactly challenge the skill of either player, and is easy to beat using cards such as Circle of Protection: Red.

Selene says: The most common "house rule" regarding deck construction is to simply adopt the Duelists' Convocation Type I or Type II deck construction rules, which you'll find beginning on p. E-1. Some care needs to be taken when adopting these for private play—some of the restrictions are not because cards are imbalancing but because they tend to drag games out too much for tournament play or would be useless given the Duelists' Convocation floor rules. For example, the "remove from your deck if not playing for ante" cards are only banned because Duelists' Convocation Type I and Type II tournaments aren't played for ante.

House rules can cover every aspect of the game, and then some. Just be sure that new players in your house are informed of the house rules before any duels get started.

Mathias says: Another fairly common "house rule" is to treat all cards which have changed in different editions as their latest edition version, so that someone with the earlier printings doesn't have an advantage or disadvantage over someone with a later printing of the same card. This can be a problem if you don't have all the cards memorized, though, since you can't always just read the card to find out what it does. However, in the Collectors' Information section (starting on p. F-1), you can find a complete listing of all the Fourth Edition cards and their wordings, as well as an indication if the wording change from previous editions to the Fourth Edition is important.

Selene says: And another common house rule is to allow "proxy cards"—that is, writing the name of a card on an extra land and treating that land as if it were the card written on it. Again, this can be a problem if you don't have all the cards memorized. It is, however, a good way to experiment with a new deck design before going out and trading for the cards you need.

Mathias says: Some other variants on playing for ante we've seen include preselected ante cards: the players agree beforehand on what the ante will be and select cards of equal value instead of turning over a random card from the deck; protected ante: if you ante a card you don't want to lose, you can remove it from the game but must ante two more random cards to replace it; easy tradeback: if a player loses a card from ante, the loser can demand it back in exchange for the winner's choice of one card of the next lower level of rarity. For example, if I won Selene's Counterspell (which is an uncommon) in the ante under this rule, I would give it back for one common of my choice. Finally, there's booster tradeback: if a player loses a card in ante, the loser can get it back in exchange for an unopened booster pack.

Miscellaneous

Other Rules

As the game of **Magic** has developed, so have the rules. Earlier editions of **Magic** used slightly different sets of rules, and the wordings on the cards have also changed over time as we've tried to make them as clear and easy to understand as possible without substantially altering the game. This means that before you start playing **Magic** with someone new, you need to talk about which version of the rules you're going to use and how you're going to deal with any peculiar side effects that may arise when you mix cards from different releases.

*Selene says: There's one change to the current cards that isn't really a rule at all, but is a noticeable change anyway—the tap symbol is different. Earlier versions of this symbol ⊘ have been replaced with a clearer one ⊙. Now that **Magic** appears in languages other than English, the symbol needs to be more universal—in some languages, the word "tap" doesn't begin with a "T"!*

In most cases, later editions of the rules have clarified the old rules rather than changing them, so conflicts shouldn't come up too frequently. When they do, we encourage you to talk things over with your opponent and decide for yourselves how you want to resolve them. If you and your opponent can't agree in the heat of battle, flip a coin to resolve the current situation and then talk it out afterwards. Keep track of your decisions so you can use them again if necessary.

If you think making the rules is strictly our job, we'll be happy to give you the official line on any rules question. Just check out p. G-1 for ways to contact us.

*Mathias says: This looks like the end of the rules, doesn't it? Not so fast! The "Glossary and Notes" and "Sequence of Play" sections that begin on the next page contain not only the definitions for words used in the **Magic** cards and rules, but also some of the more detailed special-case rules that were left out of this part so as not to overwhelm a new player. Take a break and go play some more games now, though; you can always look things up in the Glossary if a question comes up during play. Enjoy!*

glossary and notes

This glossary doesn't just contain definitions; it also includes extra information about many of the terms. A lot of this information was a little too technical or complex to be included in the basic rules explanation, but it's stuff you should eventually know. Terms and explanations appearing in italics are, in most cases, expanded definitions which have not appeared in previously published glossaries.

Activation cost

Many permanents have special abilities in the form of "[cost]: [effect]." Anything in front of the colon is the activation cost for that effect. For example, if a card says "⊙: Add ● to your mana pool" then the activation cost is ⊙. Some permanents have additional costs, which are paid at the same time as the activation cost but are not part of the activation cost. For example, Strip Mine says

"⚑: Sacrifice Strip Mine to destroy target land." In this case, the activation cost is still ⚑ and the sacrifice is an additional cost, paid at the same time. A few permanents have usage costs which are not activation costs; you can tell the difference because they aren't written as "[cost]: [effect]." See also Cost.

Ante

Magic, like marbles, is often played "for keeps"—at the beginning of the game, each player turns over the top card from his or her deck, and these cards become the prize for winning the game. These prize cards are called the ante. Playing for ante is usually optional.

Artifact

An artifact is a magically created device or non-living creature with magical powers. Artifact cards have either "Artifact" or "Artifact Creature" as a spell type. (Older cards may have other variants.) An artifact spell does not become an artifact until the spell is cast and resolved. If a non-creature artifact becomes tapped for any reason, it stops working; any continuous effects cease, and it may not be activated again until it becomes untapped, even if its activation cost does not have ⚑ in it. Most artifacts requiring an activation cost can be used immediately after casting.

Artifact creature

An artifact which is also a creature is called an artifact creature; this is indicated on the card by the words "Artifact Creature" on the card. It is not always necessary for an artifact to have the words "Artifact Creature" on it to make it an artifact creature; certain spells can turn a non-creature artifact into an artifact creature. Artifact creatures, though not summoned, are subject to summoning sickness just like other creatures. Unlike non-creature artifacts, if an artifact creature becomes tapped, it does not stop working; any continuous effects remain active, and effects with activation costs not involving ⚑ may still be used. Artifact creatures are affected by spells that affect either artifacts or creatures. Finally, artifacts (including artifact creatures) are always "cast," not "summoned."

Attack

The attack is one possible action you can take during your main phase. You only get one attack per turn, and you attack your opponent with your creatures. No permanent spells or sorceries may be cast during the attack. The complete attack sequence is as follows:

1. Announce your attack. This is your opponent's last chance to use pre-attack effects.
2. Declare and tap your attacking creatures.
3. Either player may use fast effects.
4. Your opponent declares blocking. Blocking doesn't make creatures tap, but tapped creatures can't block.
5. Either player may use fast effects. If a fast effect removes or taps a blocking creature at this point, the attacking creature is still blocked. A tapped blocker deals no damage but still receives damage from the attacker it blocked.
6. Assign damage. Players may use only interrupts or damage prevention fast effects; no other kinds of fast effects are allowed. See also *damage prevention*.
7. Creatures that take lethal damage and aren't regenerated go to the graveyard. Any effects that happen when a creature goes to the graveyard are triggered.
8. *Any effects that happen "at the end of combat" take place.*

Attacking creature

The term "attacking creature" applies only during the attack. An attacking creature is any creature participating in the attack on the attacking side, whether tapped or not; creatures not participating in the attack are not attacking creatures. Before the attack begins and after the attack ends there are no attacking creatures, so spells or effects which require an attacking creature as a target may not be used.

Banding

Banding is a special ability some creatures have that allows them to form a group with another creature (or other creatures) while attacking or defending and to distribute damage differently when doing either. When attacking, you can form a band of attacking creatures out of any number of creatures that have banding; you can even include one creature that doesn't have banding. You must declare which creatures you want to band when you declare your attack; attacking bands can't form or disband after your opponent declares blockers. When your banded group of creatures attacks, your opponent's creatures have to block this band as one or let it through as one. If a defending creature blocks any of the banded creatures, then it blocks them all. Any damage this defending creature deals gets distributed among the creatures in your attacking band as you desire. Banding doesn't allow creatures in a band to "share" any other special abilities. When defending, if even one creature in a defending group has banding (during damage dealing), then the controller of the defending group gets to decide how the damage from the attacker blocked by the group gets distributed among the creatures in that group.

Bands with other

This is an obsolete term found on early edition cards. Some out-of-print creatures have a specialized version of banding called "bands with other _____." Any group of two or more creatures with the same type of bands with other _____ ability can attack as a band, or can count as a single creature when determining what creatures can attack as a band. (Note, though, that creatures without that ability cannot be included, even if their type matches the type named in the ability.) Also, if two or more creatures with the same type of bands with other _____ ability block the same attacker(s), the defending player gets to assign damage just as if one blocker had real banding.

Basic land

See land.

Batch

A series of non-interrupt fast effects that build on one another as players respond to each other's spells. Batches are resolved by first-in, last-out for all effects. Any damage done to creatures or players isn't applied until the end of the batch, but creatures that are destroyed through means other than damage are sent to the graveyard immediately and regeneration and/or death effects are checked when this occurs.

Block, blocked, blocking

Creatures cannot directly attack other creatures, so a creature can only attempt to attack the opposing player. When that happens, the defending player can block with his or her own creatures. Attacking creatures that are opposed by defending creatures in this fashion are blocked and the defending creature is called a blocking creature. Once an attacking creature is blocked, it stays blocked, no matter what happens to the blocker. Casting a spell which would have made the block illegal or giving the attacking creature an evasion ability will not "unblock" it; you should do those things before the block is declared. Only creatures can block; Circles of Protection, for example, prevent damage but do not block.

Bury

A card that is buried must be sent to the graveyard without possibility of regeneration.

Card

If a spell specifies that it affects a "card," then it cannot affect creatures which are represented by tokens rather than cards. A few spells affect cards in the graveyard, the ante, your library, or your hand, but if the spell doesn't specify one of these, it can only affect cards in play.

Caster

The caster of a permanent is the player whose deck the card came from, even if the card came into play by some means other than normal casting. In other words, caster is a synonym for owner.

Casting cost

When a card refers to the casting cost of another spell, it means the total number of mana points needed to cast the spell, regardless of color. For the purposes of these cards, a spell costing 2 ♣ ♣ has a casting cost of 4. If the spell in question is an X spell not currently being cast, then X=0. Token creatures (see also *token*) have a casting cost of 0. *Note that the X=0 rule only applies before and after a spell has been successfully cast; when the spell is being cast, X equals the actual number of mana points spent. Also, a few spells have additional costs listed in the text of the card; these costs are paid at casting time, but are not part of the casting cost.*

Color

The color of a card is determined by the type of mana you need to cast it, as specified in the upper right corner of the card. If a card takes more than one color of mana to cast, it is considered all of those colors at once. If the card requires no particular color of mana or no mana at all to cast, as with artifacts and lands, then the card is colorless. The colors in **Magic** are black, blue, green, red, and white; colorless doesn't count as a color.

Any damage generated by a particular source is the same color as that source; see also **source of damage**.

Colorless mana

Colorless mana is the sixth type of mana, distinguished from the five types of colored mana. Cards that provide colorless mana indicate this through words, not symbols; whereas a card providing red mana would indicate so by the  symbol, cards providing colorless mana would indicate so by specifying the addition (for example, "Add 2 colorless mana to your mana pool"). Colorless mana may be used (along with any combination of the other types of mana) to pay costs which require mana of any type. These are the costs that are listed in the gray circles as a mana cost, such as ③. See also mana.

Concede

A player can concede the game at any time. In a two-player game, the game ends immediately and the other player wins. If a game is played for ante, the winning player collects the ante.

Continuous artifact

This is an obsolete term found on early edition cards. To play these cards under the current rules, simply change the card type from "Continuous Artifact" to "Artifact."

Continuous effect

Some permanents have effects which apply all the time. If there is no cost or condition associated with an effect listed on a card, then it is a continuous effect. Continuous effects of lands, creatures, and enchantments can only be stopped by getting rid of the card; continuous effects of non-creature artifacts stop while the artifact is tapped.

Controller

Usually, the controller of a spell is the player who cast that spell. Sometimes, though, a spell or effect can give you temporary control over your opponent's card. If you take control of a card this way, you just take control of the card itself; you don't get control of any enchantments already on the card. If a card says "you" on it, it means the card's controller; if it meant the card's owner, it would specify "owner." A card under temporary control of another player is returned to its original owner or its owner's graveyard when it leaves play, when the controlling enchantment or effect is removed, or when the game is over, whichever comes first.

Cost

The cost of a spell is the casting cost plus any other costs defined in the text of the spell. For example, Drain Life has a casting cost of 2 (1 💀), but an additional cost of 💀 for each point of damage dealt. Some spells require a sacrifice or payment of life as part of the cost. Similarly, the cost of an effect is the activation cost plus any other costs defined in the text of the effect. Some effects call for the removal of counters; this is also a cost. All costs must be paid at the time the spell or effect is announced (all targets must be chosen at this time as well; see target). This payment cannot be interrupted or otherwise interfered with.

Counter (noun)

A counter is a marker used as a reminder on certain cards. Counters can be coins, poker chips, beads, pieces of paper, or whatever you like. See also *poison counter* and *token*.

Counter (verb)

Countering a spell or effect means preventing that spell or effect from being cast. Countered spells go to the graveyard; the caster of the countered spell still has to pay the casting cost. A countered spell isn't successfully cast.

Creature

A creature is a monster or other ally called in to aid the wizard in a duel. Creatures are usually brought into play by a summon spell. Note that some spells affect creatures and others affect spells—a "summon creature" card is a spell while being cast, and it becomes a creature only after it has been successfully cast and resolved. If a creature has a power that is a continuous effect, the effect functions as long as the creature remains in play, even if the creature becomes tapped. Cards in the graveyard or in your hand are not creatures; if a spell refers to a "creature" in the graveyard or in your hand, this is shorthand for "a summon or artifact creature card." See summoning sickness, attack, power, *and* toughness.

Damage

Wounds and magically caused injuries are recorded as damage. Creatures usually do damage when they attack, and many different spells cause damage. Each point of damage done to a player results in a loss of one life unless the damage is prevented or redirected. Any time that a creature has damage equal to or exceeding its toughness, it is considered to have taken lethal damage and goes to the graveyard unless saved. Some spells and effects say to destroy, bury, remove from the game, or sacrifice a creature; these are not considered damage.

Damage dealing

During an attack, the point at which the creatures damage each other and (possibly) the defending player is called damage dealing. Before any of the creatures deal damage, players have a chance to use fast effects to destroy or neutralize them (see attack *for the full sequence of steps). Normally, each creature deals damage equal to its power. Blocking creatures only damage the creatures they blocked. Attacking creatures that were blocked only damage their blockers; if all of their blockers are gone, they just attack empty air and do no damage. Unblocked attacking creatures are the only ones that can damage a player. (See* trample *for an exception.) Any creature that regenerates during a combat before the damage dealing starts is unable to deal or receive damage during this step. For example, you block an attacking Hill Giant (a 3/3 creature) with your Clay Statue (a 3/1 creature that can regenerate for ②), and your opponent zaps the Statue with a Lightning Bolt, destroying it. You pay ② to regenerate the Statue. Since it regenerated, the Statue will not deal or receive damage in the damage dealing part of this combat. The Hill Giant doesn't get to deal damage. If the Hill*

Giant were a War Mammoth (a 3/3 creature with trample) instead, then it would deal its trample damage directly to the defending player. If a blocker is tapped— for example, because someone cast Twiddle on it, or it tapped to use a special ability—then that blocker will not deal damage to the creature it blocks in this step. The tapped blocker can still be damaged or destroyed by the creature it blocked, which still deals its damage. Attacking usually requires a creature to tap, so attacking creatures deal damage whether they are tapped or not. If a creature was somehow removed from the combat before the damage dealing step, then that creature is no longer an attacking or blocking creature, so it cannot deal or receive damage from the combat. Any spell that removes a creature from play removes it from the combat. Also, if a creature changes controllers during combat, it is removed from the combat. If there are several attacking and blocking creatures, then resolve the combats in the following order: The attacker decides which combat to resolve first and must then declare how he or she wishes to assign the damage from the attacking creature (or creatures; see banding*) in that combat. The defending player must then declare how he or she wishes to assign the damage from the blocking creatures in that combat (usually there is only one attacking creature, and thus not much choice; see* banding*). The attacker then decides which combat to resolve next and the process continues. See also* first strike.*

Damage prevention

Any time one of your creatures is damaged, you get the chance to prevent the damage, redirect it, or regenerate the creature. You can't do any of these things, however, until it's time to resolve all the damage in a chain of fast effects; see also "Resolving Fast Effects" on p. **B-48**. Damage prevention effects target the damage itself, not the source of the damage; see also *target*. During the damage resolution step, only damage prevention and interrupt effects may be used. *Damage prevention only works on "fresh" damage—that is, it only works at the time the damage is being applied.* For example, if you have a Healing Salve (which can prevent up to 3 damage to a creature or player) and one of your creatures takes a point of damage from a Prodigal Sorcerer, you must decide then and there whether to use the Salve. If you decide not to, then that point of damage can no longer be prevented; it will stay on the creature until the heal phase at the end of the turn or until the creature regenerates, whichever comes first. If the creature takes another point of damage later in the turn and you use the Healing Salve, the new damage will be prevented but the earlier point of damage will stay on the creature (see also *regeneration*). Spells like Unsummon (an instant that returns a creature to its owner's hand) and Giant Growth (an instant that gives a creature +3/+3 until the end of the turn) are not damage prevention, and so are not legal to use during a damage prevention step; they can save a creature from dying in some cases, but they have to be played as part of the chain of fast effects. If you wait until damage resolution begins, it's too late. For example, if your opponent has a Merfolk (a 1/1 creature) and you cast a Lightning Bolt to deal 3 damage to it, your opponent can cast a Giant Growth on the Merfolk—the Giant Growth will resolve first in the batch, and the Merfolk will live since the damage is always applied after all fast effects in the batch have resolved. If, however, your opponent waits until after the Lightning Bolt resolves and the damage prevention step begins to cast the Giant Growth, it will be too late, since the Giant Growth is not a damage prevention effect. Damage prevention or redirection is useless if a creature is "destroyed" by an effect, since "destroy" isn't equal to any amount of damage, but regeneration can save a destroyed creature. None of these can save a creature that is "buried." A damage prevention step happens any time that a creature is sent to the graveyard or damaged or a player is damaged. The rules about using spells and effects during damage prevention take precedence over any other rule governing what you can or can't do during a given part of the turn.

Defending (player, creature)

The defending player is the subject of an attack. On some older cards, the phrase "defending creature" appears; it is a synonym for "blocking creature."

Destroy

A permanent that is destroyed is sent to the graveyard but may be saved by regeneration or by effects that prevent destruction. When a spell or effect destroys a creature, it ignores the creature's toughness entirely; destruction is not the same as damage and cannot be prevented by damage prevention effects.

Discard

This means to take a card from your hand and put it on top of your graveyard.

Discard phase

The discard phase comes immediately after the main phase. If the player whose turn it is has more then seven cards in hand at this time, he or she must discard down to seven. It is legal to use fast effects during this phase before but not after discarding.

Draw (noun)

If both players have less than one life at the end of a phase or at the beginning or end of an attack, the game is considered a draw—no one wins. If you were playing for ante, you both take back your own ante.

Draw (verb)

This means to take a card from your library and add it to your hand.

Draw phase

The third phase of a turn is the draw phase. Usually, all that happens in this phase is that you draw a card, but it is legal to use fast effects both before and after drawing.

Duel

Each game of **Magic** is called a duel. To minimize the effects of an unlucky shuffle, you'll most often play "best two of three" or "best three of five" rather than just a single duel.

Enchant world

Enchant World cards are a special type of enchantment. They follow all the rules for normal enchantments plus one additional rule: Only one Enchant World enchantment can be in play at any time. If a second Enchant World card is brought into play, the first one is immediately buried.

Enchantment

An enchantment is one of the four types of permanents. Enchantments are labeled either "Enchantment" or "Enchant _____" (where _____ is filled in with the type of permanent that the enchantment may be played on or "world"). Enchant _____ spells can only be cast on a permanent of the appropriate type; if that permanent leaves play, the enchantment is buried. Enchant _____ spells also continue to check to see if the card they are on is still a legal target. If at any time the card they are on ceases to be a legal target, then bury the enchantment.

End phase

When you've finished with everything you want to do in your turn, you must tell your opponent. This is the end phase of the turn. Both players can use fast effects at this time. At the very end of the end phase, after both players have said that they don't want to use any more fast effects, all the effects which indicate that they happen at the end of the turn take place automatically. If there is more then one such effect to occur, the player whose turn it is decides what order they will happen in. As soon as all of these effects are resolved, the phase ends; you can't squeeze in more fast effects at the last moment.

Evasion abilities

Some creatures have special abilities that prevent them from being blocked (or that restrict which creatures can block them) during an attack. These are called evasion abilities or, sometimes, stealth abilities. The most common evasion abilities are flying and landwalk. Evasion abilities are always on; you can't "turn them off" and allow the creature to be blocked, even if it would benefit you to do so.

Fast effect

Interrupts, instants, and non-continuous effects of permanents are called fast effects. Unless otherwise specified on the card, you can use fast effects during the Upkeep, Draw, Main, Discard, and End phases of any player's turn. Non-interrupt fast effects can be cast in reaction to other non-interrupt spells and other non-interrupt fast effects, forming a "batch"; once all players have said they are done with fast effects, everything in the batch resolves in the "last in, first out" order (i.e., LIFO), with all damage resolved at the very end of the batch. No new effects may be used when you're in the middle of resolving a batch, unless they are triggered by something that happens in that batch, such as a creature's destruction. See damage prevention for details regarding creature destruction during fast effects.

First strike

Creatures with the first strike ability deal their damage first in an attack. If any creatures have first strike, steps 6 and 7 in the attack sequence (see attack) happen twice. After all of the first strike damage has been assigned, damage prevention occurs as usual, and then any creatures dealt lethal damage go to the graveyard. After this step, any surviving creatures without first strike deal their damage. Creatures killed by the first strike damage do not get to deal damage, but any special effects caused by their attack or block will still happen. For example, a Thicket Basilisk (one of the special powers of which is that any non-wall creatures that block the Basilisk are destroyed at the end of combat) attacks and is blocked by two White Knights, 2/2 creatures with first strike. The Knights deal 4 damage to the Basilisk, killing it, so the Basilisk doesn't get to deal damage. But at the end of the attack, the Basilisk's special ability will still destroy both of the Knights.

Flying

A creature with the flying ability can only be blocked by other flying creatures. This is an evasion ability, so you can't have your creatures "fly low" and allow them to be blocked, even if it would be helpful for you to do so. Flying creatures can *block* non-flying creatures, though—they just can't be blocked by them.

Forestwalk

See landwalk.

Graveyard

Your graveyard is your discard pile, which is always face up. Cards in the graveyard are *cards*; they aren't artifacts, creatures, or whatever they would be if they were in play. Any card that breaks this rule will specifically say so. Cards in the graveyard have no "memory" of how they got there or what enchantments or counters were on them when they were destroyed. They can't be healed or regenerated. You may look through your opponent's graveyard at any time. *Each player's graveyard is separate, but if a spell refers to "the graveyard" it means all graveyards combined. Cards that you own always go to your own graveyard, no matter who controlled them last. If a spell says that it affects a creature in the graveyard, it can be used on any Summon or Artifact Creature card, regardless of whether that card was ever in play or not. It cannot be used on other types of cards, even if that card would become a creature when brought into play. Similarly, if a spell says that it affects an artifact in the graveyard, it can be used on any Artifact or Artifact Creature card, and so on. Any "permanent effects" on a card end when that card goes to the graveyard (i.e., enchantments, etc.). See also* damage prevention, bury, *and* **remove from the game**.

Hand

A hand is the cards a player has drawn from his or her library but not yet played. Cards in your hand are just cards; they become spells at the time you attempt to cast them, and may become creatures, artifacts, or enchantments if the casting succeeds. If a spell or effect returns a card to a player's hand, the card always goes back to its owner's hand, no matter who controlled it at the time it was returned. You can never have another player's card in your hand.

Heal phase

The last part of every turn is the heal phase. No fast effects can be used during this phase; all damage is removed from every player's creatures and all "until end of turn" effects go away simultaneously; also referred to as the Heal Creatures phase.

Islandwalk

See landwalk.

Instant

An instant is the most common type of fast effect spell. The card for an instant spell is placed in your graveyard as soon as the spell is resolved. See also fast effect and p. B-95.

Interrupt

An interrupt is a special type of fast effect. Interrupts are the only effects that can be used while another spell is in the process of being cast, so only an interrupt can target a spell or counter another spell. Unlike other fast effects, an interrupt is always resolved immediately after it is announced (unless it is itself interrupted or the caster of the original spell interferes by interrupting his or her own spell before allowing the other player's interrupt to resolve). Another difference between interrupts and other fast effects is that changes made by interrupt spells last as long as the target remains in play, even though the interrupt card is placed in the graveyard as soon as the spell is resolved. This permanent change only applies to interrupt spells, not to special abilities that say to "play as an interrupt." See also p. B-95.

Kill

Kill is often used as an informal synonym for destroy when referring to a creature. Some older cards also use this term.

Land

Land is a type of card that typically generates mana. You may play one and only one land card during your turn. Land is colorless and is a permanent, though it's never a spell. When a spell turns a land of any type into a *basic land*—a forest, island, mountain, plains, or swamps—it loses its original abilities and takes on all the properties of that land, including the type of mana generated. *Land is not mana and mana is not land; land is merely the most common source of mana. Tapping a land for mana is always played as an interrupt; tapping a land for any other effect is just a normal fast effect. Playing a land is not casting a spell, so it doesn't follow the spell timing rules. You may not "respond to" your opponent's playing a land, and you may not play a land as a response to an opponent's action or while a spell is being cast. When a land is tapped, any continuout effects it may have are still active, and any effects which do not include ☯ may still be used.*

Landwalk

A creature with a landwalk ability—swampwalk, forestwalk, and so forth—cannot be blocked if the opponent has any land of that type in play. It can't even be blocked by another creature with the same type of landwalk. *See* evasion abilities.

Legend

A legend is a special type of creature and follows all the rules for creatures plus one additional rule: Only one legend of any given name can be in play at any time. If a second legend with the same name comes into play, it is immediately buried. If more than one legend with matching names come into play at the same time, all of them are buried. Any creature labeled "Summon Legend" or "Summon (something) Legend" is a legend.

Legendary land

This is an obselete term found of some early edition cards. A legendary land follows all the normal rules for lands but as with legends, only one legendary land of a particular name may be in play at any one time. If a second legendary land with the same name comes into play, it is immediately buried.

Library

Your library is your draw pile. If your library is ever empty when you need to draw a card, you lose the game. Once the game has started, no one (including you) may look through your library, count the cards in it, or shuffle it unless a card specifically gives a player that ability.

Life

Each player starts the game with 20 life. Each point of damage done to the player subtracts one life point if it is not prevented or redirected. If a player has less than one life at the end of a phase or the start or end of an attack, that player loses the duel. You can go below zero life and not lose if you manage to gain back enough life to put you above zero life before the end of the phase. There is no limit to how many life you can gain or lose; it's possible (though unlikely) for a player to have hundreds or even thousands of life at the end of the game.

Main phase

Most of the action during a turn takes place in the main phase. Not only are fast effects legal during this phase as in others, but during your main phase, you can also cast permanent or sorcery spells, declare one attack, and play one land. You can do as many or as few of these actions as you like, and you may mix them in any order. For example, you could summon a creature, then attack, then play a land and summon another creature.

Mana

The magical energy used for casting spells and activating special powers is called mana. Most mana comes from tapping land, but some mana comes from other sources. Mana is not land, and land is not mana. Tapping a land for mana is always played as an interrupt. There are six types of mana, consisting of the five colored types—Black, Blue, Green, Red, White—and colorless mana.

Mana burn

See mana pool.

Mana pool

When you generate mana (whether by tapping lands or in some other way), the mana goes briefly into your mana pool, an imaginary holding place for mana. You can then use the mana in your mana pool to cast a spell. Your mana pool empties at the end of each phase and at the beginning and end of an attack; if any unused mana remains in your mana pool when it empties, you take 1 damage for each point of mana you didn't use. This kind of damage is called *mana burn*. Mana burn is a colorless source of damage. *You will usually generate mana just before you need it for a spell and will generate only as much as you need so that you won't have any extra; however, some mana sources like Dark Ritual give you more than one mana, which may leave you with extra. You can prevent mana burn damage using damage prevention spells or effects, but you'll need to tap for new mana to pay for them, since the mana that was in your pool is already considered gone.*

Mono artifact

This is an obsolete term found on early edition cards. To play these cards under Fourth Edition *rules, add an activation cost of ☉ to the effect and change the card type to "Artifact."*

Mountainwalk

See landwalk.

Owner

Any reference in **Magic** *to the owner of a card means the player whose deck the card came from, as opposed to the player who happens to be controlling it at a given point in the game. (If you're borrowing cards from a friend to play with, you're still considered the "owner" for game purposes.) A few very special cards can change the ownership of a card; these are always removed from the deck before the game starts if you're not playing for ante.*

Permanents

All artifacts, lands, creatures, and enchantments in play are permanents, as are any tokens representing permanents (see also *tokens*). Spells that will become permanents aren't considered permanents until successfully cast. *Specifically, a spell that targets a permanent cannot target a spell that will become a permanent; it must wait until the first spell has resolved and created the permanent before it can target it.*

Phase

Each player's turn in **Magic** *is divided into several parts, called phases, as follows:*

1) *Untap phase*
2) *Upkeep phase*
3) *Draw phase*
4) *Main phase*
5) *Discard phase*
6) *End phase*
7) *Heal phase*

Each of these phases happens every turn, even if you don't have anything to do during that phase, and every player can use fast effects in each of phases 2–6.

There is no time "between phases" for things to happen; all actions and effects take place during one or another of the phases.

Plainswalk

See landwalk.

Play (in play)

Cards that have been played in your territory or in your opponent's territory are considered in play. Cards in either player's hand, library, or graveyard aren't in play; neither are cards that have been removed from the game. Cards that aren't in play aren't valid targets for targeted effects unless the targeting spell specifically says so; see also *target*.

Poison counter

A few cards give players poison counters. These can be represented by any convenient objects; see counter. If a player gets ten poison counters, that player loses immediately, even if his or her opponent has negative life. It doesn't matter whether the counters came from the same card or from several different cards.

Poly artifact

This is an obsolete term found on early edition cards. To play these cards under Fourth Edition *rules, just change the card type to "Artifact."*

Power

A creature's power is the amount of damage it deals in combat. It is the first of the two numbers written in the lower right of the creature card. If a spell or effect reduces a creature's power to 0 or less, that creature deals no damage. *Furthermore, a creature with zero or less power is treated as having a power of 0 for all purposes except for raising the power back up again. For example, a Yotian Soldier enchanted with Weakness has a power of -1. If it attacks, it will deal no damage; if it is hit with a Swords to Plowshares, its controller will receive zero life; and so on. Casting Giant Growth on that Soldier, however, would give it +3 power, raising it up to a power of 2. Also, if a card says to give a creature a specific power (rather than modifying its existing power), then treat the creature as though the first number in the lower right hand corner of the card were actually changed.*

Protection

A creature with protection from a particular color of magic cannot be blocked by creatures of that color or targeted by spells, enchantments, or effects of that color, and all damage done to it by sources of that color is reduced to zero whether targeted or not. Additionally, giving a creature protection from a given color (with a ward, for example) destroys any enchantments of that color already on the creature. Protection is not immunity; the creature is still vulnerable to non-targeted non-damage-dealing effects. For example, Wrath of God (a white spell which buries all creatures) will bury a creature with Protection from White. Protection cannot prevent a creature from being sacrificed.

Rampage

When defense is chosen, an attacking creature with "Rampage: *" gets +*/+* until the end of the turn for each creature beyond the first assigned to block it. The * varies but is defined on the rampaging creature's card. Even if some of the blockers are killed or removed after blocking, the rampaging creature keeps the bonus until the end of the turn. Rampage, like trample, has no effect unless the creature attacks.

Regeneration

A creature on the way to the graveyard due to either lethal damage or to a "destroy" effect can be saved by regeneration. Regeneration prevents destruction; if a creature regenerates, then it wasn't destroyed and no special effects that would have happened due to its destruction will take place. Regeneration also allows a creature to ignore all of the damage it has taken so far this turn, and regeneration taps the creature as a side effect if it wasn't already tapped. Regeneration can only be used during damage prevention and only on a creature that is on its way to the graveyard.

Remove from game

When a spell or effect removes a card from the game, that card isn't put into the graveyard. Instead, it should be set aside until the game is over. Spells and effects that affect the graveyard can't affect this card. *And because the card doesn't go to the graveyard, none of the special graveyard effects occur. See also* token.

Sacrifice

Certain cards require you to sacrifice a permanent in play, usually as part of the cost of generating a particular effect. You can only sacrifice a permanent you control, and you can't sacrifice a permanent that is already on its way to the graveyard. Sacrificed permanents get buried immediately; they can't regenerate. Since a sacrifice is a cost, it happens instantaneously as soon as you declare it; it can't be prevented by other effects. Even if the permanent requiring the sacrifice is countered or destroyed, the sacrifice still takes place. It is legal to sacrifice a creature represented by a token. A sacrifice isn't a targeted effect; see also *target*.

Sorcery

Like an instant, a sorcery spell is placed in the graveyard immediately after it is resolved. Sorceries, however, may only be cast during your own turn, during the main phase, and may not be cast during an attack or as a reaction to another spell.

Source of damage

The source of a given amount of damage is the card that dealt that damage, whether or not another card helped it do so. For example, if you put a Firebreathing enchantment on your Grizzly Bears to increase their power, all the damage those Bears deal is considered damage from the Bears, even though the Firebreathing helped. So although Bears are green and the Firebreathing is red, all the Bears' damage is damage from a green source. *On the other hand, if you tap a land enchanted with Psychic Venom, the enchantment deals two damage to you; since the Psychic Vemon is dealing the damage, this damage is from a blue source. If the enchantment said that the land itself deals two damage, that damage would be damage from a colorless source (because lands are considered colorless). Read cards carefully; the card will always say what the source of damage is. See also* color.

Spell

*Cards in **Magic** come in two types: lands and spells. Casting a spell always involves playing a card from your hand. Special abilities of cards already in play are not spells and cannot be affected by things that affect spells. Some spells bring a permanent into play; these cards are considered spells while being cast and become creatures, artifacts, or enchantments only if the spell manages to resolve successfully.*

Stealth abilities

See evasion abilities.

Summon

Creatures are usually brought into play by means of a summon spell. Summon Creature cards are spells while being cast; if the spell is successful, the card then remains in play and represents the creature that was summoned. Artifacts and artifact creatures are cast instead of summoned, so anything that affects a summons won't affect the casting of an artifact.

Summoning sickness

A creature of yours may not attack or use any special ability whose activation cost includes the ⊕ symbol unless the card or token representing the creature was in play under your control at the beginning of your turn (see also *token*). *This should be interpreted as meaning "continuously under your control since your last untap phase."* This inability is usually called summoning sickness. Creatures suffering from summoning sickness can be used to defend *and can also use abilities that don't have ⊕ in their costs. Finally, only creatures suffer from summoning sickness; non-creature artifacts and lands may be used immediately after being brought into play.*

Swampwalk

See landwalk.

Tap (tapping)

Tapping a permanent means turning it sideways. Many cards with special abilities require tapping the card as part or all of the cost for that ability; this is represented by the symbol ⊕. Note that tapping the card does not in itself generate the effect; the controller of the card has to announce that he or she is using the effect and then tap the card when paying the cost. If something else happens to tap a card which has a ⊕ ability, the ability is not activated.

Tapped

A sideways card is referred to as tapped. Non-creature artifacts are completely deactivated for as long as they remain tapped, but tapped creatures and lands still function normally.

Target

A target is the specific card, token, or player at which a spell is aimed. Some spells require one or more targets; you can't cast such spells if there are no valid targets in play. Usually, the type of target required will be obvious; an "Enchant Land" card must be played on a land, for example. Spells that affect a whole class of cards, such as all creatures in play, don't require a target and can therefore be cast at any time. If a spell targets a permanent, that spell can't be cast until the spell for the permanent is successfully cast; see also *permanent*. If a spell is aimed at a single target and that target is removed from play or becomes invalid before the spell resolves, that spell fizzles and has no effect. If a spell is aimed at multiple targets and one or more of those targets is removed or becomes invalid before the spell resolves, that spell still affects any of its original targets that are still valid and in play. If a target becomes invalid and then becomes valid again before the spell resolves, the spell will not fizzle. Creature combat—attacking and blocking—isn't considered a targeted effect. *If a spell or effect requires a target, you must announce the target at the time you cast the spell, and you can't change it later; this must be done at the same time that the cost of the spell is paid. If no legal targets exist at this time, then the spell or effect may not be used.*

Territory

The part of the table in front of you, where you play most of your cards, is called your territory. Each player has his or her own territory.

Token

Occasionally, a card will ask you to use a token to represent a permanent, such as a creature. Use anything you like for the token: coins, poker chips, playing cards, or whatever, though it's best to find something with a clearly defined top and bottom so it's easy to tell if it's tapped. These tokens are permanents, and are affected by spells and effects that affect the appropriate type of permanent, but they aren't considered cards. If any effect takes a token out of play, remove it from the game. You can't send a token to the graveyard, return it to your hand, or otherwise maintain it out of play. *To clarify, a token can be sent to the graveyard; it just can't stay there. If a token is sent to the graveyard, remove it from the game immediately after placing it in the graveyard. This will trigger effects that depend on something going to the graveyard but not those that require a card to remain in the graveyard.*

Toughness

A creature's toughness is the amount of damage it can take before it is destroyed. If a creature's toughness is reduced to 0 or less, the creature dies. Damage prevention effects can only prevent damage; they can't prevent effects that reduce a creature's basic toughness. See also *damage prevention*.

You don't check whether a creature's toughness has been reduced to 0 or less until after all effects in a batch have been resolved; it's possible for a creature to survive if its toughness is first lowered and then raised by two different spells in the same batch. Also, if a card says to give a creature a specific toughness (rather than to modify its existing toughness), then treat the creature as though the second number in the lower right corner of the card were actually changed.

Trample

Normally, an attacking creature which is blocked cannot damage the defending player. A creature with the trample ability gets around this limitation by dealing a special type of damage in combat, called trample damage. If a blocking creature has taken damage greater than its toughness, any excess unprevented trample damage will "spill over" from the creature to its controller at the end of damage prevention, even if the creature that was damaged regenerated. If a single creature receives both normal damage and trample damage at the same time, apply the trample damage last. Since the excess damage isn't redirected until the creature goes to the graveyard or regenerates, you can't take the spillover dam-

age yourself and then save the creature by preventing one damage to it. Trample only functions when the creature is attacking, not when it's blocking.

Turn

Every turn consists of seven phases; see phase. When one player's turn finishes, the next player's turn begins immediately. There is no time "between turns." Some spells may be used during any player's turn; others may only be played during your own turn. Effects which wear off at "end of turn" last until the heal phase of the current turn, no matter whose turn it is.

Untap

Turning a card back from the sideways tapped state to the normal upright position is called untapping the card. Untapping a card does not undo any of the effects caused by tapping the card; it merely makes the card available to be tapped again.

Untap phase

The first part of each turn is the untap phase. All you do in this phase is untap cards; you can't use fast effects. All of your cards untap simultaneously. You must untap all of your cards; if you forget to untap something, then when someone notices the mistake you must back up to the untap phase and replay the turn from there. Some cards give you the option of keeping them tapped; these cards do not untap during the untap phase.

Upkeep cost

Some cards have an upkeep cost. If you control a card with an upkeep cost, you must pay the cost or suffer the effects of not paying it during the upkeep phase of your turn before you can use any non-continuous special abilities of that card.

Upkeep phase

Usually referred to as simply "upkeep," the second part of each turn is the upkeep phase. This is the first chance to use fast effects during the turn. Also, all upkeep costs are dealt with during this phase. The player whose turn it is chooses in what order he or she will deal with the upkeep effects and can use fast effects both before and after each of them. If your permanent with an upkeep cost leaves play before the cost has been paid, you don't have to pay the cost. You can't end the phase if one of your permanents has an upkeep cost which hasn't been dealt with.

Wall

Any card labeled Summon Wall counts as a wall, no matter what the name of the card is—for example, Carnivorous Plant is a wall, though "wall" does not appear in its name. Walls are creatures and follow all the same rules as any other creature with one exception: unless it otherwise specifies, a wall may not attack. Even a wall with power greater than zero, like the Carnivorous Plant, may not attack—but it can deal damage to any creature it blocks. Just like any other defender, a wall can normally only block one attacking creature at a time. Finally, remember that walls can be affected by any spells that affect creatures, even if this seems illogical or silly. For example, you can get rid of a Wall of Stone by casting Terror on it.

Winning

If, at the end of any phase of either player's turn or at the beginning or end of an attack, your opponent's life total is 0 or less, you win. If a player's life total reaches 0 or less at any other time, that player has until the end of the phase to get back to 1 or more life. If both players are reduced to 0 or less life during the same phase (even if one player is at zero and the other is at -100), the duel is a draw and both players keep their ante. If you can't draw a card when required to do so, you lose the duel immediately. *Certain cards may define other ways to win or lose.*

You, your

Cards which use "you" or "your" in their text always mean the current controller of the card. This is usually, but not always, the player who cast the spell. If a card just affects "you" then it can't affect your creatures. For example, a Circle of Protection—which says "prevent all damage against you"—can only stop damage to the player, not damage to that player's creatures. See also controller.

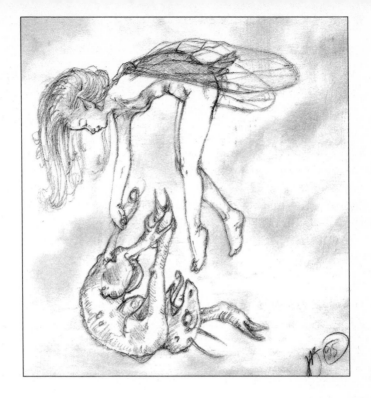

sequence of play: a quick reference guide

Each of your turns consists of these seven phases, in order. All of these phases happen every turn, even if you don't need to do anything during some of them. There is no time "between phases" or "between turns"—everything in the game happens during a phase.

"You" means the player whose turn it is.

1. *Untap.* You must untap all of your cards, unless you are specifically prevented from doing so by existing effects. No fast effects can be used.

2. *Upkeep.* All effects and damage that say "during upkeep" happen now. You choose the order in whch they occur, but you cannot end the phase as long as you have anything in play with an upkeep cost that hasn't been dealt with yet. Fast effects are allowed.

3. *Draw.* You must draw a card. If you cannot draw a card because your library is empty, you lose. Fast effects are allowed.

4. *Main.* During the main phase, you may cast as many spells as you want, of any type. You may also play one land and make one attack (See p. **B-87**). You can do each of these either before, after, or between spells, but not during a spell. Other players may use fast effects but not other types of spells.

5. *Discard.* If you have more than seven cards in your hand, you must discard until you have only seven. If you have seven or fewer, you may not discard, even if you want to. Fast effects are allowed.

6. *End.* Tell your opponent that you are finished. This is the last chance for anyone to use fast effects this turn. Once everyone is finished with fast effects, anything that specified "at end of turn" happens.

7. *Heal Creatures.* Remove all damage points from everyone's surviving creatures. At the same time, all "until end of turn" effects expire. No fast effects can be used.

> Any time a player or creature takes damage or is "destroyed"
> there is an opportunity to use damage prevention
> or regeneration effects. This is an exception to the
> "no fast effects" statements above.

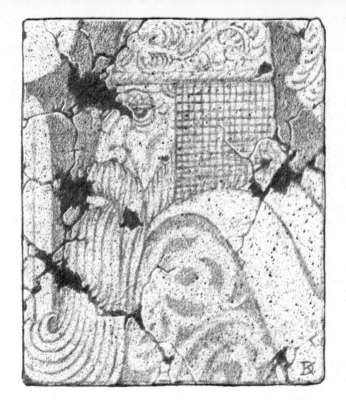

detailed attack sequence

1. *Announce attack.* Tell your opponent that you are attacking. The attack hasn't actually started yet. Your opponent may use fast effects now; if he/she does, it cancels your announcement and you may do something else instead of attacking, if you prefer. If you choose not to attack after your opponent responds to your attack declaration with a fast effect, you may announce an attack later in your main phase or you may simply decide to skip your attack this turn.

2. *Declare attackers.* Tell your opponent which creatures are attacking, and tap them or pay any special attack costs as needed. Previously tapped creatures cannot attack. If you want any of your creatures to use the banding ability, you must form them into groups and declare banding now. No fast effects may be used.

3. *Fast effects.* Any player may use fast effects. These resolve normally. After the effects are resolved, any player may use more fast effects, and so on.

Don't go on to the next step until no one wants to use any more fast effects. If someone takes control of one of the attacking creatures, it is no longer an attacker.

4. *Declare blockers.* Your opponent must tell you which creatures are blocking each of your attacking creatures and must pay any special blocking costs as needed. Tapped creatures cannot block; blocking does not make a creature tap. Once a block is declared, the attacking creature remains blocked no matter what happens to the blocker later. No fast effects are allowed.

5. *Fast effects.* The same as step 3. Note that making a blocked attacker unblockable now is useless; it is still blocked and will still exchange damage with its blocker. If control of one of the creatures changes, it is no longer an attacker/blocker.

6. *Damage dealing and prevention.* First, attackers and blockers deal their power in damage to each other and unblocked attackers deal their power in damage to the defending player. All of this happens at the same time. If there is a choice about how to divide up any damage, the player controlling the damage-dealer chooses. But:

> • If any of the creatures have first strike, they are the only ones who get to deal damage at first. After step 7, repeat steps 6 and 7 a second time, this time for damage from surviving creatures without first strike.
> • An attacker or blocker which regenerated during an earlier step cannot deal any damage or be dealt any damage.
> • A blocked attacker with no remaining blockers cannot deal any damage.
> • A tapped blocker cannot deal any damage.
> • Banding and trample change some of the above; see the rules for details. Then a damage resolution step occurs, during which players may use only damage prevention (including damage redirection and regeneration) and interrupt effects. No other fast effects are allowed.

7. *Bury the dead.* Any creatures that still have lethal damage go to the graveyard. Any special effects caused (or permitted) by creatures going to the graveyard happen now. No other fast effects are allowed.

8. *End.* Any effects that happen "at the end of combat" take place. No fast effects may be used.

general rulings summary

The rules of **Magic: The Gathering** have undergone a series of changes
since they were first released, due in part to their original incompleteness.
The complexity of card interactions forced rulings to be made by interpreting
the cards; several of these rulings are now general enough to affect many
cards or situations, and the most important of these rulings appear below.

Land

Playing a land is not a fast effect, so it cannot be done in response to anything
nor can it be responded to.

If a land has a special ability that does not require an activation cost at all,
then that ability is always "on," even when the land is tapped.

Damage Prevention

A single damage prevention step occurs after resolving any single spell or effect that destroys or buries one or more permanents (except in the case of "at end of turn" effects, which are discussed under "Rules about Phases," and triggered effects, which are discussed under "Triggered Effects"); all permanents destroyed or buried by that spell or effect are processed in that single damage prevention step. A single damage prevention step also occurs after resolving a batch of spells and/or effects in which any creature or player is damaged or in which any creature's toughness is lowered to the point where it takes lethal damage. Finally, a single damage prevention step occurs after resolving a damage dealing step in combat (either damage dealing from first strike or normal damage dealing) in which any creature or player is damaged.

A creature has taken "lethal damage" whenever it has taken damage equal to or greater than its current toughness (including having its current toughness reduced to zero or less).

The Graveyard and Going to the Graveyard

A permanent is "on the way to the graveyard" only during a damage prevention step and only if it has taken lethal damage or is being sent to the graveyard due to a destroy or bury spell or effect.

Cards sent to the graveyard are always put on the top of the graveyard. If multiple cards go to the graveyard at the same time, the owner of the cards chooses the order in which they are put in the graveyard. Token creatures sent to the graveyard are momentarily put in the graveyard before being removed from the game; hence, token creatures sent to the graveyard generate effects that are triggered by creatures being put into the graveyard.

You cannot reorder cards in the graveyard unless a spell or effect specifically allows or instructs you to do so.

Cards that Are Out of Play

Unless specifically stated, spells and effects do not interact with cards that are not in play. For example, a spell that says "destroy all islands" only affects islands in play.

Cards that are not in play have no memory of whether they were ever in play nor of anything that may have happened to them while they were in play (including the effects of interrupt spells).

Rules about Phases

The "active player" is the player whose turn it is. Except during the untap and heal creatures phases, when the active player says "I'm done with the current phase," the non-active player can declare fast effects in response to this announcement. Responding to such an announcement cancels the ending of the current phase and thus gives the active player additional opportunities to take actions during that phase.

Certain effects or required actions can only be used or must be used during a particular phase (for example, paying upkeep costs during upkeep or drawing a card during the draw phase). Any such effect or required action that does not have an activation cost can only be used once during that phase. Play all such effects and required actions as instants. Such effects and required actions can be played in any order provided that all such required actions are played or the source of such actions is removed before the phase ends. You must always pay the entire upkeep cost on a permanent or none of it.

If a permanent has an upkeep cost, you may not use any ability of that permanent that requires an activation cost until you have paid the upkeep cost of that permanent.

Untap costs are an exception to the once-per-phase rule; untap costs can be paid multiple times during upkeep. You must always pay the entire untap cost on a permanent or none of it.

Effects that last "until end of turn" end during the heal creatures phase. Effects that happen "at end of turn" are processed at the end of the end phase. The active player chooses the order in which "at end of turn" effects are processed. Only one damage prevention step occurs for all "at end of turn" effects.

Activation Costs

In general, abilities of permanents that do not include ◈ in the activation cost can be used, even when the permanent is tapped; however, this rule does not apply to non-creature artifacts.

Normally, when you use an effect, you pay for it once to generate the effect once. However, if you pay the entire cost multiple times simultaneously, multiply the effect that many times. In this case, make all decisions (such as choosing targets) only once for the entire effect. For example, to have your Brothers of Fire deal 1 damage each to two different targets, pay ① ◐ ◐ to have it deal damage to the first target and then another ① ◐ ◐ to have it deal damage to the second. To have it deal 2 damage to a single target, however, you can pay ② ◐ ◐ ◐ ◐ all at once.

When You Can Play a Spell or Use an Ability

If a spell or ability has no target, you can still play it, even if it will have no effect. If a spell or ability requires a target, you can only play it if there is a legal target and only if there are the correct number of legal targets. One exception to these rules is that spells or abilities that prevent or redirect damage or regenerate creatures can only be played during a damage prevention step when a player or creature has taken damage, or when a creature is on the way to the graveyard, respectively. This is because those spells or abilities target the damage, not the target receiving the damage.

The legal targets of a spell or ability are specified in the text of the spell or ability immediately following the word "target." For example, an ability that says "tap target creature" can be played on a creature regardless of whether that creature is currently tapped or untapped. An ability that says "tap target untapped creature" can only be played on a creature that is currently untapped.

Resolving Spells and Effects

When you resolve a spell or effect, try to complete as much of the effect as possible, except where one part of the effect is a prerequisite for another. For example, consider an effect that says "Tap target creature. Effect deals 1 damage to that creature." Even if the target creature is already tapped when this effect resolves, the effect will still deal 1 damage to that creature. By contrast, consider an effect that says "Tap target creature to have [effect] deal 1 damage to that creature." If the target creature is already tapped when this effect resolves, the second part of the effect is ignored because the first part of the effect is a prerequisite for the second. Note, however, that some spells or effects that appear to have a prerequisite may not actually have one. The first part of a spell or effect sometimes requires sacrificing a permanent, paying life, or removing counters from a card. These are costs that must be paid when the spell or effect is played (and thus are still paid even if the spell or effect is countered or fizzles), rather than prerequisite effects.

Except in the case of certain enchantments, after a spell or effect resolves, you do not constantly recheck to see if the target of that spell or effect remains valid; the effect continues to work even if the target becomes illegal after the spell or effect resolves. For example, words like "target creature" do not mean that the target has to remain a creature for the effect to continue working. A good way to think of this is as if the first instance of "target creature" in an effect actually said "target creature, which is a token or a card" and all later references to that creature actually said "that token or card." This rule does not apply to Enchant _____ cards (Enchant Creature, Enchant Land, etc.), which continuously recheck to see if their target is legal and are buried if their target becomes illegal.

The characteristics of the source of an effect (for example, color, power and toughness, controller, etc.) are determined when the spell or effect is announced. These characteristics can only be modified by interrupts that target the spell or effect. (These characteristics cannot be modified by interrupts that target the source of an effect, so after an effect using the ability of a permanent has been announced, interrupts that affect that permanent do not modify the effect.) All other characteristics are determined when a spell or effect resolves. A spell or effect containing the phrase "when <permanent> is placed in the graveyard" lock in which player is the controller of <permanent> when <permanent> is on the way to the graveyard, so anything affecting "<permanent>'s controller" would affect its current controller and not necessarily its owner.

A spell that will not become a permanent goes to the graveyard once it has been resolved or countered; it does not go to the graveyard when played.

Triggered effects that are triggered by an event that occurs during the resolution of a spell or effect do not occur in the middle of resolution; rather, they occur immediately after the spell or effect resolves completely.

Spells and effects that affect both players at the same time always resolve their effect on the active player first. A player can never lose the game during the resolution of a spell or effect, however, so if all players lose the game (other than as a result of being reduced to 0 life or less) during the resolution of a single spell or effect, the game is a draw.

Counters

All counters with the same name represent the same type of counter, so any effect that affects a certain type of counter affects all counters of that type, regardless of the source of the counter.

Forced Effects

If a card instructs or forces a player do something, that player must try to follow the instructions using his or her existing resources (for example, creatures already in play, mana already in that player's mana pool, etc.), but that player is not required to cast spells or use effects to get those resources unless specifically instructed by the cards to do so.

Triggered Effects

Triggered effects are effects that only happen or can only be used when a certain event occurs—for example, when a creature is placed in the graveyard. Only one damage prevention step occurs for all triggered effects that are triggered by the resolution of any single spell or effect.

timing

Tom Wylie

Overview

"I attack with my Craw Wurm."

"Ack! Bad Touch! Well, not so bad. I'll just kill it with Terror before damage dealing."

"You can do that?"

"Sure, says right here that I can play fast effects during the attack."

"Oof. Well, I'll Unsummon the Wurm to my hand before your Terror kills it."

"I don't think you can do that."

"The book says I can respond to your instants...."

Sound familiar? Your first few games of **Magic** were probably pretty simple, with you and your opponent playing one spell at a time and just attacking (or taking your lumps) without trying to be fancy about it. But sooner or later, someone tried to play an effect "illegally," when the opponent wasn't expecting it, and a conversation like the one above began. Maybe you played a spell during the attack; maybe your opponent used her Prodigal Sorcerer at the end of your turn instead of on her turn. As with any dispute, you probably turned to the rulebook for help, but since the rulebook tends to be abbreviated due to the limited space available, it may not have properly addressed the question you were asking. This article attempts to explain the timing rules in greater detail, such that the answers to almost any question can be found herein.

This explanation of the rules focuses on fast effects, which are assumed to take center stage in the timing scene. Throughout these rules, all discussions of "instants" should be read as referring to "instant spells and abilities that are played as instants"; that is, non-interrupt fast effects. Also, references to the *active player* refer to the player whose turn it is.

Instants can be played at almost any time, and often are used in response to one another in groups of effects referred to as "batches." Thus, most timing conflicts result when both players try to play instants at the same time or before the other player can do something. This article will present the rules for playing and resolving instants before detailing how other classes of effects, such as sorceries and interrupts, fit into this backdrop. It will then cover the different phases of the turn, and this will be followed by a brief discussion of specialized timing steps such as damage prevention. Finally, we'll look at timing protocol: how to avoid playing an effect before it's your turn and what should happen when someone does get ahead of him- or herself.

A word of warning before we begin: This article is intended to cover absolutely everything about timing. If something isn't making sense, skip ahead to the next example, read it, and then reread the confusing explanation. The text itself is intended to simply lay down the rules, so it may often seem a bit cryptic without a practical application of the rules detailed.

Instants

There are two major rules concerning how instants are played. First, they do not do anything immediately when cast but instead wait for responses before resolving. Second, they can be used in response to any non-interrupt effect. These two qualities result in instants being grouped into *batches* of effects, with each instant in the batch being used in response to the one before it. Only when both players are done adding effects to a batch do the effects in the batch begin resolving. Note that the term "respond" is merely used here in respect to ordering the play of instants. It is not required that the play of an effect be motivated by anything in particular.

As with all fast effects, instants can be played during either player's turn; there is never a phase or other timing step when only one player can play effects. This freedom of use, combined with the fact that instants form into batches, is why instants form the basis of the timing system.

> Example: A batch might consist of a creature being targeted by Lightning Bolt, Unsummon, and Terror in succession. None of these effects does anything when cast; each waits for responses to be played and resolved.

> Another batch could include a Lightning Bolt, with some other creature being Unsummoned "in response" to the Bolt, even though the Unsummon's and Bolt's effects have nothing to do with one another.

Constructing Batches of Effects

At their most basic level, phases are defined in terms of giving each player a chance to start a batch of effects. Each phase has its own rules to differentiate it from the others—these rules will be examined later—but each phase is essentially a series of opportunities to play effects.

Each phase begins in a "null state," from which the active player can start a batch of effects. The active player has two choices when faced with a null state: play an effect to start a batch or announce intention to end the phase. If the active player decides to end the phase, then the opportunity to play effects passes to the opponent. The opponent then has essentially the same choices: play an effect to start a batch or allow the phase to end. If the opponent also declines to start a batch, then the phase ends. If either player starts a batch of effects, then it is constructed and resolved under the rules outlined below. Once the batch has finished resolving, the phase returns to the "null state" that it began in, with the active player again having the choice of playing effects or trying to end the phase. This process continues until both players are willing to let the phase end.

If either player starts a batch of effects, the active player has the opportunity to respond with another instant or to pass. If the active player opts not to respond, then the opponent is given the same choice to respond or to pass. If either player responds with an instant, that instant is added to the batch and the process of responding is repeated, with the active player again having the first opportunity to respond. Once both players have declined to respond to an effect, the batch is considered complete, and begins to resolve.

> Example: Carrington's upkeep phase begins, so he gets the first chance to do something. Carrington decides to start a batch by playing Terror on one of Hannah's creatures. The Terror doesn't resolve immediately but instead, it waits for both players to respond. Carrington decides not to follow his Terror up with another effect.

Hannah responds to the Terror by playing Unsummon on its target, and the response cycle begins again. Both Carrington and Hannah pass, so the batch is now complete, consisting of the Terror and the Unsummon.

Playing Effects

If an effect requires any costs, these must be paid as the effect is played. Costs include but are not limited to paying mana, making sacrifices, and paying life. If an ability is used, the cost may also include tapping the permanent that has the ability or removing counters from that permanent.

If an effect requires one or more targets, then all targets must be chosen as the effect is played. To determine whether an effect is a targeted effect, look in the card text for the word "target" in a phrase that describes just what is targeted—for example, "target creature." Effects that target more than one thing cannot target the same thing twice but must target that many different things. Note that whether the effect will actually do something to a target is unimportant; all that matters is that it match the target specification on the card.

Decisions about what the effect will target are made simultaneously with any other decisions required by the effect and with paying any costs required. If an effect requires any decisions at all, it should be assumed that these decisions are made while the effect is being played unless the card text clearly indicates otherwise.

Example: Phantasmal Terrain instructs the caster to choose a basic land type. Twiddle either taps or untaps its target, and the caster must decide which of these it does (it does not simply toggle the target's tapped state). Reverse Damage requires choosing a source of damage to convert damage from that source into life gain. None of these say when to make the decision, and all of these choices can be made based on information available when the spell is played, so all of them are made at that time.

Example: Primal Clay can have one of three forms. Normally, the form would be chosen as you played it, but Primal Clay instructs you to choose the form as it comes into play, so the choice is made as it resolves instead.

Example: Balance reduces all players to the same number of lands, creatures, and cards in hand. So, in some sense, it involves a choice: if you have more land than your opponent, you will have to choose which land(s) to lose. Balance, however, won't count lands and so forth until it resolves, so it can't know how much to make you lose when played. All choices about what to lose are therefore made when Balance resolves, not when it is played.

Example: Because costs are paid at the same time as targeting decisions are made, it is not possible for a Royal Assassin, which destroys "target tapped creature," to destroy itself. If it's already tapped, then it can't pay the cost for its effect, and if it's untapped, you would be looking for a tapped creature at the same time as the cost was being paid, so the Assassin wouldn't qualify as a valid target.

Resolving Effects

Once everyone has finished adding effects to a batch, the effects resolve one at a time, starting with the last effect played and working back to the effect which started the batch. Once the batch has started resolving, no more effects may be added to it. The following guidelines govern what an effect will actually do when it resolves. These rules apply equally to all effects, such as interrupts, unless they specify effects in a batch.

Any targeted part of an effect will recheck the target when the effect resolves. If the target has disappeared or is no longer a legal target for the effect, then the entire effect *fizzles*, and doesn't do anything. If an effect targets multiple things, the various targets are checked individually, so fizzling against one target won't cause the whole effect to fail. If an effect combines targeted and non-targeted elements, the non-targeted portion will fizzle if and only if all of the targeted elements fizzle. An effect which fizzles completely is still considered to have been successfully cast; it just wasn't usefully cast. If a target becomes invalid after the effect has resolved, this will not cause the effects to wear off prematurely. The effect will continue until the conditions described on the card are met.

Example: Terror is played on a creature, followed by Unsummon being played on the same creature. The Unsummon resolves first (since it was the last one cast), and it returns its target to its owner's hand. The Terror then resolves and finds that its target has disappeared, so the Terror fizzles.

Example: Ashes to Ashes removes two non-artifact creatures from the game (targeted elements) and also deals 5 damage to the caster (non-targeted element). Hannah plays Ashes to Ashes on two creatures, which are then Unsummoned, killed, or otherwise made invalid targets in response. Had Ashes to Ashes affected one or both targets, Hannah would have taken the full 5 points of damage, but since the spell fizzles against both, no damage is dealt.

Example: Crumble's effect has two parts—bury an artifact (targeted) and give that artifact's controller life (non-targeted). If Crumble is played on a Yotian Soldier, which is Unsummoned in response, Crumble will fizzle due to it being now targeted against an invalid target. The non-targeted element thus fizzles as well, and no life is granted by Crumble.

Example: Giant Growth is played on a creature; its effects last until end of turn. Playing Green Ward on the creature *later* in the turn will not cause the Giant Growth to wear off, even though it would be an illegal target for future Giant Growths.

Example: Xenic Poltergeist is a creature that temporarily turns a non-creature artifact into an artifact creature. The very nature of the effect thus makes the artifact an illegal target for the second application of the effect. If a Poltergeist animates an Amulet of Kroog, the Amulet is now an artifact creature, so it may not be affected again that turn. This does not, however, cause the effect to wear off—it lasts for the stated duration (until the Poltergeist's controller's next upkeep).

Some effects resolve in stages, with the success of one element being a prerequisite for processing another element. If the prerequisite fizzles, or otherwise doesn't do anything, then the second part of the effect will automatically fail. Note that if the prerequisite is to do damage or to destroy something, the effect will normally finish resolving before damage prevention begins, so preventing the damage or destruction during the later damage prevention step won't prevent the rest of the effect from happening.

Most effects which have prerequisities are written as "do something to do something else," but you have to take care when reading such cards. If the "do something" is to sacrifice something, pay life, or remove counters from the card, then it is a *cost* rather than part of the effect and would have been done when the effect was played. In these cases, only the "do something else" is considered to be the effect.

Example: Coral Helm's ability instructs you to "Discard a card at random from your hand to give target creature +2/+2 until end of turn." Discarding is thus a prerequisite for enhancing the target's statistics for the turn. Although the Helm can be used while your hand is empty, the effect won't do anything if you have nothing to discard when it resolves.

Example: Osai Vultures gain a carrion counter during any turn in which something died, and the controller of the Vultures can "Remove two carrion counters to give Vultures +1/+1 until end of turn." Since removing counters is a cost, the actual effect is to give the Vultures +1/+1, and the counters are removed when the effect is played rather than when it resolves.

Damage dealt to a creature or player by an effect in a batch is not applied immediately. Instead, all damage dealt by the effects in a batch waits until the batch has finished resolving and is then applied all at once. Also, creatures do not check their toughness against the damage they've taken until the end of the batch, after any damage from the batch has been applied. Thus, a creature whose toughness is dropped to 0 will not die immediately but will be affected normally by effects that resolve later in the batch. Only if its toughness is still less than 1 at the end of the batch will it die.

> Example: Carrington is out of black mana when Hannah decides to poke his Drudge Skeletons with her Prodigal Sorcerer. Carrington responds to this by playing Unsummon on the Skeletons. Hannah responds to that by playing Holy Light, which will give all non-white creatures -1/-1 until end of turn. No more fast effects are played. The Holy Light resolves first, making the Skeletons 0/0, but they do not die immediately, since they won't check their toughness until everything has finished resolving. The Unsummon resolves next, returning the Skeletons to Carrington's hand. The Prodigal Sorcerer's poke then fizzles because it no longer has a target.

Fitting Non-Instant Effects into the Picture

Having established how instants work, we now turn our attention to other effects, examining how they fit into the batch structure of instants.

Interrupts

The most basic interrupt in the game is to tap a land for mana, but interrupts also include all interrupt spells and any abilities which say they are played as interrupts (usually mana sources other than land). Whenever a player has the opportunity to play an instant, he or she may decide to play an interrupt instead, though interrupts are never added to batches. Once an interrupt has been successfully cast, it resolves immediately. Either player may then respond with another interrupt, with the active player deciding first whether to do so. Both players can continue to play interrupts for as long as desired, but no instants may be played at this time, since instants may not respond to interrupts. Note that this is not the only time that interrupts can be played (see below).

Once both players are finished with interrupts, whoever played the first of the interrupts still has the opportunity to play the next non-interrupt effect. Interrupts simply halt the normal flow of the game and do not otherwise disturb the process of playing instants and non-fast effects.

> Example: Carrington's main phase begins with Hannah's Prodigal Sorcerer tapped. Carrington decides to start a batch by stabbing the Sorcerer with his Royal Assassin (tap to destroy target tapped creature). Carrington decides that's enough and that he's done. Hannah

now has the chance to respond, and she decides that the best response would be to untap the Sorcerer with Twiddle. To do this, she needs 🜚, so she puts off her instant to play an interrupt (tapping a land for mana). Carrington can take advantage of this to play interrupts, but that's all. Once both players are done with interrupts, it is still Hannah's turn to play instants, so she plays Twiddle on the Sorcerer to untap it. (This will cause the stab from the Royal Assassin to fizzle when it resolves and finds the Sorcerer untapped.)

Note that the intent of the timing rules is preserved: Carrington said he was done, so he had to let Hannah play the next instant. If Hannah had begun interrupts by tapping for mana and the interrupts had concluded with Carrington's priority in playing instants restored, he would have been able to take advantage of Hannah's need for mana by playing a tapping instant such as Twiddle on the Sorcerer before Hannah could play her Twiddle to untap the Sorcerer. (Because effects in a batch resolve last to first, Carrington's Twiddle would, in this case, resolve next to last, tapping the Sorcerer, which would then be destroyed by the Royal Assassin's stab.)

Non-Fast Effects

There are two sorts of non-fast effects: sorceries and spells that become permanents when they resolve (summons, artifacts, etc.). While lands are permanents, playing a land is not considered to be a spell at all, but a step unique to the main phase.

Sorceries and spells that become permanents may be played by the active player whenever the main phase is at a null state—that is, whenever the active player is allowed to start a batch of effects. They may not be played during the attack. Once played, sorceries and spells that become permanents follow the same rules as instants, so any rules about batches of effects apply equally to non-fast effects.

Note that during the main phase, the active player may always decide to start a batch with a sorcery or a spell that becomes a permanent, even if the other player wants to start a batch with a fast effect.

Example: Carrington successfully casts Benalish Hero while Hannah has a Prodigal Sorcerer in play. Because the Hero is not yet in play, any instants responding to the summoning will not be able to target the Hero. Assuming that there is no response to the summons, the Hero enters play, and the phase returns to the "null state." Carrington is now able to start a batch by playing any instant, sorcery, or spell that becomes a permanent, even if Hannah wants to use a fast effect such as her Sorcerer's poke. Carrington decides to start the batch by playing Holy Armor on the Hero. Hannah was hoping to use her Sorcerer to kill the Hero, but that's hopeless now, since the damage from the poke won't resolve until after the armor is in place. Thus, the Hero will survive the damage.

Example: Hannah's main phase has started. Deciding that she wants to play a Fireball, she taps a whole bunch of lands for mana. Carrington is thinking of using Mana Short, an instant which would tap all of Hannah's lands and empty her mana pool; however, Carrington could not play this in response to the lands being tapped for mana, since you cannot respond to interrupts with instants. Once the interrupts are finished, Hannah still has control over playing the next effect, so plays the Fireball. The fact that Carrington wants to play an instant doesn't stop Hannah from playing the sorcery. Carrington could respond to the Fireball by playing his Mana Short, but the Fireball has already been paid for so he can't stop it with the Mana Short. If Carrington had been worried about Hannah casting something like a Fireball, he should have played the Mana Short during Hannah's upkeep or draw phase, before she had the chance to cast a sorcery.

The Phases of the Turn

Each phase has its own timing rules which modify the flow of the phase. These rules generally affect the active player's ability to end the phase, typically by prohibiting her from doing so before taking some action or actions. In addition to the phase-specific rules detailed below, the following rules apply to any effect which occurs or is used during a given phase.

Some effects state that they happen at the beginning of a certain phase or at the end of a certain phase. For example, Ivory Tower states that its effect applies at start of upkeep, and Black Vise says that it kicks in at end of upkeep. When a phase begins, all "start of phase" effects which apply are handled one at a time, in the order chosen by the active player. Only when all such effects have been resolved does the phase reach the "null state" which allows players to start batches of effects. At the end of the phase, once both players have declined to start a batch of effects, any "end of phase" effects are resolved one at a time, again in the the order chosen by the active player. Only when these effects have finished resolving do the players check for mana burn. Since the processing of "start of phase" and "end of phase" effects does not include a null state, no effects may be played at these times.

There are also effects which only happen during certain phases rather than being usable at any time. Some of these effects happen automatically (Unstable Mutation, Cursed Rack, Howling Mine) while others only occur at the option of the player who controls the effect (Sylvan Library, Shapeshifter). These effects follow all the timing rules of instants, so they may either start a batch or be used in response to other effects. The automatic effects are referred to as "upkeep effects," "draw effects," and so on. The active player cannot choose to ignore automatic effects; if she ever tries to announce end of phase when there are such effects left to deal with, she must focus on these effects instead. The active player is allowed to put off dealing with such effects to take other actions, however, and if one of these effects is removed before it is dealt with (typically by destroying the source), then it can be safely ignored. Optional effects played during specific phases are also played as instants.

> Example: Carrington begins his turn with Unstable Mutation played on his Drudge Skeletons and no other upkeep effects or costs to worry about. His upkeep phase begins uneventfully and immediately enters the "null state." If he doesn't want to play an instant, he can't try to end the phase but must play the Mutation's upkeep effect. Neither player responds to this, so the Skeletons get their counter and die at the end of the batch (if this reduces them to 0 toughness). Once that batch has been resolved and the upkeep phase has returned to the "null state," Carrington is free to try to end his upkeep. Note that Carrington could have started his upkeep by casting Red Elemental Blast on the Unstable Mutation. This would have eliminated the upkeep effect of the Mutation, and he would have been able to try to end the phase without doing anything else.

Untap Phase

No fast effects are allowed during the untap phase. The active player makes any decisions about what will or won't untap, then everything which is going to untap does so, and then the phase is over. Remember that everything the active player controls untaps unless an effect specifically stops a permanent from untapping or allows the player to decide not to untap it.

Upkeep Phase

Three classes of effects can change the flow of the upkeep phase: upkeep effects, upkeep costs, and untap costs. Effects of all three classes are played as instants, using the timing rules outlined earlier. Upkeep effects and upkeep costs must be played at some point during the upkeep phase, though the active player is free to remove whatever generates the effect or cost before dealing with it. In the case of upkeep costs, "dealing with it" can consist of not paying the cost and accepting the consequences. If a permanent has an upkeep cost, then abilities of that permanent that have an activation cost may not be used until that upkeep cost has been dealt with, which means waiting for the payment, or lack thereof, to resolve (not paying the cost will typically make it impossible to use the ability). Untap costs, such as Brass Man or Paralyze, are purely optional. If a permanent has multiple upkeep costs or untap costs applied to it, the player must pay all those costs or none of them.

Draw Phase

The draw phase has one built-in, phase-specific effect: the free draw for the turn. This is treated as a phase-specific effect, so it is played as an instant.

Main Phase

The main phase has two specific steps: playing a land and conducting an attack. Both of these steps are optional. Whenever the active player has the opportunity to start a batch of effects, she may play a land. Neither player may respond to this, so the land simply enters play, and the phase returns to the null state.

The active player may also choose to announce intention to attack instead of starting a batch, just as she would announce intention to end the phase. The opponent may then choose to start a batch of effects rather than allow the attack to begin. If the opponent does so, a batch of effects is constructed and resolved normally, and the phase returns to the null state. The active player is not required to announce the attack again immediately, or at all, but may instead play effects or simply decide to skip the attack entirely. Once the attack is over, the main phase returns to the null state. Each player can play effects before and after the land is played, as well as before and after the attack. If the active player controls any creatures that are required to attack or has otherwise been forced to conduct an attack, then ending the main phase without conducting the attack is not permitted.

> Example: Hannah has played Siren's Call on Carrington's creatures, which forces all of them—including tapped creatures, which will be destroyed if they don't attack—to attack this turn (except for Carrington's walls and any creatures which have summoning sickness). Carrington must go through the attack at some point during the turn, so he cannot end the main phase until he has announced and completed an attack. Hannah must have played the Siren's Call before the attack had actually started, but she still had the opportunity to do so even after Carrington announced his intention to attack. In that case, since she would have played it in response to Carrington's intent to attack, it would have aborted the attack, but Carrington would still be required to attack at some point later in the turn.

Discard Phase

The discard phase has an end-of-phase effect that requires the active player to discard down to seven cards.

End Phase

The end phase is the last opportunity for either player to play fast effects during the turn. In addition, any effects that happen "at end of turn" are treated as end-of-phase effects of this phase.

Heal Creatures

As with the untap phase, no effects are allowed during healing of creatures. Simultaneously, all damage heals and all "until end of turn" effects wear off.

Casting Effects

We have been assuming for simplicity's sake that once a spell is played, it will be successfully cast and will resolve at some point in the future. This, however, is not necessarily the case. Once an effect has been played (all costs are paid, any targets are chosen, and so on), the effect must go through a casting period, during which both players are allowed to play interrupts. Interrupts played at this time can counter or modify an effect, usually the effect they interrupt. Even effects which are played as interrupts have this casting period, so it's possible to interrupt an interrupt.

Basics of Interrupting Effects

Once an effect has been played, the player controlling that effect (called the controlling player hereafter) gets the first opportunity to play interrupts. The controlling player continues to play interrupts one at a time, with those interrupts resolving as they are cast, for as long as desired. When the controlling player is done with interrupts, the opponent may play one interrupt, which will resolve immediately. The controlling player may then play any number of interrupts, followed by the opponent being able to play another interrupt. This process continues until everyone has finished playing interrupts, with each interrupt resolving as soon as it is successfully cast.

Both non-targeted interrupts and interrupts that target permanents may be played freely in this manner. If, however, *both* players want to target an effect being cast with interrupts, all of the controlling player's interrupts targeting that effect must resolve before any of the opponent's do. This means that during an effect's casting period, the opponent may not play interrupts that target the effect (referred to for the remainder of this passage as "targeted interrupts") until the controlling player has finished doing so, though the opponent can play other interrupts before then. When the controlling player is done targeting the effect with interrupts, the opponent may play one targeted interrupt (following any number of other interrupts). The resolution of this interrupt will wait while the controlling player plays any number of interrupts, including any number of additional targeted interrupts. Once the con-

trolling player is finished with targeted interrupts a second time, the opponent's targeted interrupt resolves, and the controlling player may never again
target that effect with interrupts. Both players can continue to play interrupts,
however, with that restriction in mind.

Example: Hannah plays Flashfires. This may seem foolish since she
controls plains and Carrington does not, but she has a trick up her
sleeve. Because she cast the spell, she gets to play interrupts first, and
she takes the opportunity to tap an island for 🜄. Once that has
resolved, she plays Magical Hack on the Flashfires, changing "plains"
to "forests" (which Carrington has but Hannah does not). The Hack
resolves immediately and changes the text of the Flashfires.

Note that Carrington could have been playing interrupts during the
casting of Magical Hack or during the tapping of the island. For
example, he could have tapped a forest for 🜎 and used that mana to
Lifelace something in play. Or he could have tried to counter the
Magical Hack. We are assuming that Carrington is doing nothing in
this case.

Once the Hack has resolved, Hannah can choose to continue playing
interrupts, but she declines. Carrington can now play an interrupt,
and taps one of his islands for 🜄, drawing it into his pool. Hannah can
now play interrupts again, but she sees no point so declines.
Carrington then plays Blue Elemental Blast, targeted at the Flashfires.
Its resolution waits for Hannah to play interrupts.

Hannah taps an island for mana then Thoughtlaces the Flashfires.
She has no more interrupts to play, so Carrington's Blue Elemental
Blast resolves (and fizzles, since the target is now invalid). The inter-
rupt process can now continue, but Hannah can no longer target the
Flashfires, having declined to target it with any other interrupts after
casting the Thoughtlace. Thus, Carrington could now target the
Flashfires (which is a blue spell now due to the Thoughtlace) with a
Red Elemental Blast, and Hannah would not be permitted to inter-
rupt the Red Elemental Blast to target the Flashfires with a
Purelace.

Interrupting One Effect to Target Another

Interrupts are not restricted to targeting the effect they are interrupting but
can target any effect which is not yet successfully cast. When deciding
whether or not the interrupt can be used and whether it resolves as soon as it
is successfully cast, look at whether you can interrupt the effect directly and
what will happen if you do.

If you control the effect you're targeting, then the situation is essentially the same as if you were targeting it directly. If your opponent has already targeted the effect and that interrupt has resolved, then you are prohibited from targeting your effect, even indirectly. If it is still legal for you to target the effect, then your interrupt will resolve as soon as it is successfully cast, just as if you had interrupted the effect directly.

If you don't control the effect you're trying to target, the situation is still basically the same as if you tried to interrupt the effect directly. If any of your interrupts which targeted that effect have already resolved, then the controlling player can no longer target it at all, and your interrupt will resolve as soon as it is successfully cast. But if the controller of the effect can still target it, then the resolution of your interrupt is put on hold indefinitely. Your interrupt will not resolve until the target effect gets to the state where the players are interrupting it directly, and the controlling player has finished interrupting it. At this point, all of your interrupts being kept on hold will resolve one at a time, in the order they were cast.

> Example: Hannah plays a Fireball against Carrington. Carrington interrupts the Fireball directly to target it with a Blue Elemental Blast. Hannah interrupts the Blast to target the Fireball with a Lifelace, which will turn it from red to green (thus making the Blast useless). Because Hannah can still target the Fireball, she can play the Lifelace, and the Lifelace resolves immediately. There are no more interrupts, so the Blast resolves, but it fizzles since its target is no longer red.

> Example: Carrington plays Tranquility and does not interrupt it. Hannah interrupts the spell to target it with Chaoslace (changing the color of the Tranquility spell from green to red). Carrington chooses not to play any interrupts, so the Chaoslace resolves, and turns the Tranquility red. Hannah now targets the spell again, this time with a Blue Elemental Blast. Because at least one of Hannah's interrupts targeting the Tranquility has resolved, Carrington cannot target the Tranquility again, even by interrupting the Blast.

So What Did That Interrupt Do, Anyway?

When interrupts resolve, they follow essentially the same procedure that an instant does except that any damage dealt by an interrupt resolves immediately and if an interrupt changes something's toughness, that creature checks immediately to see whether or not it's dead. A targeted interrupt will generally do one of two things: it will modify the target in some way, or it will counter or destroy it.

Directly modifying a spell, or the effect generated by an ability, will change the outcome of that effect. But changing the source of an ability will not change the effect itself: once the effect was played, it was divorced from the source completely. Changing an effect or its target in such a way as to render the target invalid will not cause the effect to abort immediately; it will still be cast normally, and only when it resolves will it re-examine the target to see if that target is legal. If the target has become legal again, then the effect will resolve normally.

Countering a spell or ability neutralizes it completely. The effect is essentially destroyed, and it is no longer possible to interrupt the effect; if the effect was a spell, the card is placed in the graveyard immediately, not when the effect would have resolved. Any interrupts which are "on hold" and targeting the effect will now resolve in the order in which they were cast, though they will typically fizzle entirely, since their target has now disappeared (and is thus invalid). Destroying the source of an ability won't counter the effect which was already generated.

> Example: Hannah plays a Fireball, and Carrington plays Thoughtlace on the Fireball. This turns the spell blue, so the damage done by it would be blue, for example. The next turn, however, Carrington taps his Prodigal Sorcerer to poke one of Hannah's creatures. Hannah interrupts the poke to Lifelace the Sorcerer, turning it green, but the fact that the Sorcerer is now green doesn't change the fact that is was blue when the poke was used. The poke, and the damage done by it, will still be blue.

> Example: Hannah plays a Disintegrate, so Carrington targets it with a Blue Elemental Blast. The Blast is being used to counter a spell, so the Disintegrate is nullified and is not considered to be successfully cast. The next turn, Carrington uses another Prodigal Sorcerer, this time to poke Hannah directly. Hannah interrupts the poke to play Red Elemental Blast on the Sorcerer. But the ability has already been used, so the effect is considered distinct from the source—thus, the Blast doesn't counter the poke. To counter the poke, Hannah would have to use an interrupt which targets the effect directly, which the Blast does not; the Blasts just target spells and permanents.

Specialized Timing Steps

The timing system outlined above doesn't work for every effect in **Magic**. Certain effects can't function properly if used during the normal timing sequence, or they require paying costs at odd times. These effects are used during specialized timing steps which exist in isolation from the normal flow of timing. These steps exist solely for the benefit of the effects in question, and ignore the timing context in which they occur, so it is possible for instants to apparently be played during such a step "illegally." If both players have effects to play during the step, the active player uses any or all effects first. Each such effect would resolve as it was paid for. Once such a step has been completed, the turn resumes.

   Example: Aladdin's Lamp can be used in place of drawing a card, so it is played during the resolution of an effect that instructs the player to draw a card. Remember that the free draw during the draw phase is considered an effect.

   Example: Brainwash requires that the enchanted creature's controller pay ③ in order to attack with the creature. This cost is paid during a specialized timing step that occurs while attackers are being chosen.

During these specialized steps, only two types of effects may be played: the effects the step is created for and interrupts which provide mana. No other effects are allowed unless the rules for the step in question specify otherwise. Note that this makes it impossible to counter most specialized effects, as counterspells don't provide mana and thus typically aren't allowed during such steps.

There is no complete list of the specialized timing steps that occur, as these steps are generated as needed in order to handle certain effects. In general, it should be assumed that any effect which clearly cannot be used during a normal batch of effects follows the rules outlined above.

The largest group of effects requiring a specialized step are *triggered effects*, i.e., those which are only used when a certain event occurs. Triggered effects are a little unusual because they involve two kinds of effects: those which happen automatically and those which must be activated. Triggered effects always trigger while something else is going on, but they wait for that step to finish before being resolved. For example, if a bunch of creatures are placed in the graveyard, any effects triggering by those placements will wait until all of the creatures are in before going off. When the step that triggered the effects has finished, all triggered effects which automatically go off will do so in the order they entered play. The active player then goes through all of her activated effects and uses as many as desired, followed by the opponent using as many activated effects as desired. Each triggered effect, whether automatic or activated, will resolve immediately when its turn comes up, but all damage and destruction resulting from triggered effects will be handled in one damage prevention step at the end. Triggered effects must be used immediately or not at all.

   Example: During Hannah's main phase, she enchants Carrington's Personal Incarnation with Creature Bond and then Terrors it once the enchantment is in place. Both players have Soul Nets in play. There are no responses to the Terror, so it resolves, and the Incarnation is put into the graveyard. Four effects are triggered by its death: the Incarnation's backlash, the Creature Bond, and the two Soul Nets. These effects are processed in the following order.

First, the continuous effects go off: the Personal Incarnation and the Creature Bond. The Incarnation entered play first, so it is processed first, and Carrington loses half of his life. This is not damage, so the effect is not delayed. The Creature Bond is then processed, but its damage is deferred until all triggered effects have resolved. Since it's Hannah's turn, she then decides first whether or not to activate her Soul Net. After that, Carrington decides whether or not to activate his Soul Net. Finally, there is a damage prevention step in which the damage from the Creature Bond is processed.

Damage Prevention

The damage prevention step is a hybrid timing step. Like normal specialized steps, it occurs whenever required—that is, whenever damage is dealt or something is buried or destroyed. But it does not have the stunted timing structure characteristic of most specialized steps, instead allowing for any number of batches of damage prevention effects. Damage prevention effects basically include those which prevent damage, those which redirect it, and regeneration. For example, cards which remove a creature from play or boost a creature's toughness are not considered damage prevention effects, so they may not be played during damage prevention.

Damage prevention effects can't be used effectively during the normal batch sequence, since at the time the effect would resolve, there wouldn't be any damage being dealt or any creatures being sent to the graveyard. These effects must wait for damage to actually be dealt or for a creature to actually be sent to the graveyard. Damage prevention steps thus happen most often at the end of any batch in which damage was dealt, or after any effect in a batch resolves and sends something to the graveyard. Such steps also occur after any damage dealing step in which any damage was dealt, and in fact this rulebook generally describes the damage prevention step in the context of the attack.

Note: Certain other effects are also used during damage prevention and can only be used at this time. For example, Eye for an Eye can only be used during damage prevention, as it has to wait for damage to actually be dealt.

Example: Carrington shoots Hannah with a Lightning Bolt; it is now her chance to respond. Powering up her Circle of Protection: Red now would be pointless and, in fact, impossible, since the Bolt hasn't done anything yet. There are no responses to the Bolt, so the batch starts resolving. The Bolt resolves first, but the damage is not dealt until later, so the Circle still can't be used. Only when the batch is finished resolving is the damage actually dealt. This is when the damage can be prevented, but since effects cannot normally be played during or at the end of the resolution of a batch, a damage prevention step is generated. It is during this step that (finally!) Hannah can use the Circle to stop the damage.

The damage prevention step is processed much like a normal phase, except that there is no mana burn at the end of the step. At the start of the step, any automatic damage prevention effects, such as protection, take effect. Any permanent which was simply sent to the graveyard, or which has taken lethal damage, is marked as being *on its way* to the graveyard. Any such permanent is eligible to be regenerated and may not be sacrificed at this point. If a creature is regenerated, or if enough of the damage being dealt to it is prevented, then that creature is no longer considered to be on its way and could be sacrificed later in the step.

Once the automatic effects have been applied, the step then enters normal "null state" in which the players can build up batches of damage prevention effects. This is exactly the process used during a normal phase, so the active player decides first whether to do anything, and so on. The resolution of each batch of effects will return the step to a "null state," so there can be multiple batches within each damage prevention step.

At the end of each damage prevention step, check to see if anything's toughness has dropped as a result of creature death. If any creature has now taken lethal damage, another damage prevention step begins to account for that creature.

Example: Carrington has four Keldon Warlords in play. Hannah hits one with a four-point Fireball and another with a Lightning Bolt. Once the batch has finished resolving, Carrington has a 4/4 creature with 4 points of damage, a 4/4 creature with 3 points of damage, and two undamaged Warlords. No damage is prevented, so the Fireballed Warlord is put into the graveyard; this drops all the other Warlords to 3/3. Thus, once damage prevention is over, the Bolted Warlord is not regenerated, it also dies, and the other Warlords drop to 2/2. Note that during the second damage prevention step, the Warlord could be regenerated, but it would be too late to prevent the damage from the Lightning Bolt.

The Lifecycle of an Effect

The complete process of playing and resolving an effect is described here for reference. For more details, refer to the appropriate rules section above.

The first step is to play the effect. This involves taking the card from the hand (if a spell), paying any costs, choosing any targets, and making any other decisions which must be made when the card is played. No effects are legal during this step, so any mana required would have to be in the player's mana pool before the effect could be played. All costs paid at this time are lost, even if the effect fizzles or is countered.

Once the effect has been played, any triggered effects go off, such as Soul Net triggering in response to a sacrificed creature. This includes a damage prevention step if necessary.

Now that the effect has been played, it enters the period during which it can be countered or otherwise affected by interrupts such as counterspells. Interrupts may be played by either player at this time, under the guidelines outlined above. The casting period ends in one of two ways: an interrupt resolves which counters the effect, or both players will decide that they're finished with interrupts. If the effect is countered, then it effectively never happens, and if the effect was a spell, its card is placed in the graveyard. Remember that the effect is distinct from the source, so if the effect was generated by an ability, changing or destroying the source will do nothing to the effect itself.

If the effect is not countered, then it is successfully cast. Any effects which would be triggered by the effect being successfully cast, such as Crystal Rod or Verduran Enchantress, are triggered now. This also includes a damage prevention step if necessary. If the effect was triggered or is an interrupt that is not required to be "on hold" due to targeting someone else's effect, it resolves immediately. If it is an "on hold" interrupt, it will resolve appropriately. In all other cases, the effect begins or builds onto a batch which resolves in the "last in, first out" order.

When an effect resolves, it attempts to do so completely, under the guidelines outlined above. If the effect is a spell, then the card is either put into play or into the graveyard, depending on the nature of the spell, as soon as it has finished resolving. Any effects which were triggered by events occuring during the resolution then go off, followed by damage prevention if required by the effect.

PLAYING THE GAME

Talking Too Fast

Every so often, one player will talk too fast and attempt to play an effe[ct] before he or she can legally do so. Talking too fast typically happens one [of] two ways: a player tries to start a batch, or respond to an effect, when it's th[e] other player's turn to play effects; or a player skips ahead to a given phase, [or] even to the end of the turn, when the other player wanted to stop and d[o] something along the way. Such situations typically result from the play[er] being too anxious to play an effect, but occasionally a simple miscommuni[-] cation will lead to this sort of mistake.

If one player does something too soon or out of turn, then his or her oppo[-] nent can back up the turn to before the effect was ever played. The prematu[re] action is retracted entirely: a spell would be returned to the player's han[d,] lands tapped for mana would be restored and the mana removed from t[he] pool, and so on. The action simply never happened, as far as the game is co[n-] cerned. Once the game state is cleaned up, the player who backed things [up] goes ahead and does whatever it is she wanted to do, and the turn progress[es] normally from there. The player who talked too fast is not obligated to repe[at] those actions that were retracted later in the turn, unless of course she w[as] compelled to take those actions in the first place.

> Example: Carrington starts his turn by untapping and then talks too
> fast by simply drawing a card and declaring an attack. Hannah
> wanted to play an effect prior to Carrington's attack, so she makes
> Carrington back up the turn to the main phase before the attack, and
> then she plays her fast effect. Carrington's attack never actually
> started, so he still gets the chance to attack, or he might play a
> sorcery before trying the attack again, or he could just decide not to
> attack at all.

Fortunately, a little cooperation between the players will go a long w[ay] toward avoiding situations where the turn must be backed up. The simple[st] way to avoid backing up is to ask the other player, "Are you done yet?" wh[en] you suspect that the game is entering a stage where both players will be wan[t-] ing to play fast effects. Note that because it is the active player who decid[es] first whether to do something or not, it will mostly be up to the opponent [to] ask, "Are you done yet?" and up to the active player to confirm with the oppo[-] nent that it's okay to advance the turn to a new phase.

The advantage to asking questions like "Are you done yet?" is that you a[re] confirming with your opponent that it's okay for you to go ahead and pl[ay] effects. If your opponent says that yes, she's done, then she's explicity turn[ed] down her chance to play effects and cannot change her mind if you go ahe[ad]

B-114

and do something. She can respond to whatever you do, of course, but by saying, "I'm done," she gives you the green light to play effects.

Example: Carrington has just completed an attack and has a Giant Spider that took 3 damage from a blocking creature. Hannah is considering poking it with her Prodigal Sorcerer to finish it off, but she knows that Carrington is playing with Web—so she doesn't want to poke prematurely. (Remember that if she just says, "I poke your Spider with my Sorcerer" after the attack, Carrington can claim she was talking too fast, and force her to back up. Carrington could then play a Web on his Spider.)

To avoid this problem, Hannah asks Carrington, "Now that the attack's over, are you going to do anything?" If Carrington declines to play an effect, she can go ahead and poke the Spider without fear that Carrington will back up the turn. And if Carrington does do something, she can keep verifying whether he's done or not after each effect. (Or, if Carrington does something other than cast Web on the Spider, Hannah could then respond to that by poking the Spider with her Sorcerer, knowing that Carrington cannot respond to the poke by playing a Web, a non-fast effect.)

If the active player indicates that she's done with her turn and the opponent opts to play fast effects before the turn ends, it should be assumed that such effects are played during the end phase following discard, unless the opponent explicitly says otherwise. The active player will be able to respond normally or to start new batches of fast effects. But since the opponent played an effect after the main phase, the active player cannot play sorceries and such. If the active player simply ends the turn without declaring an attack, it should not be assumed that the player called for an attack in which no creatures were actually assigned to attack. The opponent can thus back the turn up to the main phase and force an attack with effects such as Siren's Call.

It is important for players to recognize that they can telegraph their moves by playing effects before the other player is ready for them, for example, by jumping ahead to play effects during end phase when the active player hasn't had the chance to attack yet. Because the overeager player is talking too fast, it's perfectly legitimate for the other player to back up the turn and use that knowledge to his or her advantage by playing an effect that she wouldn't have played otherwise. A player who doesn't like tipping his or her hand should probably get into the habit of asking "Are you done yet?" when it's crucial to know whether the other player is, in fact, done with effects.

excuse me, Mr. Suitcase?

Paul Peterson

Now you've done it. You broke down and bought a deck of those cards everyone is playing with. You immediately ran over to your friend's house to challenge Mr. Suitcase-of-Cards to a game or two of **Magic**. After playing thirty games for ante and losing thirty cards, you've become a little disillusioned.

That's fine. Don't give up. What you need to do is make your **Magic** deck more competitive. That's where I come in. I'll show you how to go through a starter deck and a couple of booster packs and end up with a deck that won't embarrass you in front of your friends.

The first step is, of course, to get the cards. One starter deck and two booster packs provide a good mix of cards to choose from, although one starter deck should be sufficient. And look, I just happen to have a starter deck and a couple of boosters right here!

The next step is to concentrate deeply on the cards in your packs, hoping that you get something good. This step is usually done as you open your packs and may include small offerings to the Wizards of the Coast.

Once you have opened the packs, sort the cards by land type and color, placing all of the mountains with the red cards and so on. Put any artifacts aside for now. Sorting the cards like this will not only show you how many cards of each color you have but will also indicate how much land of each type you have to support those cards.

Most players find that the best way to "tune" their starter decks is to immediately get rid of at least one color—preferably two or three. You probably lost those first thirty games because you never seemed to have the right mana to go with the cards in your hand, yet all the while your opponent was zinging you with creatures and spells. By removing one or more colors, you vastly improve your chances of having the right mana at the right time.

The first criterion to consider in eliminating a color is the number of cards you have in that color. If you only have four blue cards in all of those packs, they probably aren't going to help you very much, no matter how impressive they are. If, by some quirk of fate, you seem to have near-perfect symmetry among the five colors, you will have to figure out which colors you prefer to get rid of. There are several ways you could do this: You could choose randomly; you could pick the colors that have the coolest-looking cards; or you could show the cards to Mr. Suitcase and keep the colors of whatever cards make him breathe faster.

Next, you should check for land support. You must make sure that you have enough land in your deck to cast the spells that you have; otherwise, you'll continue to run into the problem of never having enough of the right mana. Having thirty really great white cards is useless if you only have one plains to power them.

So how much land is enough? An average, balanced deck requires about half as many lands as spells, so roughly a third of your total cards should be land. This is a good starting point, and after you've played for a while you can adjust the proportions to suit your own style. A quick look through my cards shows that, although I have nine green cards and twelve white cards, I only have three forests and four plains. I could reduce the number of green and white non-land cards to bring the ratio back up—and I might do so later—but since I'm trying to get rid of colors anyway, I'll just remove them for now.

It is also a good idea to try to keep the number of cards roughly equal in each color you are using. This will help ensure that you don't end up with a handful of cards you can't play. If you have only six black spells and three swamps in a sixty-card deck, the chances that you will get a useful combination of swamps and spells are not very good. If, on the other hand, you have roughly the same number of cards for all of your colors, you should get equal numbers of each land, which will enable you to cast the spells in your hand.

The next step in tuning your deck requires that you know something about the cards. If you've played **Magic** a few times before—say, with one of Mr. Suitcase's decks—then you should be fine. Otherwise, take the cards you have left after removing two or three colors, shuffle them together with the artifacts, and practice. Offer to play Mr. Suitcase again (not for ante, this time). See how the various cards work together; find combinations that work well together. My deck has in it a Dark Ritual, which costs one black mana to cast to produce three black mana. This card works extremely well with the Drain Life I have. Drain Life does a point of damage to one target for each point of black mana you put into the spell beyond the original casting cost. The Dark Ritual increases my supply of black mana to pump into the Drain Life.

Try to play against as many other colors as possible. Are any of your cards more or less useless against certain colors? For example, I have a Red Elemental Blast in my deck that will counter a blue spell or destroy a blue card in play. This card is helpful against The Flood (Mr. Suitcase's all-blue deck) but is fairly useless when battling his green and black Creepy-Crawlies deck.

You should now be fairly familiar with the cards you have. It's time to tune the deck some more. Go through your deck and pull out any of the cards that don't seem to work well. This includes any cards that you never seem to use, for one reason or another. Maybe they cost too much mana to cast, or maybe they produce an effect that is not useful in your deck. I played several games with other tuned starter decks to test my deck, and I found several cards that didn't work very well. For example, in red I have a Goblin King. The King is a 2/2 creature that makes all goblins in play +1/+1 and gives them mountain-walk. But I only have one goblin in my entire deck and the King costs two red mana and one colorless to summon, which is more than most 2/2 creatures. In black, I have a Lord of the Pit and a Cursed Land. The Lord of the Pit is a

huge, nasty 7/7 flying creature with the trample ability. It's a great card, but it costs seven mana to cast and requires you to sacrifice one of your creatures per turn to it, and I don't seem to have a lot of creatures as it is. The Cursed Land enchants one land to do a point of damage to that land's controller every turn, but it costs four mana to cast. This makes it difficult to get out early, the time it would be most useful. The likelihood of my making efficient use of these cards is fairly low, so I can take them out of my deck.

One thing to keep in mind while tuning your deck is the number of creatures in it. Creatures are probably the most efficient way to deal damage to your opponent. They are also an excellent way for beginning players to learn the game. And while it is possible to create an effective deck without any creatures, you are unlikely to be able to do so working from just a starter deck. You should therefore be sure that you have enough creatures and spells that help your creatures in your deck. You should find a ratio that works well for your deck—a good ratio of creatures to other non-land cards is anything over half. In a sixty-card deck, this will give you about one-third creatures, one-third land, and one-third other spells.

It became obvious while testing my deck against other tuned starter decks that my deck was very low on creatures and that having that Lord of the Pit didn't help matters. The shortage was even worse after tuning because several of my "problem cards" were creatures. If your deck is low on creatures, see if there is one color in particular that you could remove or replace to fix the problem. After looking through the colors, I noticed that my black cards contained very few creatures other than the Lord of the Pit. There were also several cards that I never seemed to use, like the Cursed Land. But seven of the nine green cards I removed from my deck earlier were creatures, and they seemed to be pretty good creatures. By removing black from my deck and adding green, I not only got rid of some cards I couldn't use, but I also increased the creature ratio in my deck substantially.

A brief word about artifacts is in order at this point. You probably only have two or three among all your cards. My strong suggestion is to keep all of them in your deck, as many of them are extremely useful. You can use any mana to cast them, and they will probably help you no matter what colors you are playing. If after playing with them for a while, however, you find that a particular artifact isn't helping, don't hesitate to remove it from your deck. My deck had a Winter Orb in it. While the Orb is in play, a player may only untap one of her lands on her turn. After playing for a while, I could see that this hurt my deck more than it helped it, so I removed it.

It's probably a good idea to test your deck again at this point to see how any changes you've made might affect it. This is especially important if you've made any major changes, such as adding and/or removing an entire color. Try to follow the above guidelines as much as possible. Keep the colors and mana balanced. My deck needed a few forests to bring my mana balance back up, so I traded a couple of my extra cards to Mr. Suitcase for some forests.

I played several games against some untuned starter decks with my newly tuned deck. As you can imagine, my distilled deck walked all over these untuned decks. This was because I had the mana I needed to cast the spells in my hand while my opponents did not. Often the cards he could cast were useless, or else they hurt him as much as they hurt me.

The next step in tuning your deck is the most fun, in my opinion. Take your deck, along with those extra cards you have, and go to wherever the local **Magic** players hang out; a local game store or comic book shop is a good place to start. Find some people with some **Magic** cards and ask if they want to do some trading. I'd recommend you bring along someone you trust who knows both the game and the relative card values so that you don't end up trading your Lord of the Pit (a valuable rare card) for a couple of extra forests. Maybe Mr. Suitcase would be a good choice—if you've forgiven him for stomping on you earlier.

Remember that certain cards are rarer than others and therefore more valuable. This can be a tremendous help to you—you can often find collectors who have tons of extra cards but who are missing a few that they need to complete their collections. They will often trade a stack of cards for a single card they need. In this type of trade, everybody wins. You get cards that improve your deck, and the collector is one step closer to finishing her collection.

Keeping rarity in mind will also help you avoid having others take advantage of you. Not all rare cards are powerful, but in the right decks, they can *all* be valuable. This is where Mr. Suitcase comes in. When someone offers you a card for one of yours, have Mr. Suitcase look over the deal and let you know if he thinks it's a fair trade. There are also card lists which you can use as a reference that show the cards' relative rarity. These lists can be found in this book, in *The Duelist* and other magazines which cover collectible card games, and at the Internet ftp site at marvin.macc.wisc.edu.

While trading, remember what colors you are playing and try to trade for cards that help your deck, not just for cards that have good art. Ask Mr. Suitcase for suggestions on cards that would help your deck, and try to get those. Of course, make sure you have enough land to support the cards you add to your deck. Many people who have a lot of cards (like Mr. Suitcase) will give away land to new players or let it go cheap, just to get rid of the stuff. After all, paper is heavy.

By now, you should have a fairly good two- or three-color deck. It is time to go back to testing it against other decks to see how it plays. As before, watch carefully to see how the cards interact. Are you still experiencing the same problems? Are you getting the mana you need? After a few games you should be ready to cull some more cards out of your deck. It is important to remember that a skinny deck is usually an effective deck; the fewer cards that are in your deck, the greater your chance of drawing any one of them. Also, you can trade the cards you take out of your deck for other cards that fit in your deck.

By continuing this process of playing, tuning, and trading (and occasionally buying new cards), your deck will continue to improve. After a while, your deck should be good enough that you can play with most players on a friendly basis. I would not recommend using your deck in the tournaments in which Mr. Suitcase plays. The competition there will have access to enough cards to assemble very specific decks which will probably be very difficult to beat with the cards you have.

But even with a limited card selection, a decent deck is not too far away. In addition to the starter deck I've used in these examples here, I have a starter deck that I've been tuning for the last six months. I never simply add cards to it to improve it; I only trade with other similar starter decks that my friends have. Over the course of this period, my deck has become so nasty that no one likes to play against it (especially for ante), so apparently this method works. If you practice enough, trade well, and tune your deck carefully, it should work for you, too.

it's in the cards
An Examination of Card Combinations
Mark Rosewater

I actually remember vividly the moment when **Magic** "got" me. I had heard rumors about the game and finally had a chance to try it out at a convention. It took a few games to get the rules straight, but by my fourth or fifth game I had the basics down—that's when "it" happened. I had a Craw Wurm in play but my opponent had a Sea Serpent blocking; all I had in my hand was a Phantasmal Terrain. And then, out of the blue, I saw the answer: I used my Phantasmal Terrain to change my opponent's only island to a mountain and the Sea Serpent died, allowing my Craw Wurm to march over and win the game. It was the first time that I truly sensed the possibilities of the cards, how things could interreact to bring about all kinds of effects. And from that moment on I was hooked.

It's been a long time since that first day, but my appreciation of card combinations has only grown. In fact, I feel that of all the aspects of **Magic**, it is the combinations that give the game its spark. After all, **Magic** is, at its heart, a card game. It seems only proper that the constant mixing of the cards serves as the game's lifeblood.

To best examine how card combinations work, I have decided to take a look at several "classic" card combinations to see how they tick. My hope is not to spoil combinations for you but, rather, to teach you how to seek out new ones all your own.

Channel + Fireball

For starters, I thought I would begin with the granddaddy of card combinations. When used with a few out-of-print cards (to provide extra mana), the Channel/Fireball combo lets a player win on the very first turn (by hitting his or her opponent with a twenty-point Fireball). What is interesting about this combination is the treatment Channel received before the combination was first discovered. A green sorcery that lets you trade life for colorless mana, Channel was dismissed by most as a useless card. I've seen the same pattern happen numerous times: a card comes out that, on the surface, seems useless. So nobody plays with it—that is, until some inventive soul finds a combination that makes the card a killer. Then you have to trade an arm and a leg to get it.

The lesson here is that no card is useless. An ability that might seem pointless in isolation could prove invaluable if paired correctly. It is the good **Magic** player who leads the pack by finding a use for a card that others have discarded. Remember, *somebody* had to play with Channel.

Thicket Basilisk + Lure (+ Regeneration or Gaseous Form)

This combination is so popular it actually has a nickname (a "Creature Sweeper," for those that are interested). The two cards—the Thicket Basilisk and the Lure—work nicely together because the Lure (a green creature enchantment) forces an opponent to block with all of his or her untapped creatures and the Thicket Basilisk destroys any creature which blocks it. Add a Regeneration or Gaseous Form (which makes a target creature neither deal nor receive damage) to keep the Basilisk alive and this trick can be used many times. Remember that Gaseous Form does, indeed, allow the Basilisk to use its special ability to destroy all blocking creatures—this ability isn't technically *damage*, so the Lured blockers will still be destroyed.

The reason I bring this combination up is that it demonstrates well how cards can become more powerful when working in conjunction with one another.

One need only look at the Basilisk and Lure working separately to realize that, as a whole, they are stronger than the sum of their parts.

This is one of the secrets of **Magic**: True power lies not in single cards but in combinations. The difference between a *fair* **Magic** player and a *good* **Magic** player is the ability to recognize and use combinations that strengthen his or her game.

Firebreathing (or Inflatable Creature) + Dwarven Warriors

Probably the most potent of the all-common combinations, this duo allows a player to hit an opponent with large amounts of unblockable creature damage. The Dwarven Warriors uses its special ability to make a creature unblockable and then the Firebreathing (a red creature enchantment) can be used to pump up the power of the unblocked creature.

The lesson behind this combination is the importance of timing. The reason it is so effective is that the Firebreathing takes advantage of a small loophole in the Dwarven Warriors' design. The Warriors can only make a creature of power two or less unblockable. But—and this is the beautiful part—"other effects may later be used to increase the creature's power beyond 2." When examining other combinations, keep this example in mind and remember that sometimes cards will only work when used in the proper order. Don't miss out on a good mix because you failed to take into account what needs to happen first to make what happens second successful.

Colossus of Sardia + Instill Energy

For a total of ten mana, this little combination allows you to attack each turn with a 9/9 trampler. Using the extra untap ability of Instill Energy (a green creature enchantment), a player can avoid paying the Colossus of Sardia's costly untap cost (of nine colorless mana).

One of the common occurrences in **Magic** is for the designers to create a powerful creature and then balance it by adding some restriction (the Colossus' expensive untap cost, for example). But often, by finding the right card, you can create a combination that circumvents this handicap and allows the creature to function unhindered. Another example might be using a Phantasmal Terrain to create an island on your opponent's side to allow a Sea Serpent to attack.

The next time you encounter a creature with a built-in handicap, think of what cards might allow you to reduce or even eliminate the creature's downside. Quite often a single card can turn an impotent creature into a game winner.

Flight (or Jump) + Grapeshot Catapult (or Hurricane)

Often referred to as "skeet shooting," this is the practice of killing a small creature by first making it fly and then doing damage to it as a flier. While this is not the kind of combination you should ever plan a deck around, it does demonstrate how cards can be combined to create an effect that neither card is capable of by itself (in this case, killing a grounded creature).

To take advantage of combinations such as this, a player needs to always think how any one spell can set up another. In this particular case, the Flight (or Jump) grants an ability to a creature that then makes it a viable target for the Grapeshot Catapult (or the Hurricane). Another example of this might be to cast Animate Artifact on an artifact in order to make it a creature, which would then be susceptible to a Fireball.

In many ways, combinations such as these are the most exciting combinations in the game, as they allow creative thinking to accomplish tasks that seem impossible. Interestingly enough, these "miracle" combinations are found most often when players are painted into a corner and are struggling to find anything that can save them.

Pestilence + Circle of Protection: Black
(+ Black Ward or Regenerating Creature)

This combination is rather straightforward. Pestilence continually inflicts universal damage (one point to every player and to each creature for each black mana spent) while Circle of Protection: Black protects the player from its harm. The Black Ward or regenerating creature (Drudge Skeletons works quite well) are used to keep a creature in play, as Pestilence leaves play at the end of the turn if no creatures remain.

Unlike previous pairings, these two cards have a different dynamic. In this mix, one card basically functions normally while the second card is used to protect the player from the effects of the first card. Ostensibly, the combination is effective because one card acts offensively while the other acts defensively. Most often the defensive cards will be Circles of Protection and Wards, but occasionally defense will be served by other cards. The key to making this type of combination work is to ensure that the defensive card halts or limits the damage to the caster while still allowing damage to flow unheeded at the opponent.

Gloom + Sleight of Mind

This combination is used to shut down a person's ability to cast spells. Gloom (a black enchantment) causes all white spells to cost three more colorless mana to cast and Sleight of Mind (a blue interrupt) can change the word "white" on Gloom to any other color of the caster's choosing. A Lightning Bolt, for example, is not quite as handy when it has a casting cost of four. And that's if there's only *one* Sleighted Gloom in play.

Like the Flight + Grapeshot Catapult combination, this is not the type of combination you build a deck around. Rather, it is an example of how one card can be added to fine-tune a card already in the deck. For example, assume you have a heavy black and blue creature deck (often referred to as a "Bruiser" deck—black and blue... get it?). To avoid white from casting Disenchants and Swords to Plowshares, you have put some Glooms in the deck. The addition of Sleight of Mind allows you to increase the deck's flexibility. If you happen to run into a player without white, the Sleights allow you to still keep the Glooms useful. As often proves true with card combinations such as this one, a second card can be used to expand the range of another card. A few Wild Growths, for instance, will turn a Ley Druid into a major mana producer, while a couple of Evil Presences can make anybody susceptible to a Karma.

Red/Blue Elemental Blast + Chaoslace/Thoughtlace

This combination is very effective in that it allows a blue/red mage to destroy any card in play for just two mana. The Lace turns any card to the color which the Blast can then destroy—but what makes this combination truly deadly is that it can act at interrupt speed, meaning that it can be used at just about any moment in the game. Note that the actual timing of interrupts can often be tricky; see the Timing article, beginning on p. B-95, for more information.

When players match different cards in various combinations, speed is an important factor they should keep in mind. If, for example, an instant is matched with a sorcery, players restrict themselves to just using the combination on their own turn. Often times, the payoff is well worth the restriction, but nonetheless, the speed of the two effects deserves to be taken into consideration.

The Rack + Black Vise (or Cursed Rack)

These two cards are a "damned if you do, damned if you don't" combination that handicaps one's opponent by forcing them to stay at exactly three or four cards (as The Rack hurts a player for having less than three cards and a Black Vise for having more than four).

The uniqueness to this duo is twofold. First, both are artifacts, and it is important to note that artifacts work well in card combinations because they can be freely mixed with any color. Second, these two cards are successful together because each one creates an environment that complements the other. Whereas other combinations target particular cards or create a singular effect, the beauty of this type of mix is that it redefines the environment your opponent has to play in. Quite often, when this combination is done correctly, your opponent will be too busy trying to survive to focus much energy on you.

Stasis + Time Elemental + Kismet
(+ Birds of Paradise + Instill Energy)

This combination is so potent that it has an entire deck built around it known as a "Stasis" deck; the entire purpose of this combination is to keep one's opponent from ever having another untap phase. Once in play, the Stasis (a blue enchantment) eliminates the untap phase while the Kismet (a white enchantment) ensures that all of the opponent's cards come into play tapped. The Time Elemental is then used to return the Stasis to the player's hand, allowing him or her the untap phase that the opponent will never have. Then the Stasis is simply brought back into play at the end of the player's turn, effectively stopping the opponent's next untap phase. Furthermore, if the opponent is tapped out when this combination first kicks in, he or she will never be able to do anything for the rest of the game!

I bring up this trio (or should I say quintuplet, if one uses the Birds and Instill Energy as easy mana when the Stasis is in play) as an acknowledgement that combinations can, at times, number more than two. I should add that the danger in creating bigger combinations is that, as the number of needed cards grows, the probability of ever getting the cards together decreases.

The other important thing to note is that one of the reasons this combination is successful is that any two pieces of it are useful by themselves. Even without eliminating an opponent's untap phase, Kismet and Time Elemental can pretty much guarantee that nothing ever gets used.

Time to Build

Now that you've had a chance to see some of the "classics," it's time to start finding some combinations of your own. The secret to accomplishing this is actually quite simple: just keep your eyes open for the possibility. Play with all of your cards in various mixes and try to find as many different opponents as you can. And when two cards come together, resulting in something special, make a mental note. Believe it or not, almost all of the discoveries I have made came simply when I had two cards in my hand and a mind open enough to recognize that they would work well together. The rest, as they say, is... **Magic**.

multiplayer Magic

Jim Lin and Dave Pettey

Are you looking for a new way to play **Magic** besides the regular two-player way? Tired of trying to figure who has to sit out when you are playing **Magic** and have an odd number of players? Not sure what to do when you have a group of players that includes both killer players and newcomers? Or are you just looking for variety to test your **Magic** skills? Multiplayer **Magic** can be an exciting and rewarding variant for you to pursue, but be warned! Much of your two-player **Magic** experience won't carry over to multiplayer **Magic**. Old strategies and decks that seemed unbeatable may not seem so exciting anymore, and ideas you left behind as "unworkable" may suddenly have a new sparkle about them.

One of the things that doesn't carry over especially well from two-player **Magic** to multiplayer **Magic** is, believe it or not, the rules. **Magic** is a two-player game, and the rules were written for such a play environment. As a result, a whole bunch of questions like "Who can I attack?" "How do I win?" "Who counts as my opponent?" and "What happens when someone gets knocked out?" need to be answered. If you've traveled among various gaming groups, you may have noticed that many of them resolve these questions completely differently from one another when they play multiplayer games. The most important thing to remember is that before beginning play, you should agree on exactly which rules you are following. The rules presented here are those which Wizards of the Coast suggests you observe in multiplayer environments. Don't be afraid to experiment, though, and find new rules or variants that work better for your specific play group.

There are a few general questions that need to be answered for almost any multiplayer game. These questions are discussed in the first few sections below, and you can create a whole plethora of interesting variants just by mixing and matching the different options that are presented here. Next, the details of several popular variants are presented: Free-For-All, Attack Left, Crossfire Team **Magic**, Emperor Team **Magic**, and Rainbow **Magic**.

Who Is Your Opponent?

Magic is usually a two-player game, and in that environment it is quite clear who your "opponent" is: the other player. In a multiplayer game, however, it is not always so clear who is your opponent and who is not. Furthermore, some of the cards (especially those from older editions) may be difficult to understand and apply in a multiplayer game. In general, note that in a multiplayer non-team game, every other player is considered your opponent; in a multiplayer team game, every player who is not your teammate is considered your opponent. Unfortunately, this is not always enough to understand all of the cards. In most cases, *Fourth Edition* cards make sense in a multiplayer game, as well as in a two-player game. Older edition cards, however, are not nearly as multiplayer friendly, and it may not be clear how cards that read "opponent"—with no further qualifications—should be played. The following lists outline how older cards should be played in a multiplayer game.

These effects apply to "target opponent." If a continuous ability, choose that opponent when the permanent is played. You may not choose another opponent later, so if that opponent leaves the game, the permanent becomes useless, and changing control of the permanent will not change who it targets. If an activated abilty, choose an opponent each time the permanent is activated. If a spell, choose the target as normal.

Arena	Mirror Universe
Black Vise	Nebuchadnezzar
Citanul Druid	Nova Pentacle
Cuombajj Witches	Powerleech
Cursed Rack	Preacher
Dwarven Catapult	Psychic Allergy
Eternal Flame	The Rack
Festival	Rag Man
Gaea's Avenger	Rainbow Vale
Glasses of Urza	Siren's Call
Invoke Prejudice	Tempest Efreet
Jihad	Underworld Dreams
Lifeblood	
Lifetap	

These effects apply to "target player." Follow the same rules as "target opponent" cards as to when the target is chosen.

Ancestral Recall	Mana Short
Disrupting Scepter	Mind Twist
Drain Power	Storm Seeker
Kismet	Word of Command
Jovial Evil	

These effects apply to all players.

Balance	Pestilence
Eureka	Timetwister
Mana Flare	Wheel of Fortune

These effects should be read as saying "any opponent."

Bronze Tablet	Psychic Purge
Farrel's Mantle	Relic Bind ("When target
Fellwar Stone	artifact an opponent
Hyperion Blacksmith	controls…")
Land Equilibrium	Water Wurm
Land Tax	Whirling Dervish
Nafs Asp	Witch Hunter (second ability)

Choose a different opponent each time the effect applies.

Clergy of the Holy Nimbus	Ernham Djinn
Demonic Hordes	Rogahh of Kher Keep

These cards require a coin toss. Target an opponent each time the coin is flipped.

Bottle of Suleiman	Mijae Djinn
Goblin Artisans	Orcish Captain
Goblin Kites	Ydwen Efreet

The following cards should say "defending player" instead of "opponent":

Dandân	Island Fish Jasconius
Delif's Cone	Merchant Ship
Delif's Cube	Orgg
Farrel's Zealot	Pirate Ship
Giant Shark	Sea Serpent
Goblin Rock Sled	Vodalian Knights
Goblin War Drums	

Special Cases

Aladdin: Can take control of any artifact, even one you already control.

Demonic Attorney: Target opponent decides whether to concede or not. If that player does not concede, you each ante an additional card.

Ghazbán Ogre: Add "If you are tied for highest life total, Ghazbán Ogre does not change controller. If other players are tied for highest life total and you are not, choose randomly which player gets control of Ghazbán Ogre."

Nettling Imp: Targets a creature not controlled by you. Forces that player to attack and may only be used during that player's turn. Imp does not target that player.

Raging River: It is the defending player who divides up the would-be blockers.

Remove Enchantments: Read the second sentence as "If cast while an opponent is attacking you…."

Scarwood Bandits: Can take control of any artifact not controlled by you. The controller of that artifact would be the one to pay to counter the effect.

Sharazad: Whoever wins the subgame loses no life. Each other player loses half of his or her life. If a draw, everyone loses life.

Sorrow's Path: Only usable if you are not the defending player.

Wall of Dust: Read "your opponent" as "their controller."

Territories

View the territories as a ring split into a number of sections equal to the number of players remaining in the game (that is, the structure changes a little each time a player dies or loses). Thus, the territories of players sitting next to each other (assuming that players that have lost have left the table) are adjacent.

You cannot just summon creatures into your teammates' (or any other player's) territory, nor can you decide to cast a general enchantment there (enchant _____ can, of course, be played into other players' territories). In general, with the exception of the additional multiplayer rule allowing creature movement, the only way you can put a permanent into someone else's territoy is if you could have played it in your opponent's territory in a two-player duel.

Whenever you gain control of a permanent, that permanent is placed in your territory. Not all of the creatures in your territory, however, are necessarily controlled by you (see below regarding creature movement).

Leaving the Game (How Do I Lose?)

Each player has 20 life, and if during the end of any phase or at the beginning or end of any attack a player's life total is 0 or less, then that player is out of the game. A player is also out of the game if he or she is forced to draw a card or cards but does not have enough cards in his or her library to do so. Additionally, a player is out of the game if at any time he or she has 10 or more poison counters.

When a player is out of the game, all of the cards that he or she owns are removed from the game as well (this makes it easy for those players to go play someone else), and all permanents in that player's territory that he or she does not own are placed in their previous controller's territory.

The Attack and Creature Movement

One of the biggest changes in play for multiplayer environments is the nature of the attack. In a two-player environment, it is very clear: You can attack your opponent and your creatures can block his or her attacks. In a multiplayer environment, however, there are many opponents that you might want to attack, and the creatures in your territory won't always be your own (see "How Do I Move Creatures?"). Several basic questions need to be answered to understand how attacking, moving, and defending work.

Who Can I Attack?

The simplest and most basic multiplayer option is to allow your creatures to attack any opponent, no matter whose territories those creatures are stationed in (even in a teammate's territory). You can attack more than one opponent during the attack but each creature can attack only one opponent during the attack. During your attack, you declare which of your creatures are attacking *and* who each of those creatures is attacking. There are, however, several variants regarding who you can attack: 1) Attack only adjacent territories. Your creatures can only attack opponents whose territories are adjacent to the territory the creature is in. 2) Attack only in one direction. Your creatures can only attack opponents whose territories are adjacent to the territory the creature is in and who are in the correct direction (usually left). 3) Only attack one player a turn. When you declare an attack, you can only attack against one other player. This variation can be used whether or not you are using the standard rules for which opponents creatures are allowed to attack or whether or not you are using variants 1) or 2).

How Do I Move Creatures?

Any of your untapped, non-wall creatures that aren't suffering from summoning sickness can move to a teammate's territory, to either help that teammate or to move closer to the action. This movement occurs during the attack and is in lieu of that creature's attack. In its simplest form, creature movement allows you to move your creatures to any of your teammate's territories instead of attacking. Moving does not cause the creature to tap, but it does cause the creature to have summoning sickness. The creatures move immediately after attackers are declared, and you should declare which creatures you are moving when you declare which creatures are attacking. Note that creatures which are moving are *not* considered to be attacking creatures. Also, remember that moving a creature does not change the control of the creature; you still control the creature and thus make any decisions about attacking, blocking, and using the creature's special abilities, as well as paying any of its activation costs, etc.

One additional rule for moving creatures should be added if you are playing a variant in which creatures can only attack opponents whose territories are adjacent to the territory the creature is in. If a creature is forced to attack but cannot attack because it is not in a territory adjacent to any opponent, the creature is instead forced to move toward the nearest opponent's territory (into a teammate's territory or back into your territory). If there are two territories that are equally close, the controller of the creature decides toward which territory the creature moves. If the creature moves succesfully, neither it nor its controller suffers any penalty for failing to attack. For example, if Siren's Call is played, the creature will not be destroyed, and Erg Raiders will not damage its controller if it moves instead of attacks. Note that if the creature is adjacent to an opponent's territory, it *cannot* move instead of attacking—it is still required to attack.

There are a few other movement variations that are also interesting: 1) Move only to adjacent territories. You can only move a creature from one territory to another adjacent territory; thus, if you are not next to any of your teammates, you won't be able to move your creatures, and even if you are next to a teammate, it may take you several turns to send your creature to help a teammate who is far away. 2) Movement requires attack ability. In this more complicated variant, a creature can only move into a teammate's territory if you could have attacked that player in a two-player game (assuming he or she was your opponent, not your teammate). For example, under this variant, you could not move a Sea Serpent into a teammate's territory unless that teammate controlled islands. It is important to remember, however, that you still control the creature—thus, even if all of your opponent's islands are later destroyed, the Serpent is not buried and can remain in front of that player (although it will not be able to move back if you move it away).

Who Can Block?

Any creature stationed in the territory of a defending player can be used as a blocker. This means that if you are playing with creature movement rules, several players may have creatures that can block an attack. If you are playing rules where table talk is not allowed between teammates (see "Table Talk"), the defending player chooses the order in which his teammates decide whether or not and how they are using their creatures to block. Note that it is legal for creatures controlled by different players to block the same creature.

Thus, the full attack sequence is as follows: 1) Declare your intention to attack. As in the two-player game, this can be cancelled by fast effects. 2) Declare which creatures are attacking and which creatures are moving. 3) Tap attackers and move creatures that are moving. 4) Fast effects. Just as in the normal attack sequence, anyone can use fast effects. 5) Declare blockers. Defending player decides which order players decide if and how their creatures in the defending player's territory block. 6) Fast effects. 7) Damage dealing and damage prevention.

How Does Banding Work?

Banding is more confusing in a multiplayer environment. When attacking, creatures can only band together to attack if all of the creatures in the band are attacking the same player and are all in the same territory. When defending, if multiple creatures block the same attacker and one of the creatures has banding, the defending player gets to distribute damage among the blocking creatures, even if he or she did not control the banding creature.

Range (Who Gets Affected by My Spells?)

In some variants, it is desirable to have a limited range on the spells you cast and the effects you use; that is, your spells and effects can only directly effect a limited number of players on either side of you. If a game is played with a "Range" of 1, then any spells or effects that target permanents may only target permanents either in your territory or in the territories adjacent to you. Spells or effects that target other spells or effects may only be used to target spells or effects that were cast either by you or by the players sitting next to you. Spells which have a general effect only affect you, the players sitting next to you, and the permanents in those territories. For the purposes of damage prevention effects (which target the damage), damage is assumed to be in the territory of the creature or player being damaged.

For a game with a "Range" of 2, the above spells, effects, and the like now affect and are applied to you and the four players nearest you (two on either side).

For example, if, in a game with a range of 1, a player two seats away from you Lightning Bolts a creature in the territory next to you, then you may use Healing Salve or Death Ward on the creature hit by the Lightning Bolt, but you could not target the Lightning Bolt itself with a Counterspell (since the caster is not within your range). Or, if you were to cast Fog in a game with a range of 1, then creatures in your territory and the territories adjacent to you would not deal damage in combat; however, any other attacking or blocking creatures would. And if you were to cast Armageddon in a game with a range of 2, then all lands in your territory and the territories of the four players within your range would be destroyed but any other lands would be unaffected by the spell.

Table Talk (What Can I Say During the Game?)

It is important to decide before starting to play a multiplayer game how much discussion should be allowed during play. Unlike a two-player duel, you may actually want to be able to reveal the fact that you have Counterspell or a Fireball in your hand, since this could be valuable information to your teammate.

The two rules that seem to be easiest to agree upon are: 1) Players may talk about anything they wish, but all conversations must be public. Thus, if you wish to inform your teammate of something, you will have to let your opponents listen in, too. 2) No talk is allowed at all. This variant is perhaps best suited to cutthroat environments.

You may wish to adopt your own rules that will fall in between these two extremes for what may and may not be discussed. For example, perhaps you can agree to only talk about the cards that are on the table or who you would like your teammate to attack.

The Games

Free-For-All, Attack Left, Crossfire Team **Magic**, Emperor Team **Magic**.

Free-For-All

Composition:	N players with no teams.
Seating:	Players sit in a circle.
Turn Sequence:	(Randomly decide who goes first.) Play proceeds clockwise around the circle.
Object:	To be the last player remaining in the game.
Attacking:	Creatures may attack any opponent (i.e., any player other than yourself).
Moving:	There are no teams and hence no creature movement.
Range:	Unlimited (infinite).
Ante:	Each player antes a card; the winner collects all of the ante.

Attack Left

Composition:	N players with no teams.
Seating:	Players sit in a circle.
Turn Sequence:	(Randomly decide who goes first.) Play proceeds clockwise around the circle.
Object:	To accumulate the most victory points. You receive one victory point whenever the player to your left leaves the game (regardless of why this occurred). You also receive one VP if you are the last player remaining. If player A and player B, who sits adjacent and to the left of player A, both leave the game at the same time, then player A and the player to the left of player A both receive one victory point.

Attacking: Creatures may only attack players to their controller's left.

Moving: There are no teams and hence no creature movement.

Range: Range of 2, unless you are playing with a large number of players (eight or more) in which case you may want to play with a range of 1.

Ante: Each player antes a card. When the player to your left leaves the game, you get his or her ante.

Crossfire Team Magic

Composition: Two teams of two players each.
> *Team A*—composed of players A1 and A2.
> *Team B*—composed of players B1 and B2.

Seating: Players sit in a circle in the following order—A1, B1, A2, and B2.

Turn Sequence: (After randomly choosing who goes first.) Play proceeds clockwise around the circle.

Object: To have at least one member of your team remaining in the game after both players on the other team are out of the game.

Attacking: Creatures may only attack players with territories adjacent to the territory the attacking creature is in. (See variant #1 for why this might matter.)

Moving: Creatures may move to and from your teammate's territory.

Range: Range of 2. (See variant #2 for why this might matter.)

Ante: If playing for ante, each player antes a card and the team that wins must decide how to split the ante. If a dispute arises over splitting ante, each player on the winning team retrieves his or her own ante and the ante of the opponent that started the game to his or her left.

Variants: 1) Changing the order of the seating can significantly alter the play—for example, instead of A1, B1, A2, and B2, try A1, A2, B1, and B2. In this variant, either player A2 or B2 should go first.

2) Crossfire Team **Magic** can easily expand to incorporate three or more teams of two each with various seatings (for example, A1, B1, C1, A2, B2, and C2). In this case, the object becomes to have at least one member of your team remaining in

the game after both players on all other teams are out of the game.

3) Each team has a life total of 40; individual players do not have separate life totals. Thus, when either player on Team A suffers damage or loses life, it is subtracted from the common total of 40 rather than from an individual player's life total. If during the end of any phase or at the beginning or end of any attack a team's life total is 0 or less, then both players on that team are out of the game.

Emperor Team Magic

Composition: Two teams of three players each (Team A and Team B).

> *Team A*—composed of players A1, A2, and A3.
> *Team B*—composed of players B1, B2, and B3.

Seating: Sit in a circle in the following order—A1, A2, A3, B1, B2, and B3 (clockwise from left to right).

Turn Sequence: It is recommended that either player A3 or B3 begins, then play proceeds clockwise around the circle (i.e., either player B1 or A1, respectively, will go second).

Object: To remove the other team's "emperor" from the game. Team A wins if player B2 leaves the game and Team B wins if player A2 leaves the game.

Attacking: Creatures may only attack players with territories adjacent to the territory the creature is in.

Moving: Creatures may only move to and from a teammate's territory which is adjacent to the territory the creature is currently in (it is possible for a creature summoned by A3 to get into A1's territory, but it would take two turns since it has to go through A2's territory first).

Range: Range of 2.

Ante: Each player antes a card. The victorious emperor receives the ante of the defeated emperor and generals receive the ante of the opposing general that started the game next to them.

Comments: The middle player on each team is referred to as the "emperor" and the other players are commonly referred to as "generals."

Variants:	1) Emperor Team **Magic** can easily expand to incorporate multiple teams of three players each with the following seating: A1, A2, A3, B1, B2, B3, C1, C2, C3, etc. In this case, the object becomes to be the last team with an emperor still in the game. Here, too, it is recommended that either player A3, B3, or C3 goes first.
	2) Emperor Team **Magic** can be easily expanded to incorporate two teams of five players with the following seating: A1, A2, A3, A4, A5, B1, B2, B3, B4, and B5, where A3 and B3 are the emperors. In this variant, a "range" of 2 is recommended, and player A4 or B4 should go first.

Rainbow Magic

This variant is a little different than the previously detailed variants and is apt to be rife with diplomacy. The basis for this variant is to have a five-player game where each player is playing faithful to one of the five colors of **Magic**. In **Magic,** each of the five colors has two friendly colors and two enemy colors; the circle of the five colors of mana on the back of a **Magic** card shows the relationships of the five colors—those adjacent to one another are friendly colors and those non-adjacent are enemy colors (see below). For each player, the object of the game is to remain in the game until their two opposed colors have left the game. For example, the White player's object is to remain in the game until both Red and Black have left the game.

Deck Composition

This variant has its own special deck construction rules. Each player should be playing a deck composed solely of lands (any type), artifacts, and spells of the color they are representing (multicolored spells may be used as long as one of the colors of the spell is the color that player is representing).

Furthermore there are certain cards that should be banned from play in this variant; these are the cards which are designed to stop decks built around one color. Some examples of cards that you may wish to ban include: Red/Blue Elemental Blasts, Wards of any color, Circles of Protection, Black/White Knights, Conversion, Flashfires, Gloom, Karma, Deathgrip, Lifeforce, Lifetap, Tsunami, Magnetic Mountain, Volcanic Eruption, and Northern Paladin. You may also want to ban other cards that are clearly opposed to a specific color.

Who Is My Opponent?

Your opponents are the players representing the colors opposed to the color you are playing. Also take note of the rules for opponents at the beginning of this article on suggestions for how to play cards when there are more than two players and more than one opponent.

Seating Arrangement (The Pentagon of Colors)

The seating is particularly important in this variant, as is the unusual turn sequence. Players should sit in the following order: White, Blue, Black, Red, and Green (clockwise from left to right). The turn sequence should proceed as follows: White, Black, Green, Blue, and Red (randomly decide who goes first); that is, after your turn, play passes to the second player to your left. To maintain the turn sequence, a player's placement in the pentagon of the colors should still be noted even when that player has left the game.

Attacking and Blocking in the Pentagon

The attack in Rainbow **Magic** is especially complicated, though interesting, in this variant. There is no movement of creatures allowed.

First, announce your attack and declare which of your creatures are attacking which of your opponents (remember, you have two opponents and your creatures can only attack an opponent who is still in the game). For example, White can announce an attack and declare some creatures to be attacking Black and others to be attacking Red. Next, there is a round of fast effects.

Now comes the really new element of the attack, defense *en passant:* the player *between* the attacking player and the defending player may choose to step in to block the creatures before they can proceed on to the chosen opponent (unless, of course, those creatures are unblockable). Once a player chooses to block a creature he or she becomes the defending player as far as the blocked attacking creature is concerned. For example, any trample damage from a creature blocked will be redirected to the new blocking player and not to the opponent of the attacker.

The players adjacent to the attacker (in the case of White attacking, these would be Blue and Green) announce their blocks. Another round of fast effects proceeds, and then damage dealing occurs for all of the defending creatures and all of the attacking creatures which have been blocked. Next, a damage prevention step occurs (as normal), and then all of the blocking creatures *become tapped;* yes, blocking *en passant* taps your blocking creatures (it is costly to aid the enemy of your friend).

Next, the usual attack sequence resumes. There is a round of fast effects, and then the opponents of the attacking player (e.g., Black and Red, in the case of

White attacking) choose how and if to block any of the creatures that were assigned to attack them and that were not already blocked *en passant*. Next, there is another round of fast effects and, finally, a second damage dealing step and a second damage prevention step, after which the combat ends.

Variants on Deck Construction

You may wish to experiment with these alternate deck construction rules (providing your own banned list of cards).

1) Pure Color Representation: A player may only use one basic land type in their deck, namely the one that produces the mana of the appropriate color for the color they are representing. Furthermore, no artifacts are allowed in any deck.

2) Muddled Color Representation: At least 50 percent of the spells must be of the color that you are representing but the remaining 50 percent may be pulled from the colors friendly to the one you are playing.

3) No Color Restriction: The layout and turn sequence is interesting enough to warrant experimentation even without playing faithful to the colors. Your deck may conform to any normal deck construction rules.

leagues and drafts

Charlie Catino, Joel Mick, Steve Conard, and Allen Varney

Magic designer Richard Garfield says, "League play is something I recommend for any player of **Magic**. In essence, a league is a method of controlling the play environment. This can be extremely valuable for groups whose members have very different resources and skill levels. If you want a new **Magic** challenge, consider setting up a league."

A league typically consists of a small number of players (usually fewer than fifty, preferably between eight and thirty-two). Each player starts with a fixed number of cards, and no other cards enter or leave the league during the season. Everyone starts out on an even footing, no matter who happens to own the largest collection of cards. A league is ideal for introducing friends to **Magic** without requiring them to make a large investment in cards.

Your First League

When you start a league, designate one person as league commissioner. The commissioner is in charge of developing league structure, explaining and enforcing rules, overseeing players, registering matches, and maintaining the overall upkeep of the league. Running a league may require a great deal of time and resources, depending on the type of league you prefer. The league commissioner should be responsible and able to fully regulate a league; a retailer can be a good choice for this position.

When developing a league, the league commissioner and the players first work together to establish standards of deck construction, such as deck size, source of cards, and the amount of land allowed from outside sources. Once a standard is established, all other construction methods can use that standard as a starting point. Thereafter, the basic league structure will work no matter how the players get their cards.

Once the league is in full swing, there may be scheduling problems which result in some players failing to be available for league play on a regular basis. To keep the league running in a smooth and timely manner, the commissioner may require a forfeit of one card from a player who does not play at least one match in a week's time; this card should be any card of the tardy player's choice. As there are always unforeseen circumstances that may come up to hinder a player from playing matches, the commissioner shouldn't be too hard-nosed about this.

With these basics in mind, here, then, is an overview of a basic league that can work quite well as your group's first league.

Basic Sealed-Deck League

Construct Sealed-Deck League decks as follows: Each player is issued one **Magic** starter deck, two eight-card booster packs *or* one fifteen-card booster pack, and four basic lands of his or her choice. This selection of cards is the player's "draft." Players construct their playing decks using *only* these cards and no others from any other source. The league players and commissioner determine the expansion or expansions used; all players should have access to the same expansion to keep both league continuity and balance.

The basic Sealed-Deck League uses the standard **Magic** rules, but the league does not follow Duelists' Convocation rules.

Each player starts with a total of seventy-nine or eighty cards and must play with at least forty of them. The other cards form the entire "sideboard" and may be used as the player sees fit. Players may exchange cards between their sideboards and decks in between games and matches, and they are not required to sideboard one-for-one as long as they stay at or above forty cards.

League Structure

The league is divided into groups of eight players. The league commissioner randomly assigns the players to their divisions.

During sign-up for the league, each player chooses a unique symbol as a signature to put on cards lost in ante. In all games, players must play for ante. When an ante card is lost, the player losing the card places his or her symbol on the card, preferably in the bottom of the text box. This allows other players, as well as the league commissioner, to follow the history of a card.

The Play

The players within each division play only each other, so each player plays a maximum of seven matches. A match is made up of three games, and all three games must be played to complete a match. A player's standing or position in the league is determined by how many cards he or she has won or lost. Players may lose a maximum of three cards per match, unless cards that affect ante or permanent ownership (such as Rebirth) are played.

Players may challenge or accept challenges from any other player in their division. It does not matter who a player plays or in what order. Once they have completed a match, the two players register the match with the league commissioner.

Alternately, the league structure could follow a free-for-all, round-robin style. In this format, each player must play one match with all the other players in the league, with three games (each played for ante) making up a match. Each player plays all other players once. If the league doesn't control who plays whom in what order, players may seek out other players in a deliberate attempt to gain an advantage. Because players play at their own pace, sometimes a given player has played so many matches and lost so many cards that other players may view him or her as ripe for the picking. In this alternative league style, order of play becomes important.

End of Play

When all players have finished their matches within the division, the commissioner ranks the players by number of cards. The player with the most cards wins and is division champion. If the league has more than one division, the division champions can participate in a playoff to produce a league champion.

In the limited environment of a division, a player in a worst-case scenario loses twenty-one cards. In the rare event that a player loses so many cards that he or she can't play a legal deck of at least forty cards, that player is dropped from the league. When this happens, all remaining players who have not yet played that player may pick one card at random from the dropped player's remaining cards.

Multiple Seasons within a League

Before the league members start the league, they should agree on whether to play one season or several. It is a lot of fun to arrange additional seasons, which allow players to continue to play with their decks. If this is to be the case, all players who survive a league season should have a chance to improve their deck a *little*. One way to do this is to allow players who have survived a season to trade in cards, with anywhere from one to four cards traded in for the new season. Players will give up cards they don't want and can draft the same number of basic lands, the same number of cards from a random collection of cards, or any combination of these. Players killed in the previous season may start over with a new starter deck and booster pack(s).

For subsequent seasons, players are divided into "circles of power," determined by the number of cards they won during all previous seasons. The next season is played out within each circle, keeping track of the number of cards gained throughout this and the following seasons as players rise and fall through the circles of power with each passing season. Circles of power are, in fact, a good way to regulate how many trade-ins a player is allowed. For instance, if a player is negative (has lost at least one card net), that player should be allowed four trade-ins. If a player is 0–9 cards up, he or she should be allowed three trade-ins. If a player is up 10–19 cards, he or she should be allowed two trade-ins, and if a player is up 20–29 cards, he or she should be allowed one trade-in. If a player is up more than that, then he or she doesn't need *any* trade-ins.

It is possible that only a few players will make it into the upper circles of power, and it is thus likely that they won't have many matches to play. These players may wish to start over with a new deck. It is certainly acceptable for players to play more than one deck during a season; however, a player cannot have more decks than the season number. (For example, if this is the third season, a player may have up to three decks.)

Cards Gained	Circle of Power
-30 to -1	Hospital
0 to +9	Initiate
+10 to +19	First Level
+20 to +29	Second Level
+30 to +39	Third Level
+40 to +49	Fourth Level
+50 to +59	Fifth Level
+60 to +69	Sixth Level
+70+	Seventh Level

Drafts

A draft is another way to give league players their cards. The league begins with all available cards in a common pool. Each player is given a set number of points with which to purchase ("draft") any card; each card must go through the draft process. When a player has drafted the permitted number of cards, that player is out of the draft.

Determine before the draft begins where the cards will go after the league is over. If the players get to keep the cards when they're done, then they might draft particular cards not to help them win the league but just to acquire the cards. The point of the draft is to create a deck that you can win with; don't draft cards just because they are rare or because you wish to spoil another player's draft. You will soon discover that negative drafting is not the best route to victory.

Card Bank

Putting the cards back into a general pool (called a card bank) after the league is finished helps alleviate drafting problems. A card bank is a set of cards that belongs to a league of players—no one person owns these cards. Each time a league begins, these cards are used in the league. One good way to start a card bank is to run a Sealed-Deck League, after which all the cards are turned in to the commissioner to add to the bank.

One major advantage of card banks is that players don't worry that they will lose a particular card when playing for ante. Also, if the league begins with a draft, players can concentrate on drafting cards that help them create a winning deck without being tempted to draft a card just because of its rarity. (Read more on drafts later.)

Card banks also impose a lighter financial burden on players than Sealed-Deck Leagues. Once the cards are purchased, players need not spend more money. As new expansions are released, players may wish to supplement the card bank by adding boosters of their choice.

What follows are some typical drafts:

Philadelphia Draft

Determine the number of players and cards each player needs to play. For example, if the league has eight players and each player must have sixty cards, then the league needs 480 cards; however, you should manipulate the card totals as you see fit. It is recommended that all players start out with 200 points each if drafting forty cards or 300 points each if drafting sixty cards. All players are required to draft the correct number of cards. When a player introduces a card, he or she automatically bids 0 points for the card unless he or she chooses to make a higher initial bid.

Open a sufficient number of starter decks and/or boosters and sort the cards by name, placing them in piles on a table or on the floor. All players form a circle. Randomly choose who introduces a card first. After the winner of the card is determined, the player to the left of the person who introduced the first card introduces the next card. Keep going clockwise around the circle, introducing cards, until all cards are accounted for. Conduct the draft as an auction, in either of two ways:

Open bid auction: Randomly choose a player to begin the draft. This person picks any card and begins the bidding at zero or more points. Bidding proceeds clockwise. There is no limit to the number or the size of bids, but each bid must be larger than the previous bid, and bids of fractions of a point are prohibited. A player cannot bid more points than his or her current total. Highest bid takes the card, and the winning player marks off the points spent from his or her current total.

Closed bid auction: All players should have lots of scraps of paper on hand. Randomly choose a player to begin the draft by choosing any card. Each player then secretly writes down a point bid for the chosen card; this number may be zero. Everyone reveals their bids simultaneously, and the high bid wins the card.

In the event of a tie, players involved in the tie use the same secret bid procedure to increase their bids. Another way to resolve ties is to set up a rule for who gets a card (for instance, the first person who was tied with the highest bidder for the card, proceeding clockwise from the person who originally chose the card).

No Points, Just Pick

This draft is as easy as it gets: each player just picks a card.

Give all the players a few minutes to look at the cards before numbering the players in a random drafting order. To begin the draft, Player 1 chooses any card. Player 2 then chooses, followed by Player 3, and so on. Once everyone has picked once, start with the player who just picked, and go in *reverse* order around the table again.

For example, suppose there are eight players. First, the players pick one card apiece in numerical order, 1 through 8; then they each pick a card in reverse order, 8 through 1. Then the cycle repeats.

Some people feel that it is an advantage to sit in either the first or the last seat, so you can alter the drafting order in the following manner if you wish:

Round one: 1 through 8, then 8 through 1;

Round two: 2 through 8, followed by 1, then 1, followed by 8 through 2;

Round three: 3 through 8, followed by 2, then 2, followed by 8 through 3 and so on. See the Rochester Draft for a fairer sequence of drafting.

Rochester Draft

Break up into groups of four or (preferably) eight players. With eight players, you will need at least nine starter decks. Open all of the decks and shuffle the cards together.

Begin drafting by drawing sixteen cards and laying them on the table in any order. Give all of the players time to look at the cards before randomly choosing the players' drafting order. Begin drafting with Player 1 choosing any single card. Player 2 then chooses, followed by Player 3, and so on. When all eight players have finished, the draft continues with Player 8 starting, followed by Player 7, working down to Player 1. At the end of round one, each player has two cards.

On the second round of the draft, Player 1 becomes Player 8, and each other player is promoted one position. Draw sixteen more cards and place them on the table, continuing the draft as before. After thirty-two rounds, each player has sixty-four cards and has drafted from the first position an equal number of times. From nine starter decks there will be twenty-eight cards left over. Each player constructs a league deck from the sixty-four cards he or she drafted.

A slightly fairer yet slightly more complicated version with eight players follows this pattern for drawing:

```
1,2,3,4,5,6,7,8,8,7,6,5,4,3,2,1
2,3,4,5,6,7,8,1,1,8,7,6,5,4,3,2
3,4,5,6,7,8,1,2,2,1,8,7,6,5,4,3
4,5,6,7,8,1,2,3,3,2,1,8,7,6,5,4
5,6,7,8,1,2,3,4,4,3,2,1,8,7,6,5
6,7,8,1,2,3,4,5,5,4,3,2,1,8,7,6
7,8,1,2,3,4,5,6,6,5,4,3,2,1,8,7
8,1,2,3,4,5,6,7,7,6,5,4,3,2,1,8
1,8,7,6,5,4,3,2,2,3,4,5,6,7,8,1
2,1,8,7,6,5,4,3,3,4,5,6,7,8,1,2
3,2,1,8,7,6,5,4,4,5,6,7,8,1,2,3
4,3,2,1,8,7,6,5,5,6,7,8,1,2,3,4
5,4,3,2,1,8,7,6,6,7,8,1,2,3,4,5
6,5,4,3,2,1,8,7,7,8,1,2,3,4,5,6
7,6,5,4,3,2,1,8,8,1,2,3,4,5,6,7
8,7,6,5,4,3,2,1,1,2,3,4,5,6,7,8
```

and repeat.

Queue Draft

Break up into groups of four to eight players. For each group of eight players, you will need at least nine starter decks. Open all of the decks and shuffle the cards together. Now decide whether to allow the players to look through the cards before drafting—the draft is far more suspenseful if the players have no prior knowledge of the cards.

Each player starts with sixty points, with which he or she *must* draft sixty cards—no more, no less. Make sure that there are at least 61 cards for each player.

This draft is called the Queue Draft because cards are drawn and placed in a queue (sort of like a waiting line). It is recommended that the queue have as many cards in it as there are players drafting, with a minimum of six cards.

Consider the following example, which is set up for eight players. First, randomly choose the drafting order of the players. The first card is drawn from the deck, and Player 1 has the option to draft that card for a cost of 7 points. If that player doesn't want the card, it is placed on the table, beginning the queue.

The second card is drawn. Player 2 may take either the first card on the table for 6 points or the newly drawn card for 7 points (or the player can pass). If Player 2 doesn't want the newly drawn card, it is placed in the queue to the right of the first card.

The third card is drawn. Player 3 has the option of taking that card for 7 points or of taking either of the first two cards at costs of 5 points (for the first card in the queue) and 6 points (for the second).

Continue drawing cards in this way until there are eight cards in the queue. The first card on the far left is assigned a cost of 0, the second card a cost of 1, and so on to the eighth card, which costs 7 points. Once there is a free (zero-point) card on the table, each player is required to buy one card in the queue, or else he or she *must* take the free card.

The players continue to draft, paying the appropriate costs. Once a card has been drafted, all higher-cost cards slide down to the left, filling the spot of the drafted card. A new card is then drawn and placed in the eighth spot.

It is highly likely that toward the end of the draft, most players will run out of points and therefore will only take free cards.

Each player constructs his or her deck from the sixty cards he or she drafts. Note that basic land is included in the draft—so make sure players draft enough land for a practical deck!

Melting Pot Draft

Break up into groups of five players. The Melting Pot Draft requires twice as many cards as is normal in most drafts, so with five players you should have at least twelve starter decks. Open all of the decks and shuffle the cards together. Deal a hand of eight cards face down so that no player can see the cards.

Randomly choose a drafting order for the players. Player 1 picks up the hand of cards then draws two more cards and places them in the hand *on the left side;* it is important that the cards remain in the exact order in which they were drawn. This player then chooses any single card and discards the card on the extreme right. The cards that are discarded are permanently removed from the draft. Player 1 then hands the cards to the next player in the draft.

Player 2 draws two cards, puts them in the hand on the left, chooses a card, and then discards the card on the far right. The hand is passed from player to player until all the cards in the stockpile are gone. Each player must draft exactly sixty cards. The administrator should ensure that there are enough cards so that, when all the cards in the melting pot are used up, each player will have sixty cards. As players get used to this form of draft, it is possible to have more than one hand of cards rotating at the same time. Ultimately, there could be up to one hand per player in the draft.

Mons Filter Draft

The Mons Filter Draft needs to have 75 cards per player; these cards will be randomly placed in three boxes. The first box will contain the majority of the cards, 60 cards per person, the second box will contain 12 cards per person, and the third box will contain 3 cards per person.

In this draft, players randomly select cards from each box. After randomly determining the drafting order of the players, Player 1 begins by picking a card from the first box. If Player 1 doesn't want the card, he or she drops it into the second box and then picks a card from that second box. If Player 1 doesn't want *that* card, he or she drops it into the third box and picks a card from that box. Players may keep any card they pick and let the draft continue with the next player in line; however, all players must keep cards picked from the third box.

All players construct their decks from the 60 cards they drafted. Each deck must be at least 40 cards. League play uses the same standard rules as **Magic** but the league does not follow the Duelists' Convocation rules.

Beginners' Draft (or "Conscriptum Novicii")

The Beginners' Draft requires sixty cards (one starter deck) per player. Open all of the decks and shuffle the cards together. After either stacking the cards in one pile or putting them into a box, determine a random drafting order. Player 1 then picks a card. If the player wants the card, he or she keeps it; otherwise, it is discarded to another newly formed pile or box. If the player chooses to discard, he or she draws a second card which he or she must keep. When the pile or box is empty of cards, players draft from the previously discarded cards until all players have sixty cards.

Variant Draft Rules

Before beginning a draft, remove all basic land from the stockpile. After the draft, players are allowed to take as much basic land as they require to finish their decks.

The commissioner may change either the number of points given to each player or the number of cards drafted per round.

For a faster draft, pair the cards. Players acquire them two at a time. Three- or four-card groups also work.

A Few Deck Construction Ideas

When starting a league, it is always a good idea to establish the method which the players will use to build their decks. For leagues in which each player uses cards from his or her own collection, there are a variety of methods to choose from. A few suggestions:

Each player might construct a deck according to Duelists' Convocation Type II tournament rules, using only cards from the current edition of **Magic** and from the last two expansions. All players can then choose not to play for ante, thus keeping all decks tournament legal, or they can choose to play for ante anyway.

If all players have access to an abundance of cards, they can choose to construct decks with certain themes—for instance, Artist Decks, where each player's deck contains cards by only one artist; or Alphabet Decks, which must include at least one card for each letter of the alphabet (Abomination, Benalish Hero, Circle of Protection, and so on).

Be creative in establishing deck construction guidelines for your league; take into account when doing so the possibility that some players will undoubtedly own better cards than other players and that your construction rules might need to take smaller collections into account.

Variant League Rules

1. Don't use a sideboard.
2. Don't play for ante. Instead, make each game or match worth a point total.
3. As long as all players are willing, the league could have specialized rules for trading. For example, a) after each game, the player who lost can try to trade to get his or her ante and only his or her ante back from the other player; or b) after each match, you may trade exactly one card for one card with your opponent.
4. Any league can use the "add four basic land of players' choice" rule.
5. Plan a quick team tournament among all players in one division. Set aside a couple of hours in an afternoon when all of the players can get together. The teams are set as follows:

> The player who finished in fourth place can choose his or her teammate from anyone who finished fifth through eighth. The player who finished third can pick from any lower-half player who is left. The player who finished second picks a partner from the two remaining players, and the last unpicked player is teamed with the first-place player.

> Then play a round-robin tournament in which each team plays each other team three games each. The team that wins the most games is proclaimed the team tourney winner.

Use any mutually agreeable method to run your league—remember, the idea is for everyone to have fun in a controlled play environment. If you have run your own league or variations of the ones listed here, feel free to email us through the Internet at leagues@wizards.com with your report. All league submissions become the property of Wizards of the Coast, Inc. We appreciate you sending in your ideas, as it helps us create a better product for you.

the Duelists' Convocation and official tournament rules

The Duelists' Convocation

Duelists' Convocation International is Wizards of the Coast's official **Deckmaster**™ games tournament organization. One of the many things we do is track Duelists' Convocation rating points. Each Convocation member is rated by how they perform when playing against other rated competitors in our official tournaments. If you consistently beat players who are ranked higher than you, then your rating will improve; if you lose to players rated lower than you, then your rating will drop. A monthly update will keep you posted as to your most current rating. Though you can take part in our tournaments even if you are not a member, only Duelists' Convocation members can be rated via tournament play. As this rating measures your skill against other players, if you are one of our top-rated members you may be invited to play in our National Championship tournament—you might even advance to the World Championship tournament to duel against the best international players!

The Duelists' Convocation also publishes and updates Wizards of the Coast's tournament play and tournament deck construction rules. These rules are one of the reasons for the long-term popularity of **Magic**: by using the Duelists' Convocation rules, players have not been able to "break" the game. (One-turn "killer" decks *do* exist, and the only way to keep the players who use them from dominating the game is to create deck construction rules which make it harder to build that kind of deck.) Updated rules appear regularly in *The Duelist* magazine and in the Duelists' Convocation's monthly newsletter. You can also get a copy of these rules through the Internet at questions@wizards.com or by calling our customer service line at (206) 624-0933. For those of you who are interested in holding a sanctioned event, sanctioning information packets are also available.

Information on the United Kingdom and European chapters of the Duelists' Convocation is available from our U. K. and Belgian offices. (To learn more about Wizards of the Coast outside of the U.S., see p. **G-1**.)

The Duelists' Convocation sanctions three types of **Magic: The Gathering** tournaments—these are the Type I, Type II, and Sealed-Deck tournaments. All of these types of tournaments feature different deck construction rules, and all officially sanctioned tournaments still use a single-elimination format. We are currently creating a new point scoring system that will work with other tournament formats and will allow you more playing time; until that system is ready, the single-elimination format is the most efficient way to proceed.

The Type I tournament is a "constructed deck" tournament; this means that you can construct your deck using any cards that you own, as long as you work within the rules. Be sure to read the rules carefully before running or playing in a Type I tournament—the Type I tournament represents more of a "power player" tournament due to its looser restrictions, which allow for nastier decks.

The Type II tournament is also a constructed deck tournament, allowing only cards still available in the most current edition of the basic set and in the latest two expansions. This type of tournament was developed with two ideas in mind: First, the **Magic** environment should be ever changing; seeing new cards appear and disappear from time to time was the original concept behind the expansion sets and with the basic edition card rotations as well. By only allowing the two latest expansion sets and disallowing cards rotated out of the basic edition, we create an ever-shifting, ever-changing playing field. Second, by using only currently available cards we assure that, if you have never had the chance to get your hands on some of the older, out-of-print expansions (or basic set cards, for that matter!), you can still compete on equal ground with even the most seasoned players. Even **Magic** veterans should find this type of tournament the perfect battleground to practice their newest strategies with the latest expansions. We think that the Type II tournament will become the staple of the tournament circuit.

The Sealed-Deck tournament takes the final strides into restricted environments, challenging you to create the best deck possible from an extremely limited card pool without the benefit of trading! There are several options available within the Sealed-Deck tournaments, based on card availability at the time of the tournament, and care must be taken on the part of the tournament's organizers to be sure that the option they have selected is feasible at that time. Sealed-Deck tournaments are a favorite of many players, from very experienced players who want the challenge of not having access to their enormous card pools to brand new players who don't have many cards to draw from in constructing decks.

All of these rules are "modular" in design. There is a standard set of Floor Rules that applies to all tournaments, and any modifications or additions for a particular tournament type appear in the rules specific to that tournament.

The Floor Rules have been updated and upgraded to be modular with the above tournament types. There have been some slight changes made from earlier releases of these rules, so be sure to read them again to familiarize yourself with current Duelists' Convocation standards.

Type I Tournament Rules
Magic: The Gathering

Includes **Magic: The Gathering** (all editions), *Arabian Nights, Antiquities, Legends, The Dark, Fallen Empires*

4/19/95

Notes

- Exclusion of the listing of any expansion set above <u>does not</u> imply that the expansion set should be banned from tournament play. Exclusion of any existing expansion set in the above listing means <u>only</u> that final decisions as to restrictions on cards from that set have not yet been made.
- The standard rules for **Magic: The Gathering** apply to tournament play, except where amended by these rules. In cases where the official tournament rules differ from the basic rules of **Magic**, the official tournament rules take precedence.
- Note on play with non-English language cards: Be advised that in all cases, any card title, card text, rules, tournament rules or rulings, or any other facet of official tournament play where translational differences may appear, will be interpreted according to the English language versions most currently in use. This applies to all tournament types used by the Duelists' Convocation, without exception.

Deck Construction Rules

1. Type I tournament decks may be constructed from **Magic** cards from the *Limited* (first edition with black border) series, *Unlimited* (second edition), *Revised* (third edition), *Fourth Edition*, any **Magic** expansion (unless expressly disallowed by the Judge prior to the event), and promotional cards released by Wizards of the Coast in magazines or through books. All cards in the Type I tournament deck must have identical card-back design. Under no circumstances will cards from the *Collectors' Edition* factory sets be permitted in Type I tournament decks.

They are easily distinguished from legal play cards by their square corners and gold borders. Use of any card not expressly permitted in a Type I tournament deck in a Type I tournament will be interpreted by the Judge as a Declaration of Forfeiture (see Standard Floor Rules #15).

<u>Optional rule:</u> It is required that all of the cards in a player's deck have the same rounding of corners. As Alpha cards (the first section of the print run from the original limited edition basic set) have slightly more rounded corners than cards from subsequent printings (making Alphas effectively marked cards), it may be ruled that if any cards from the original Alpha card set are used in the Type I tournament deck, the <u>entire</u> deck must be constructed of Alpha cards. If this option is exercised, it must be advertised to the players in advance so that they may reconfigure their playing decks as necessary.

2. The Type I tournament deck must contain a minimum of 60 (sixty) cards. In addition to the Type I tournament deck, players may, but are not required to, construct a Sideboard of exactly 15 (fifteen) additional cards, which must always contain that number of cards while play is in progress. The use of the Sideboard is further explained in the Standard Floor Rules (rule #5).

3. There may be no more than 4 (four) of any individual card, by card title, in the Type I tournament deck (including Sideboard), with the exception of the five basic land types (plains, forest, mountain, island, swamp).

4. *The Restricted List*

No more than 1 (one) of each of the cards on the Restricted List are allowed in the Type I tournament deck (including Sideboard). If more than 1 (one) of any individual card from the Restricted List is found in a player's deck and Sideboard, that will be interpreted by the Judge as a Declaration of Forfeiture. The Restricted List may be modified by the Director of the Duelists' Convocation as necessary. If the card is originally from a **Magic** expansion, following its title will be a two-letter code denoting which expansion it is from. AN=*Arabian Nights*, AQ=*Antiquities*, LE=*Legends*, DK=*The Dark*, and FE=*Fallen Empires*. The Restricted List is as follows:

Ali from Cairo (AN)	Mind Twist
Ancestral Recall	Mirror Universe (LE)
Balance	Mishra's Workshop (AQ)
Berserk	Mox Emerald
Black Lotus	Mox Jet
Braingeyser	Mox Pearl
Candelabra of Tawnos (AQ)	Mox Ruby
Channel	Mox Sapphire
Chaos Orb	Recall (LE)
Copy Artifact	Regrowth
Demonic Tutor	Sol Ring
Falling Star (LE)	Sword of the Ages (LE)
Feldon's Cane (AQ)	Timetwister
Fork	Time Walk
Ivory Tower (AQ)	Underworld Dreams (LE)
Library of Alexandria (AN)	Wheel of Fortune
Maze of Ith (DK)	

In addition, any "Summon Legend" card is restricted to one each, as are each of the Legendary Lands from the *Legends* expansion set.

5. *The Banned List*

The following cards are banned from Type I tournament decks, and use the same expansion set abbreviations as above:

Bronze Tablet (AQ)	Jeweled Bird (AN)
Contract from Below	Rebirth (LE)
Darkpact	Shahrazad (AN)
Demonic Attorney	Time Vault
Divine Intervention (LE)	Tempest Efreet (LE)

Several of the cards on the Banned List are not allowed because they clearly state to remove them from your deck if not playing for ante, and ante is not required to be wagered in a Type I tournament (see Standard Floor Rules, rule #6). Any future cards that make the same statement will subsequently be banned. This list may be modified by the Director of the Duelists' Convocation as necessary.

Type I Tournament Floor Rules

The Type I tournament uses all of the Standard Floor Rules.

Modifications to Standard Floor Rules

Note: Rule numbers below correspond to Standard Floor Rules rule numbers.

5. The only deck alteration allowable while a duel is in progress is with the use of a Ring of Ma'rûf (AN). The Ring of Ma'rûf may only be used to retrieve a card from the player's sideboard or to retrieve a card that began the duel in the player's deck (e.g., a creature removed from play by a Swords to Plowshares). Cards other than the tournament deck and sideboard should not be allowed at the tournament. In the event that a player uses a Ring of Ma'rûf to retrieve a card from his or her sideboard, the Ring of Ma'rûf used is placed into the player's sideboard to take the place of the retrieved card, thus maintaining exactly fifteen cards in the sideboard. Otherwise, Standard Floor Rule #5 is unchanged.

Type II Tournament Rules
Magic: The Gathering

4/19/95

Notes

- The standard rules for **Magic: The Gathering** apply to tournament play, except where amended by these rules. In cases where the official tournament rules differ from the basic rules of **Magic**, the official tournament rules take precedence.

- Note on play with non-English language cards: Be advised that in all cases, any card title, card text, rules, tournament rules or rulings, or any other facet of official tournament play where translational differences may appear, will be interpreted according to the English language versions most currently in use. Determinations of "latest limited edition" sets will be made according to the latest limited edition sets released in the English language if there is a conflict in international play. Otherwise, use the latest limited editions common to players from all countries anticipated to participate. In any case where there may be discrepancies, the allowable sets/expansions should be advertised in advance.

Deck Construction

1. Type II tournament decks may be constructed from **Magic** cards from the most current edition of the basic set and the latest 2 (two) limited

edition **Magic** expansions only. Cards from previous versions of the basic set that still appear in the most current edition are allowed, with one exception. Cards from any *Collectors' Edition,* with square corners and differing card-back design, are disallowed from play, as these features make cards from this set effectively marked cards. All cards currently out of print from the basic set appear on the Banned List. Use of any card not expressly permitted in the Type II tournament deck in a Type II tournament will be interpreted by the Judge as a Declaration of Forfeiture (see Standard Floor Rules #15).

a. When new editions of the basic set and/or new limited edition expansions are released, there will be a grace period of one calendar month from the date of release of the English language version of that edition/expansion allowed for players to abide by the new deck construction rules, within certain restrictions. When a new edition of the basic set is released, players may construct decks using the card set from EITHER the old edition or the new one, not a combination (i.e., cards appearing in *Revised* [third edition] OR *Fourth Edition,* with no crossover unless the card appears in BOTH editions) during the grace period. When a new limited edition expansion is released, players may either use cards from the previously legal two expansion sets or from the incoming legal two expansion sets during the grace period (i.e., expansion sets A&B were the legal expansions, expansion C is the new release. During the grace period, sets A&B OR B&C would be allowable, but not sets A&C). In either case, once the grace period has expired, the new deck construction rules will be strictly enforced.

Optional rule: It is required that all of the cards in a player's deck have the same rounding of corners. As Alpha cards (the first section of the print run from the original limited edition basic set) have slightly more rounded corners than cards from subsequent printings (making Alphas effectively marked cards), it may be ruled that if any cards from the original Alpha card set are used in the Type II tournament deck, the entire deck must be constructed of Alpha cards. If this option is exercised, it must be advertised to the players in advance so that they may reconfigure their playing decks as necessary.

2. The Type II tournament deck must contain a minimum of 60 (sixty) cards. In addition to the Type II tournament deck, players may, but are not required to, construct a Sideboard of exactly 15 (fifteen) additional cards, which must always contain that number of cards while play is in progress. The use of the Sideboard is further explained in the Standard Floor Rules (rule #5).

3. There may be no more than 4 (four) of any individual card, by card title, in the Type II tournament deck (including Sideboard), with the exception of the five basic land types (plains, forest, mountain, island, swamp).

4. *The Restricted List*

No more than 1 (one) of each of the cards on the Restricted List are allowed in the Type II tournament deck (including Sideboard). If more than 1 (one) of any individual card from the Restricted List is found in a player's deck and Sideboard, that will be interpreted by the Judge as a Declaration of Forfeiture. The Restricted List may be modified by the Director of the Duelists' Convocation as necessary. The Restricted List is as follows:

Balance	Maze of Ith
Channel	Mind Twist
Ivory Tower	

5. *The Banned List*

For ease of use, all cards from the basic set that no longer appear in the most current edition are listed here. Other cards may be banned as well. The Banned List may be modified by the Director of the Duelists' Convocation as necessary. The following cards are banned from the Type II tournament deck:

Ancestral Recall	Demonic Hordes
Atog	Demonic Tutor
Badlands	Dwarven Demolition Team
Basalt Monolith	Dwarven Weaponsmith
Bayou	Earthbind
Berserk	False Orders
Black Lotus	Farmstead
Blaze of Glory	Fastbond
Braingeyser	Forcefield
Bronze Tablet*	Fork
Camouflage	Gauntlet of Might
Chaos Orb	Granite Gargoyle
Clone	Guardian Angel
Consecrate Land	Ice Storm
Contract from Below*	Icy Manipulator
Copper Tablet	Illusionary Mask
Copy Artifact	Invisibility
Cyclopean Tomb	Jade Statue
Darkpact*	Jandor's Ring
Demonic Attorney*	Juggernaut

Kird Ape	Rocket Launcher
Kudzu	Sacrifice
Lance	Savannah
Lich	Scrubland
Living Wall	Sedge Troll
Mijae Djinn	Serendib Efreet
Mox Emerald	Shatterstorm
Mox Jet	Sinkhole
Mox Pearl	Sol Ring
Mox Ruby	Taiga
Mox Sapphire	Tempest Efreet*
Natural Selection	Time Vault
Nettling Imp	Time Walk
Plateau	Timetwister
Psionic Blast	Tropical Island
Raging River	Tundra
Rebirth*	Two-Headed Giant of Foriys
Reconstruction	Underground Sea
Regrowth	Vesuvan Doppelganger
Resurrection	Veteran Bodyguard
Reverse Polarity	Volcanic Island
Roc of Kher Ridges	Wheel of Fortune
Rock Hydra	Word of Command

* : Banned from play, as card states to remove from deck before playing if not playing for ante. This tournament type does not require that ante be wagered.

Type II Tournament Floor Rules

The Type II tournament uses all of the Standard Floor Rules.

Modifications to Standard Floor Rules

Note: All of the Standard Floor Rules apply unmodified to this tournament type.

Sealed-Deck Tournament Rules
Magic: The Gathering

4/19/95

Notes

- The standard rules for **Magic: The Gathering** apply to all tournament play, except where amended by these rules. In cases where the official tournament rules differ from the basic rules of **Magic**, the official tournament rules take precedence.

• Note on play with non-English language cards: Be advised that in all cases, any card title, card text, rules, tournament rules or rulings, or any other facet of official tournament play where translational differences may appear, will be interpreted according to the English language versions most currently in use. Determinations of "latest limited edition" sets will be made according to the latest limited edition sets released in the English language if there is a conflict in international play. Otherwise, use the latest limited editions common to players from all countries anticipated to participate. In any case where there may be discrepancies, the allowable sets/expansions should be advertised in advance.

Deck Construction

1. Decks may be constructed using the contents of 1 (one) sealed deck of the latest edition of **Magic: The Gathering** cards (60 cards), and <u>one</u> of the following additions:

a. The contents of 3 (three) sealed booster packs of the latest 8 (eight) card booster pack limited edition expansion set (for a starting total of 84 cards); or

b. The contents of 2 (two) sealed booster packs of the latest 15 (fifteen) card booster pack limited edition expansion set (for a starting total of 90 cards); or

c. The contents of 2 (two) sealed booster packs of the latest edition of **Magic: The Gathering** basic set (for a starting total of 90 cards).

Optional rule: At the Judge's discretion, players may add exactly 4 (four) basic lands of their choice to the deck. These land cards must be issued by the tournament staff after the deck construction period (see Sealed-Deck Floor Rules, SD2) and in such a way as to take care that each player receives only four additional lands and not more (using the player sign-in list may be a good way to ensure this, as will checkmarking the player's index card as they receive their lands). This pool of basic lands can be generated from an individual collection or by having each player donate one of each basic land to create the pool as part of any entry fees at the tournament.

2. The tournament deck must contain a minimum of 40 (forty) cards, with no imposed maximum. In Sealed-Deck play, any cards from the starter deck and booster(s) not used in the tournament deck will function as that player's Sideboard. The total number of cards in a player's deck and Sideboard combined may change during the course of play, as Sealed-Deck tournaments require the wagering of ante (see Modifications to Standard Floor Rules #6: Sealed Deck). The use of the Sideboard is further explained in the Standard Floor Rules (rule #5).

3. Due to the natural limiting effect of Sealed-Deck play, as well as the fact that ante must be wagered in the Sealed-Deck tournament, there are neither Restricted nor Banned Lists for this style of tournament.

Sealed-Deck Floor Rules

Sealed-Deck tournaments will use the Standard Floor Rules, except where noted in the Modifications to Standard Floor Rules section below. There are four additional Floor Rules specific to a Sealed-Deck tournament, noted by SD#. These are:

SD1. Players are responsible for providing their own sealed decks and boosters for use in the tournament, except in cases where the decks and boosters are provided for them by the tournament organizers. If an entry fee is charged for the tournament, the fee for a player shall not exceed the Manufacturer's Suggested Retail Price for the cards allotted to and received by the player, plus an additional amount within the normal sanctioning parameters allowable by the Duelists' Convocation office sanctioning the event.

SD2. Prior to the first round's pairings, the Judge should allow a period of 45 (forty-five) minutes for players to construct their decks. All players in the tournament must open and construct their tournament decks during the same 45-minute period. The Judge must announce a warning to the players at the forty-minute mark that only five minutes remain in the deck construction period. Players must have their decks constructed prior to the end of this allotted time. If a player has not completed deck construction at the end of this allotted time, this may be interpreted by the Judge as a Declaration of Forfeiture (see Standard Floor Rules #15). In the event all players in the tournament have completed deck construction prior to the end of the 45 minutes, the tournament may commence without delay.

SD3. Players may not open their sealed deck or booster(s) prior to the beginning of the time period allotted for by the Judge.

SD4. At no time prior to or during the tournament will trading of cards from the Sealed-Deck tournament deck or Sideboard be permitted.

Modifications to Standard Floor Rules: Sealed Deck

Note: Rule numbers below correspond to Standard Floor Rules rule numbers.

5. As written, but cards from the Sideboard need not be traded into the deck on a one-for-one basis; any number of cards may be added to or subtracted from the deck, provided that the playing deck contains a minimum of 40 cards when finished. Additionally, the requirements of Sideboards containing exactly 15 cards are dropped for obvious reasons.

6. In Sealed-Deck tournaments, it IS required that players wager ante. Cards won as ante may be introduced into the playing deck at any time that a Sideboard use is allowed (i.e., in between duels or matches). A player unable to field a deck of at least 40 cards no longer has a legal deck and will be removed from the tournament.

13. *Note:* Floor Rule #13 (Judge's right to terminate an excessively long match) may come into play more often in a Sealed-Deck tournament, as many decks constructed from such a limited environment when played against each other may grind into a near stalemate situation. It is therefore recommended that if any time limits are imposed per round, it may be desirable to extend the limit to 60 or 90 minutes, depending on the tournament. This extension is entirely at the Judge's discretion and must be advertised in advance or announced to all players at the beginning of the tournament.

Standard Floor Rules
Magic: The Gathering

4/19/95

Note

- Note on play with non-English language cards: Be advised that in all cases, any card title, card text, rules, tournament rules or rulings, or any other facet of official tournament play where translational differences may appear, will be interpreted according to the English language versions most currently in use. This applies to all tournament types used by the Duelists' Convocation, without exception.

Standard Floor Rules

1. Officially sanctioned tournaments will be presided over by a Judge, who may be assisted by as many Assistant Referees as needed. NEITHER THE JUDGE NOR THE ASSISTANT REFEREES MAY PLAY IN A TOURNAMENT THAT THEY ARE ADJUDICATING. A Judge may be required to interpret rules, to terminate an excessively long match, to interpret a Declaration of Forfeiture (see Floor Rule #15), or to make any other adjudication as necessary during the tournament. The Judge is also responsible for maintaining the tournament records and providing an accurate tournament report for the Duelists' Convocation office that sanctioned the event. Assistant Referees will aid by answering rules questions on the floor, assisting with matching players for a new round, and being available to the Judge for any other assistance required. In necessary cases, the Judge may overrule any decision made by an Assistant Referee. The decision of the Judge is always final.

2. The number of players in an officially sanctioned tournament should ideally be a power of two (i.e., 32, 64, 128, etc.). In the event that the number of players is not a power of two, byes may be assigned randomly during the first round only and must be done in such a fashion that the number of players in the second round is a power of two.

3. Officially sanctioned **Magic: The Gathering** tournaments will use a standard single-elimination bracketing system with random pairings for each round. An index card (or reasonable facsimile) will be prepared for each player with the player's name, Duelists' Convocation membership number, and other tournament information on it. Cards will be shuffled and paired randomly for each round of the tournament. Alternately, tournaments with the capabilities may use a computerized system for generating random pairings for each round, provided that the Judge can keep accurate records of each player's progression throughout the tournament.

Note: The single-elimination bracketing system will be changed to another system in the near future (at the time of this writing) to accommodate more playing time for all participants in an officially sanctioned tournament. Contact your local Duelists' Convocation branch office to receive a copy of the latest official tournament rules.

4. A duel is one complete game of **Magic**. A match is defined as the best two out of three duels. A player may advance in the tournament after successfully winning one match and reporting this victory to the Judge.

5. Players must use the same deck that they begin the tournament with throughout the duration of the tournament. The only deck alteration permitted is through the use of the Sideboard (see Deck Construction Rules for the appropriate tournament type). If players intend to use a Sideboard during the course of a match, they must declare to their opponent prior to the beginning of that match that they will be using the Sideboard. Players may exchange cards from their deck for cards from their Sideboard on a one-for-one basis at any time between duels or matches. There are no restrictions on how many cards a player may exchange in this way at any given time. Prior to the beginning of any duel, players must allow their opponent to count, face down, the number of cards in their Sideboard. If a player's Sideboard does not total exactly 15 (fifteen) cards, the Judge or an Assistant Referee must be consulted to evaluate the situation before the duel can begin. If a player claims to not be using a Sideboard at the beginning of the match, ignore this counting procedure for that player, but no deck alteration of any kind will be permitted by the Judge for that player for the duration of that match. Any violation of this rule may be interpreted by the Judge as a Declaration of Forfeiture.

6. Players are not required to wager ante during the tournament. Players may play for real ante, provided that both participants in the match give their consent, though this agreement does not allow the inclusion of the banned ante cards in the tournament deck. Ante cards won in a tournament must be kept separate from the tournament deck and Sideboard and may not be used in the tournament in any capacity. If loss of ante cards from a player's deck reduces the deck below 60 (sixty) cards, the player no longer has a legal tournament deck and will be removed from the tournament.

7. Mulligan Rule: If a player draws either a) no land or b) all land cards on the initial draw of seven cards to begin a duel, he or she may restart the duel. To do this, the player must show his or her opponent that he or she has either no land or all land, reshuffle the deck, allow the opponent to re-cut the deck, and draw seven new cards. The player's opponent has the option to do the same, even if the opponent's hand does not qualify for this rule. For example, if player A draws no land and wishes to reshuffle,

player B may opt to also try to improve the hand he or she drew. A player may only use this rule once per duel.

8. A player may use plastic card sleeves or other protective devices on cards in the tournament deck with the permission of the Judge *and with the permission of their opponent.* If *for any reason* a player's opponent wishes the removal of the sleeves/protective devices, the opponent may state so at the beginning of any duel and the player must immediately comply. The Judge may wish to disallow a player's card sleeves if they are obviously marked, worn, or otherwise in a poor condition that may interfere with shuffling or game play. The exception to this rule is that sleeves may always be used to mark a player's card as belonging to that player in the event the card is in the opponent's playing field.

9. The use of "proxy" cards in the tournament deck is not allowed. A proxy card is one that has been placed into the deck to represent another card that, for one reason or another, the player doesn't want to play with—i.e., using a swamp with the word "Nightmare" written on it because the player doesn't want to play with their actual Nightmare.

10. Players must at all times keep the cards in their hand above the level of the playing surface. If a player is in violation, the Judge may issue a warn-

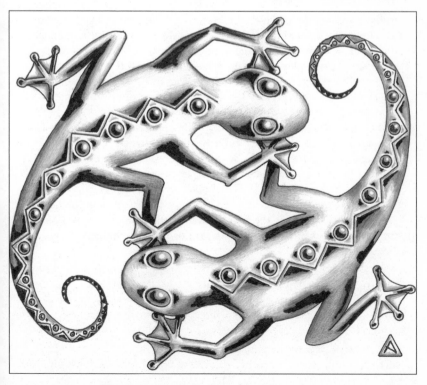

ing to the player or interpret the violation as a Declaration of Forfeiture, at the Judge's discretion.

11. Players may not have any outside assistance (i.e., coaching) during a match. If a player is in violation, the Judge may issue a warning to the player or interpret the violation as a Declaration of Forfeiture, at the Judge's discretion.

12. Unsportsmanlike conduct will not be tolerated at an officially sanctioned tournament. Players, Judges, and Assistant Referees will conduct themselves in a polite, respectable, and sportsmanlike manner. A player behaving in an excessively belligerent, argumentative, hostile, or unsportsmanlike manner may receive a warning or have this behavior interpreted as a Declaration of Forfeiture, at the Judge's discretion. Repeat offenses of this type by a particular member should be reported to the Duelists' Convocation office sanctioning the event for investigation and possible action. Behavior of this type on the part of an Assistant Referee should be reported to the Judge, who may issue the offender a warning or remove the individual from the tournament. Behavior of this type on the part of a Judge should be reported to the Duelists' Convocation office sanctioning the event for investigation and possible action.

13. In the event of an excessively long match, the Judge may need to adjudicate the outcome prior to its actual conclusion. In some cases, the Judge may wish to impose a time limit for each round of the tournament. In either case, the time limit will not be less than 45 (forty-five) minutes of playing time for a complete match. In the event of a long match, the Judge must give the players involved a time warning not less than 10 (ten) minutes prior to the end of the allotted time. If at the end of the allotted time the match is not completed, the Judge will award the victory as follows: if the players are currently playing the first or third duels of the match, to the player with the highest life total in the current duel; if playing the second duel of the match, to the player who won the first complete duel. SEMI-FINAL OR FINAL ROUNDS SHOULD NEVER BE ADJUDICATED BY A TIME LIMIT. It is HIGHLY recommended to allow matches to play to their conclusion (comebacks from 20–1 are not unheard of), but in cases where this is not possible, Judges will use the above format.

14. Players must take their turns in a timely fashion. Whereas taking some time to think through a situation is acceptable, stalling for time is not. If the Judge feels that a player is stalling to take advantage of a time limit, the Judge may issue warning or interpret the stalling as a Declaration of Forfeiture, at the Judge's discretion.

15. Failure to adhere to the above rules, or to any other rules specific to a particular tournament, may be interpreted by the Judge as a Declaration

of Forfeiture. Only the Judge may make an interpretation of a Declaration of Forfeiture. This is a more pleasant way of stating that if a player breaks the rules, the Judge will remove the individual from the tournament.

16. *Note:* The Director of the Duelists' Convocation reserves the exclusive right to add, delete, alter, transmute, polymorph, switch, color-lace, sleight of mind, magical hack, or in any other way change these or any other official Duelists' Convocation rules, whole or in part, with or without notice, at any time that it is deemed necessary or desirable. This right is non-negotiable.

Magic: a collecting history

T. Brian Wagner and Victor K. Wertz

We released the first cards for **Magic: The Gathering** to the general public on August 5, 1993, with a first printing of nearly 10 million cards, which we made available as either sixty-card "starter decks" or fifteen-card "booster packs." After the first 2.6 million cards (commonly called Alpha cards) had already gone out, however, we found some problems and made corrections for the final 7.3 million cards (often referred to as Beta cards).

Most of the fixes involved minor typos or miscredited artwork, yet we also took this opportunity to add in two cards that we had accidentally left out of the first run of cards—Circle of Protection: Black and Volcanic Island.

We also worked to clarify the rules. A fantasy story by Richard Garfield was removed from the initial rulebook to make room for a brief summary of play, and the rulebook was expanded to forty pages. For further clarification, we added a list of commonly asked questions and an index—this new rulebook, with all of its corrections and additions, appeared in starter decks beginning with the Beta print run.

While the presses were temporarily stopped, the folks who work for Carta Mundi, the Belgium company that prints all of the **Magic** cards, made some changes of their own, particularly in the packaging: They improved the process of shrinkwrapping the starter deck display boxes and added UPC barcodes to the bottoms of the individual deck boxes. Finally, before restarting the presses, Carta Mundi sharpened the dies used to cut the cards, which resulted in a less-rounded corner on the Beta cards. These cards were released on October 4, 1993.

After the original black-bordered *Limited Edition* print run of 10 million cards sold out much faster than anticipated, we changed the black borders on the card faces to white and added the phrase *Unlimited Edition* to the packaging. The *Unlimited Edition* was released on December 1, 1993, and approximately 35 million cards were printed.

Shortly thereafter, we released 13,500 *Collectors' Edition* sets of **Magic: The Gathering**. These limited edition sets contained 363 cards, including one each of the 302 different cards, with multiple land cards making up the difference. Ten thousand sets were sold in the U.S. and Canada, while 3,500 *International Collectors' Edition* sets were produced for sale overseas. Unlike other **Magic** cards, the *Collectors' Edition* cards have square corners and the card backs have gold bolders. Additionally, these cards have gold lettering on the back of each card that marks them as either *Collectors' Edition* or *International Collectors' Edition* cards. These cards are not allowed in tournament play and generally are not used for regular games. The sets were released on December 8, 1993.

We periodically augment **Magic: The Gathering** with additional expansion sets. These generally contain between 75 and 400 cards, all centered around some theme within Dominia. The first expansion set, *Arabian Nights,* was released on December 17, 1993, and had a print run of 5 million cards. The second expansion set, *Antiquities,* was released on March 4, 1994, and had a print run of 15 million cards. The third expansion set, *Legends,* was released on June 10, 1994, and had a print run of 35 million cards. The fourth expansion set, *The Dark,* was released on August 8, 1994, and had a print run of 62 million cards. At this writing, the latest expansion set is *Fallen Empires*, which was released on November 15, 1994. More expansion sets are on the way and will offer players views of areas and times of Dominia yet to be explored.

The "Unlimited" name was not really accurate, and soon afterwards we released the "Revised" edition, removing some cards deemed too powerful or too confusing and adding some cards from the *Arabian Nights* and *Antiquities* expansion sets. Once again, the rules were changed and clarified. These cards have the same white border as the *Unlimited Edition* but can be differentiated from the previous edition by the omission of the "beveled" edge on the *Revised Edition* cards.On November 15, 1994, we released a special "gift box" edition of **Magic**. Each gift box contained two 60-card starter decks, 30 glass counters and a bag to put them in, and a greatly expanded and clarified copy of the rules, all in a larger box. We will continue to produce gift boxes which will contain cards from the most current edition of **Magic**.Richard Garfield's original vision of the game was that the selection of cards in the basic set would always be changing; therefore, we periodically rearrange the assortment of cards. Cards that appeared in previous expansion sets (*Arabian Nights, Antiquities, Legends, The Dark,* and *Fallen Empires*) are "rotated" in and certain other cards are removed. For example, the *Fourth Edition* was released in April of 1995; the card list included in this chapter is from the selection of cards in *Fourth Edition*. You can identify *Fourth Edition* cards by the return of the "beveled" edge and the change in the copyright notice at the bottom of the card (previously, the illustration was copyright the respective artist; now copyright is held by Wizards of the Coast). The packaging for *Fourth Edition* has likewise changed—starter decks now display the five mana symbols instead of the five colored stones and booster packs feature one of five selected pieces of art from the game (Brass Man, Hurloon Minotaur, Mana Vault, Mesa Pegasus, or Spirit Link). At the time of this writing, *Fourth Edition* is the current edition of the basic set, but you can be assured that changes will continue to be made in the future to reflect the ever-changing world that Richard Garfield envisioned.Occasionally, we make available special "promotional/preview" cards through various publications and venues. The first promotional card was the Nalathni Dragon card, originally made available to attendees of DragonCon 1994. It was then released to members of the Duelists' Convocation and included in issue #3 of *The Duelist*. Other promotional cards include Arena, Sewers of Estark, Windseeker Centaur, Giant Badger, and Mana Crypt, all of which were made available through the HarperPrism **Magic: The Gathering** novels by sending in a coupon and proof of purchase to HarperPrism.

In addition to all of these official cards, we have discovered the occasional counterfeit card. These cards can usually be identified by their lower-quality printing and card stock. Also, many counterfeit cards are color copies glued to land cards and can be identified by the double-layer look visible on the edge of the card. These cards are virtually worthless to most collectors.

With the proper information, it's easy for you to determine the rarity of any given card; however, you should note that the rarity of a card doesn't necessarily determine its value. To many players, a card that is more useful in game play is more important than a rare card. Additionally, the condition of a card is of vital importance to many collectors. Finally, some people value cards by a specific artist and simply aren't interested in other factors.

At the present time, your best sources for information on card values are independent card-collecting magazines and the Internet. Three magazines that provide card value listings for collectible card games are *Scrye, Inquest,* and *Conjure.* On the Internet, the Usenet group `rec.games.deckmaster. marketplace` and the mailing list `gg-marketplace-l` are valuable sources of information. These are sources independent of Wizards of the Coast, as we are not allowed to comment on card values or prices.

The following pages provide a complete list of the 378 different cards included in the current *Fourth Edition* print run of **Magic: The Gathering**. In addition to providing all of the card names, the list includes color, spell type, artist, and frequency; separate listings provide complete *Fourth Edition* card texts, indicate differences in wording from previous editions, and explain any rulings differences.

Card lists and collecting information will also be published regularly in *The Duelist* (the official **Deckmaster** magazine) and the *Duelists' Companion* (the newsletter for Duelists' Convocation members). They will also be maintained on the official Wizards of the Coast World Wide Web page; you may send email to `questions@wizards.com` for more information.

Through regular mail, you can also receive complete card lists that contain information on almost every card that we have ever printed. Currently, the following five lists are available: *Fourth Edition, Arabian Nights/Antiquities, Legends, The Dark/Fallen Empires,* and *Discontinued/Promo.* To receive one of these lists, send a self-addressed stamped business-sized (#10) envelope (SASE) to Wizards of the Coast, P.O. Box 707, Renton, WA 98057-0707. Be sure to mark the envelope, indicating which particular card list you wish to receive. You may send multiple SASEs in one envelope if you wish.

Fourth Edition Card List and Errata List

The following list contains all of the cards in *Fourth Edition,* as well as any differences between *Fourth Edition* and previous editions of the cards. Wizards of the Coast recommends that all cards be played using the most recent version of their wording. Where previous wordings and *Fourth Edition* wordings differ functionally, this is noted by the symbol ⚔ preceding card titles. Multiplayer changes (e.g., Rag Man) are ignored for ⚔ purposes. For cards that are currently out of print, any changes between various editions of the out-of-print cards or any errata about out-of-print cards are listed under the latest edition that contained the card. In the following list, several standard changes are referred to:

M: "Mono Artifact" instead of "Artifact" and no ⚙ in the activation cost

P: "Poly Artifact" instead of "Artifact"

C: "Continuous Artifact" instead of "Artifact"

G: "Gain(s)" instead of "Get(s)"

B: "Do" or any form of that verb instead of "Deal" or any form of that verb

T: "Any target" instead of "Target creature or player"

R: "Regenerate(s)(.)" instead of "Regenerate"

S: "Schuler" instead of "Shuler" in the artist credit

D: "Denise Detwiler" instead of "Dennis Detwiller" in the artist credit

A: "Tap to" with no activation cost instead of an activation cost of "⚙"

Abomination
Black / Summon Abomination / Mark Tedin / Uncommon
***Fourth Edition* Text:** At the end of combat, destroy all green and white creatures blocking or blocked by Abomination.
Differences: The *Legends* version has different wording: "All green or white creatures blocking or blocked by Abomination are destroyed at the end of combat."

Air Elemental
Blue / Summon Elemental / Richard Thomas / Uncommon
***Fourth Edition* Text:** Flying

Alabaster Potion
White / Instant / Harold McNeill / Common
***Fourth Edition* Text:** Give target player X life, or prevent X damage to any creature or player.
Differences: The *Legends* version has different wording: "Target player gains X life or prevents X damage to any one creature or player."

⚔ Aladdin's Lamp
Artifact / Artifact / Mark Tedin / Rare
***Fourth Edition* Text:** X̄, ⚙: Instead of drawing a card from the top of your library, draw X cards but choose only one to put into your hand. Shuffle the leftover cards and put them at the bottom of your library. X cannot be 0.

Differences: The *Revised* and *Arabian Nights* versions say "in" instead of "into," add "You must" before "shuffle," and do not say "X cannot be 0." The *Arabian Nights* version also has change M and a casting cost of 5 5 instead of 10.

Rulings Differences: Aladdin's Lamp no longer allows X to be 0. *The Revised and Arabian Nights versions of Aladdin's Lamp allowed X to be 0.*

Aladdin's Ring

Artifact / Artifact / Dan Frazier / Rare
***Fourth Edition* Text:** 8 , ⟳: Aladdin's Ring deals 4 damage to target creature or player.

Differences: The *Revised* version has changes B and T. The *Arabian Nights* version says "Do" instead of "Aladdin's Ring deals" and has changes M and T.

Ali Baba

Red / Summon Ali Baba / Julie Baroh / Uncommon
***Fourth Edition* Text:** ➋: Tap target wall.
Differences: The *Arabian Nights* version says "a" instead of "target."

Amrou Kithkin

White / Summon Kithkin / Quinton Hoover / Common
***Fourth Edition* Text:** No creature with power greater than 2 may be assigned to block Kithkin.

Differences: The *Legends* version has different wording: "Creatures with power greater than 2 may not be assigned to block Kithkin. Blocker's power may be increased after blocking has been assigned."

⚔ Amulet of Kroog

Artifact / Artifact / Margaret Organ-Kean / Common
***Fourth Edition* Text:** ➋ , ⟳: Prevent 1 damage to any creature or player.

Differences: The *Antiquities* version says "target" instead of "creature or player" and has change M.

Rulings Differences: Amulet of Kroog no longer targets the creature or player being damaged. *The Antiquities version stated that Amulet of Kroog targeted the creature or player receiving damage, not the damage being dealt.*

Angry Mob

White / Summon Mob / Drew Tucker / Uncommon
***Fourth Edition* Text:** Trample / During your turn, Angry Mob has power and toughness each equal to 2 plus the total number of swamps opponents control. During other turns, Angry Mob has power and toughness 2/2.

Differences: *The Dark* version has different wording: "Trample / During your turn, the *s below are both equal to the total number of swamps all opponents control. During any other player's turn, * equals 0."

⚔ Animate Artifact

Blue / Enchant Artifact / Douglas Shuler / Uncommon
***Fourth Edition* Text:** Target artifact becomes an artifact creature with power and toughness each equal to its casting cost; target retains all its original abilities. Animate Artifact does not affect artifact creatures.

Differences: Previous versions say "is now" instead of "becomes," "both power and toughness equal" instead of "power and toughness each equal," and add "as well" after "abilities." The *Revised* version also says "Has no effect on" instead of "Animate Artifact does not effect." The *Unlimited* and *Limited* versions do not have "artifact" before "creature" and do not have "Animate Artifact does not affect artifact creatures." The *Unlimited* and *Limited* versions add "This will destroy artifacts with 0 casting cost" at the end; these versions also say "Enchant Non-Creature Artifact" instead of "Enchant Artifact" and have change S.

Rulings Differences: Animate Artifact can now be played on artifact creatures. *The Limited and Unlimited versions did not allow*

Animate Artifact to be played on artifact creatures.

Animate Dead

Black / Enchant Dead Creature / Anson Maddocks / Uncommon

***Fourth Edition* Text:** Take target creature from any graveyard and put it directly into play under your control with -1/-0. Treat this creature as though it were just summoned. If Animate Dead is removed, bury the creature in its owner's graveyard.

Differences: The *Revised* version has different wording: "Any creature in any graveyard comes into play on your side with -1 to its original power. At end of game, or if this enchantment is discarded without removing target creature from play, target creature is returned to its owner's graveyard. Target creature may be killed as normal." The *Unlimited* and *Limited* versions have different wording: "Any creature in either player's graveyard comes into play on your side with -1 to its original power. If this enchantment is removed, or at end of game, target creature is returned to its owner's graveyard. Target creature may be killed as normal."

Animate Wall

White / Enchant Wall / Dan Frazier / Rare

***Fourth Edition* Text:** Target wall can now attack.

Differences: Previous versions add "Target wall's power and toughness are unchanged by this enchantment, even if its power is 0" at the end.

Ankh of Mishra

Artifact / Artifact / Amy Weber / Rare

***Fourth Edition* Text:** Each time a player puts a land into play, Ankh of Mishra deals 2 damage to that player.

Differences: Previous versions have different wording: "Ankh does 2 damage to anyone who puts a new land into play." The *Unlimited* and *Limited* versions also have change C.

✗ Apprentice Wizard

Blue / Summon Wizard / Dan Frazier / Common

***Fourth Edition* Text:** ◐, ⟳: Add ③ to your mana pool. Play this ability as an interrupt.

Differences: *The Dark* version says "This ability is played" instead of "Play this ability."

Rulings Differences: *Fourth Edition* has errata: Apprentice Wizard should read "add three colorless mana to your mana pool. Play this ability as an interrupt."

Armageddon

White / Sorcery / Jesper Myrfors / Rare

***Fourth Edition* Text:** Destroy all lands.

Differences: Previous versions have different wording: "All lands in play are destroyed."

Armageddon Clock

Artifact / Artifact / Amy Weber / Rare

***Fourth Edition* Text:** During your upkeep, put one doom counter on Armageddon Clock. At the end of your upkeep, Armageddon Clock deals X damage to each player, where X is the number of doom counters on Armageddon Clock. / During any upkeep, any player may pay ④ to remove a doom counter from Armageddon Clock.

Differences: The *Revised* and *Antiquities* versions have different wording: "Put one counter on Armageddon Clock during each of your upkeeps. At the end of your upkeep, each player takes damage equal to the number of counters on the Clock. Any player may spend ④ during any upkeep to remove a counter." The *Antiquities* version also has change C.

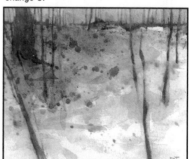

Ashes to Ashes

Black / Sorcery / Drew Tucker / Uncommon

***Fourth Edition* Text:** Ashes to Ashes removes two target non-artifact creatures from the game and deals 5 damage to you.

Differences: *The Dark* version has change B.

Ashnod's Battle Gear
Artifact / Artifact / Mark Poole / Uncommon
Fourth Edition Text: ②, ↻: Target creature you control gets +2/-2 as long as Ashnod's Battle Gear remains tapped. / You may choose not to untap Ashnod's Battle Gear during your untap phase.
Differences: The *Antiquities* version has different wording: " ②: Give a creature of yours +2/-2 as long as Ashnod's Battle Gear is tapped. You may choose not to untap Ashnod's Battle Gear during untap phase" and change M.

Aspect of Wolf
Green / Enchant Creature / Jeff A. Menges / Rare
Fourth Edition Text: Increase target creature's power and toughness by half the number of forests you control, rounding down for power and up for toughness.
Differences: Previous versions say "Target creature's power and toughness are increased" instead of "Increase target creature's power and toughness" and "have in play" instead of "control."

Backfire
Blue / Enchant Creature / Brian Snōddy / Uncommon
Fourth Edition Text: Backfire deals 1 damage to target creature's controller for each 1 damage dealt to you by that creature.
Differences: The *Legends* version has different wording: "For each point of damage done to you from target creature Backfire does one point of damage to target creature's controller."

Bad Moon
Black / Enchantment / Jesper Myrfors / Rare
Fourth Edition Text: All black creatures get +1/+1.
Differences: Previous versions add "in play" after creatures and have change G.

⚔ Balance
White / Sorcery / Mark Poole / Rare
Fourth Edition Text: Each player sacrifices enough lands to equalize the number of lands all players control. The player who controls the fewest lands cannot sacrifice any in this way. All players then equalize cards in hand and then creatures in play in the same way.
Differences: The *Revised* version has different wording: "Whichever player has more lands in play must discard enough lands of his or her choice to equalize the number of lands both players have in play. Next, equalize the cards in hand and then creatures in play the same way. Creatures lost in this manner are considered buried." The *Unlimited* and *Limited* versions have different wording: "Whichever player has more lands in play must discard enough lands of his or her choice to equalize the number of lands both players have in play. Cards in hand and creatures in play must be equalized the same way. Creatures lost in this manner may not be regenerated."
Rulings Differences: *Fourth Edition* has errata: Players should equalize cards in hand by discarding, not by sacrificing.

⚔ Ball Lightning
Red / Summon Ball Lightning / Quinton Hoover / Rare
Fourth Edition Text: Trample / Ball Lightning can attack the turn it comes into play. / At the end of any turn, bury Ball Lightning.
Differences: *The Dark* version has different wording: "Trample / Ball Lightning may attack on the turn during which it is summoned. Ball Lightning is buried at the end of the turn during which it is summoned."
Rulings Differences: Ball Lightning is now buried at the end of any turn. The Dark *version stated that the card was only buried at the end of the turn it was summoned.*

⚔ Battering Ram

Artifact / Artifact Creature / Jeff A. Menges /
Common

Fourth Edition Text: Banding when attacking /
At the end of combat, destroy all walls blocking Battering Ram.

Differences: The *Antiquities* version has different wording: "Bands, but only when
attacking. / Any wall blocking Battering Ram
is destroyed. Walls destroyed this way deal
their damage before dying."

Rulings Differences: Battering Ram now
destroys walls that block it at the end of combat. *The* Antiquities *version implied that the
wall was destroyed during damage dealing.*

Benalish Hero

White / Summon Hero / Douglas Shuler /
Common

Fourth Edition Text: Banding

Differences: Previous versions say "bands"
instead of "banding." The *Unlimited* and
Limited versions also have change S.

Bird Maiden

Red / Summon Bird Maiden / Kaja Foglio /
Common

Fourth Edition Text: Flying

Differences: The *Arabian Nights* version had
two versions of the card with size variations
in the uncolored mana symbol.

⚔ Birds of Paradise

Green / Summon Mana Birds / Mark Poole /
Rare

Fourth Edition Text: Flying / ☉: Add one
mana of any color to your mana pool. Play
this ability as an interrupt.

Differences: The *Revised* version says "This
ability is played" instead of "Play this ability."
The *Unlimited* and *Limited* versions say "This

tap may be played" instead of "Play this ability" and have change A. *Limited* (Alpha) says
"//" instead of a line break and does not have
"of any color."

Rulings Differences: Birds of Paradise can
now add mana of any color to your mana
pool. *The "Alpha" version could only add colorless mana.*

Black Knight

Black / Summon Knight / Jeff A. Menges /
Uncommon

Fourth Edition Text: Protection from white,
first strike

Black Mana Battery

Artifact / Artifact / Anson Maddocks / Rare

Fourth Edition Text: ②, ☉: Put one charge
counter on Black Mana Battery. / ☉: Add ☠
to your mana pool and remove as many
charge counters as you wish. For each
charge counter removed from Black Mana
Battery, add ☠ to your mana pool. Play this
ability as an interrupt.

Differences: The *Legends* version has different wording: "②,⚒: Put one counter on
Black Mana Battery. / ⚒: Add ☠ to your
mana pool. Remove as many counters as
you wish. For each counter removed add ☠
to your mana pool. This ability is played as
an interrupt."

⚔ Black Vise

Artifact / Artifact / Richard Thomas /
Uncommon

Fourth Edition Text: At the end of target
opponent's upkeep, Black Vise deals that
player 1 damage for each card in his or her
hand in excess of four.

Differences: The *Revised* version has different wording: "If opponent has more than
four cards in hand during his or her upkeep,
Black Vise does 1 damage to opponent for
each card in excess of four." The *Unlimited*
and *Limited* versions have different wording:
"If opponent has more than four cards in
hand during upkeep, Black Vise does 1 damage to opponent for each card in excess of
four" and change C.

Rulings Differences: Black Vise now targets
an opponent and deals damage at the end of
that player's upkeep. *Previous versions stated that Black Vise affected "opponent"; thus,*

in a two-player game, stealing Black Vise would change who it affected. Also, Black Vise affected opponent "during" upkeep instead of at "end of" upkeep.

Black Ward
White / Enchant Creature / Dan Frazier / Uncommon
Fourth Edition Text: Target creature gains protection from black. The protection granted by Black Ward does not destroy Black Ward.
Differences: Previous versions do not have "The protection granted by Black Ward does not destroy Black Ward."
Rulings Differences: The protection granted by Black Ward now cannot destroy Black Ward. *Previous versions of Black Ward would destroy themselves under the right circumstances.*

Blessing
White / Enchant Creature / Julie Baroh / Rare
Fourth Edition Text: ✳: Target creature Blessing enchants gets +1/+1 until end of turn.
Differences: The *Revised* version has different wording: "✳: +1/+1." The *Unlimited* and *Limited* versions do not have "Blessing enchants" and have change G.

Blight
Black / Enchant Land / Pete Venters / Uncommon
Fourth Edition Text: If target land becomes tapped, destroy it at end of turn.
Differences: The *Legends* version says "it is destroyed" instead of "destroy it."

Blood Lust
Red / Instant / Anson Maddocks / Common
Fourth Edition Text: Target creature gets +4/-4 until end of turn. If this reduces crea-

ture's toughness to less than 1, creature's toughness becomes 1.
Differences: The *Legends* version says "creatures" instead of "creature," "below" instead of "to less than," and "is" instead of "becomes." The *Legends* version also has change G.
Rulings Differences: Blood Lust now only affects one creature. *The* Legends *version could be read to mean that it affected multiple creatures.*

Blue Elemental Blast
Blue / Interrupt / Richard Thomas / Common
Fourth Edition Text: Counter target red spell or destroy target red permanent.
Differences: Previous versions have different wording: "Counters target red spell being cast or destroys a red card in play."
Rulings Differences: Blue Elemental Blast can now target any red permanent in play, including tokens. *Previous versions stated that Blue Elemental Blast could only target red spells being cast or red cards in play.*

Blue Mana Battery
Artifact / Artifact / Amy Weber / Rare
Fourth Edition Text: ②, ⟳: Put one charge counter on Blue Mana Battery. / ⟳: Add 💧 to your mana pool and remove as many charge counters as you wish. For each charge counter removed from Blue Mana Battery, add 💧 to your mana pool. Play this ability as an interrupt.
Differences: The *Legends* version has different wording: "②, ⟳: Put one counter on Blue Mana Battery. / ⟳: Add 💧 to your mana pool. Remove as many counters as you wish. For each counter removed add 💧 to your mana pool. This ability is played as an interrupt."

Blue Ward
White / Enchant Creature / Dan Frazier / Uncommon
Fourth Edition Text: Target creature gains protection from blue. The protection granted by Blue Ward does not destroy Blue Ward.
Differences: Previous versions do not have "The protection granted by Blue Ward does not destroy Blue Ward."
Rulings Differences: The protection granted by Blue Ward now cannot destroy Blue Ward.

Previous versions of Blue Ward would destroy themselves under the right circumstances.

Bog Imp
Black / Summon Imp / Ron Spencer / Common
***Fourth Edition* Text:** Flying

Bog Wraith
Black / Summon Wraith / Jeff A. Menges / Uncommon
***Fourth Edition* Text:** Swampwalk

➤ Bottle of Suleiman
Artifact / Artifact / Jesper Myrfors / Rare
***Fourth Edition* Text:** 1 : Sacrifice Bottle of Suleiman. Flip a coin; target opponent calls heads or tails while coin is in the air. If the flip ends up in opponent's favor, Bottle of Suleiman deals 5 damage to you. Otherwise, put a Djinn token into play. Treat this token as a 5/5 artifact creature with flying.
Differences: The *Revised* and *Arabian Nights* versions have different wording: " 1 : Flip a coin, with opponent calling heads or tails while coin is in the air. If the flip ends up in opponent's favor, Bottle of Suleiman does 5 damage to you. Otherwise, a 5/5 flying Djinn immediately comes into play on your side. Use a counter to represent Djinn. Djinn is treated exactly like a normal artifact creature except that if it leaves play it is removed from the game entirely. No matter how the flip turns out, Bottle of Suleiman is discarded after use." The *Arabian Nights* version has change M.
Rulings Differences: Bottle of Suleiman now sacrifices itself as it is used. *The* Arabian Nights *and* Revised *versions stated that Bottle of Suleiman was discarded when the effect resolved.*

Brainwash
White / Enchant Creature / Pete Venters / Common
***Fourth Edition* Text:** Target creature cannot attack unless its controller pays an additional 3 .

Differences: *The Dark* version has different wording: "Target creature may not attack unless its controller pays ③ in addition to any other costs required for the creature to attack."

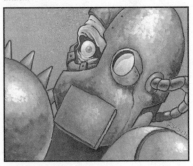

⋏ Brass Man
Artifact / Artifact Creature / Christopher Rush / Uncommon
***Fourth Edition* Text:** Brass Man does not untap during your untap phase. / ①: Untap Brass Man. Use this ability only during your upkeep.
Differences: The *Revised* version has different wording: "Brass Man does not untap as normal; you must pay ① during your upkeep phase to untap it." The *Arabian Nights* version has different wording: "Brass Man does not untap as normal; you must pay ① during your untap phase to untap it."
Rulings Differences: Controller can now pay to untap Brass Man during his or her upkeep phase; also, Brass Man has an activation cost to untap. *The* Arabian Nights *version stated that Brass Man could be untapped during the untap phase; also, the* Arabian Nights *and* Revised *versions of Brass Man did not have an activation cost.*

⋏ Bronze Tablet
Artifact / Artifact / Tom Wänerstrand / Rare
***Fourth Edition* Text:** Comes into play tapped. ④, ⊙: Remove Bronze Tablet and target card opponent owns from the game. You become owner of opponent's card, and opponent becomes owner of Bronze Tablet. Opponent may prevent this exchange by paying 10 life; if he or she does so, destroy Bronze Tablet. Effects that prevent or redirect damage cannot be used to counter this loss of life. Play this ability as an interrupt.

Remove Bronze Tablet from your deck before playing if not playing for ante.
Differences: The *Antiquities* version has different wording: "④: Target any card opponent has in play; remove it and Bronze Tablet from game. You become owner of that card, and your opponent becomes owner of Bronze Tablet. Exchange is permanent; play as interrupt. Opponent can prevent exchange by spending 10 life; this discards Bronze Tablet. Damage-preventing effects cannot counter such loss of life. Bronze Tablet comes into play tapped. Remove this card from deck if not playing for ante." The *Antiquities* version also has change M.
Rulings Differences: *Fourth Edition* has errata: Bronze Tablet should only target cards in play, not any card opponent owns.

Brothers of Fire
Red / Summon Brothers / Mark Tedin / Common
***Fourth Edition* Text:** ① ② ②: Brothers of Fire deals 1 damage to target creature or player and 1 damage to you.
Differences: *The Dark* version has changes T and B.

The Brute
Red / Enchant Creature / Mark Poole / Common
***Fourth Edition* Text:** Target creature gets +1/+0. / ② ② ②: Regenerate target creature The Brute enchants.
Differences: The *Legends* version does not have "target creature The Brute enchants" and has changes G and R.

Burrowing
Red / Enchant Creature / Mark Poole / Uncommon
***Fourth Edition* Text:** Target creature gains mountainwalk.

Carnivorous Plant
Green / Summon Wall / Quinton Hoover / Common

Carrion Ants
Black / Summon Ants / Richard Thomas / Uncommon
***Fourth Edition* Text:** ①: +1/+1 until end of turn

Differences: The *Legends* version's flavor text has the attribution: "General Chanek Valteroth."

Castle

White / Enchantment / Dameon Willich / Uncommon
***Fourth Edition* Text:** Untapped creatures you control get +0/+2 when not attacking.
Differences: The *Revised* version has different wording: "Your untapped creatures gain +0/+2. Attacking creatures do not get this bonus." The *Unlimited* and *Limited* versions have different wording: "Your untapped creatures gain +0/+2. Attacking creatures lose this bonus."

Cave People

Red / Summon Cave People / Drew Tucker / Uncommon
***Fourth Edition* Text:** When attacking, Cave People gets +1/-2 until end of turn.
1 🔴 🔴, 👁: Target creature gains mountainwalk until end of turn.
Differences: *The Dark* version says "If declared as an attacker" instead of "When attacking" and "get" instead of "gets."

Celestial Prism

Artifact / Artifact / Amy Weber / Uncommon
***Fourth Edition* Text:** 2, 👁: Add one mana of any color to your mana pool. Play this ability as an interrupt.
Differences: The Revised verison has different wording: "2, ⟁: Provides 1 mana of any color. This use is played as an interrupt." The *Unlimited* and *Limited* versions have different wording: "2: Provides 1 mana of any color. This use can be played as an interrupt." The *Unlimited* and *Limited* versions also have change M.

Channel

Green / Sorcery / Richard Thomas / Uncommon
***Fourth Edition* Text:** Until end of turn, you may add colorless mana to your mana pool at a cost of 1 life per one mana. Play these additions as interrupts. Effects that prevent or redirect damage cannot be used to counter this loss of life.
Differences: The *Revised* version has different wording: "Until end of turn, you may add colorless mana to your mana pool at a cost of 1 life per point of mana. These additions are played with the speed of an interrupt. Effects that prevent or redirect damage may not be used to counter this loss of life." The *Unlimited* and *Limited* (Beta) versions have different wording: "Until end of turn, you may add colorless mana to your mana pool, at a cost of 1 life each. These additions are played with the speed of an interrupt. Effects that prevent damage may not be used to counter this loss of life." The *Limited* (Alpha) version has different wording: "Until end of turn, you may add colorless mana to your mana pool for 1 life each. These additions are played with the speed of an interrupt. Life spent this way is not considered damage."

⋏Chaoslace

Red / Interrupt / Dameon Willich / Rare
***Fourth Edition* Text:** Change the color of target spell or target permanent to red. Costs to cast, tap, maintain, or use a special ability of target remain unchanged.
Differences: Previous versions say "one card either being played or already in play" instead of "target spell or target permanent" and add "entirely" before "unchanged."
Rulings Differences: Chaoslace can now target any permanent in play, including tokens, but cannot target lands as they are being played. *Previous versions of Chaoslace could only target cards; this included targeting lands as they were being played.*

Circle of Protection: Artifacts

White / Enchantment / Pete Venters / Uncommon
***Fourth Edition* Text:** 2: Prevent all damage against you from one artifact source. If a source deals damage to you more than once in a turn, you may pay 2 each time to pre-

vent the damage.
Differences: The *Antiquities* version says "prevents" instead of "prevent" and "must" instead of "may" and has "you want" before "to prevent." The *Antiquities* version also has change B.

Circle of Protection: Black

White / Enchantment / Jesper Myrfors / Common
***Fourth Edition* Text:** ①: Prevent all damage against you from one black source. If a source deals damage to you more than once in a turn, you may pay ① each time to prevent the damage.
Differences: The *Revised, Unlimited,* and *Limited* (Beta) versions say "Prevents" instead of "Prevent," "must" instead of "may," and "1 mana" instead of "①." These versions also add "you want" before "to prevent" and have change B. This card does not appear in the *Limited* (Alpha) version.

Circle of Protection: Blue

White / Enchantment / Dameon Willich / Common
***Fourth Edition* Text:** ①: Prevent all damage against you from one blue source. If a source deals damage to you more than once in a turn, you may pay ① each time to prevent the damage.
Differences: Previous versions say "Prevents" instead of "Prevent," "must" instead of "may," and "1 mana" instead of "①." Previous versions also add "you want" before "to prevent" and have change B.

Circle of Protection: Green

White / Enchantment / Sandra Everingham / Common
***Fourth Edition* Text:** ①: Prevent all damage against you from one green source. If a source deals damage to you more than once in a turn, you may pay ① each time to prevent the damage.
Differences: Previous versions say "Prevents" instead of "Prevent," "must" instead of "may," and "1 mana" instead of "①." Previous versions also add "you want" before "to prevent" and have change B.

Circle of Protection: Red

White / Enchantment / Mark Tedin / Common
***Fourth Edition* Text:** ①: Prevent all damage against you from one red source. If a source deals damage to you more than once in a turn, you may pay ① each time to prevent the damage.
Differences: Previous versions say "Prevents" instead of "Prevent," "must" instead of "may," and "1 mana" instead of "①." Previous versions also add "you want" before "to prevent" and have change B. The *Limited* (Alpha) version credits the artist as Anson Maddocks instead of Mark Tedin.

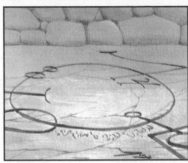

Circle of Protection: White

White / Enchantment / Douglas Shuler / Common
***Fourth Edition* Text:** ①: Prevent all damage against you from one white source. If a source deals damage to you more than once in a turn, you may pay ① each time to prevent the damage.
Differences: Previous versions say "Prevents" instead of "Prevent," "must" instead of "may," and "1 mana" instead of "①." Previous versions also add "you want" before "to prevent" and have change B. The *Unlimited* and *Limited* versions have change S.

Clay Statue

Artifact / Artifact Creature / Jesper Myrfors / Common
***Fourth Edition* Text:** ②: Regenerate
Differences: The *Antiquities* version has change R.

⚒ Clockwork Avian

Artifact / Artifact Creature / Randy Asplund-Faith / Rare
***Fourth Edition* Text:** Flying / When Clockwork

Avian comes into play, put four +1/+0 counters on it. At the end of any combat in which Clockwork Avian is assigned to attack or block, remove a counter. / X, ⊖: Put X +1/+0 counters on Clockwork Avian. You may have no more than four of these counters on Clockwork Avian. Use this ability only during your upkeep.

Differences: The *Antiquities* version has different wording: "Flying / Put four +1/+0 counters on Avian. After Avian attacks or blocks a creature, discard a counter. During his or her upkeep, controller may buy back lost counters for 1 per counter; this taps Avian."

Rulings Differences: Clockwork Avian now loses counters at the end of combat; also, there is an activation cost to obtain more counters. *The* Antiquities *version implied that Clockwork Avian lost counters when declared as an attacker or blocker; also, the cost to obtain more counters did not include an activation cost.*

⋏ Clockwork Beast

Artifact / Artifact Creature / Drew Tucker / Rare

Fourth Edition Text: When Clockwork Beast comes into play, put seven +1/+0 counters on it. At the end of any combat in which Clockwork Beast is assigned to attack or block, remove a counter. / X, ⊖: Put X +1/+0 counters on Clockwork Beast. You may have no more than seven of these counters on Clockwork Beast. Use this ability only during your upkeep.

Differences: The *Revised* version has different wording: "Put seven +1/+0 counters on Beast. After Beast attacks or blocks a creature, discard a counter. During the upkeep phase, controller may buy back lost counters for 1 per counter; this taps Beast." The *Unlimited* and *Limited* versions have different wording: "Put seven +1/+0 counters on Beast. After Beast attacks or blocks, discard a counter. During the untap phase, controller may buy back lost counters for 1 mana per counter instead of untapping Beast; this taps Beast if it wasn't tapped already."

Rulings Differences: Clockwork Beast now loses counters at the end of combat; also, there is an activation cost to obtain more counters. *Previous versions implied that Clockwork Beast lost counters when declared as an attacker or*

blocker; also, the cost to obtain more counters did not include an activation cost.

⋏ Cockatrice

Green / Summon Cockatrice / Dan Frazier / Rare

Fourth Edition Text: Flying / At the end of combat, destroy all non-wall creatures blocking or blocked by Cockatrice.

Differences: Previous versions have different wording: "Flying / Any non-wall creature blocking Cockatrice is destroyed, as is any creature blocked by Cockatrice. Creatures destroyed in this way deal their damage before dying."

Rulings Differences: Creatures blocking or blocked by Cockatrice are now destroyed at the end of combat. Also, Cockatrice now cannot destroy attacking walls that it blocks. *Previous versions implied that creatures blocking or blocked by Cockatrice were destroyed during damage dealing. Also, previous versions destroyed attacking walls.*

⋏ Colossus of Sardia

Artifact / Artifact Creature / Jesper Myrfors / Rare

Fourth Edition Text: Trample / Colossus does not untap during your untap phase. / 9: Untap Colossus. Use this ability only during your upkeep.

Differences: The *Antiquities* version has different wording: "Trample / Colossus does not untap normally during untap phase; you may spend 9 during your upkeep phase to untap Colossus."

Rulings Differences: Colossus now has an activation cost to untap. *The* Antiquities *version did not have an activation cost.*

Conservator

Artifact / Artifact / Amy Weber / Uncommon
***Fourth Edition* Text:** 3, ⊙: Prevent up to 2 damage to you.
Differences: Previous versions have different wording: "3, ⌁: Prevent the loss of up to 2 life." The *Unlimited* and *Limited* versions also have change M.
Rulings Differences: Conservator now only prevents damage, and only prevents damage dealt to controller. *Previous versions stated that Conservator prevented both damage and loss of life, and could be used to help any player.*

Control Magic

Blue / Enchant Creature / Dameon Willich / ~~Uncommon~~
***Fourth Edition* Text:** Gain control of target creature.
Differences: The *Revised* version has different wording: "You control target creature until enchantment is discarded or game ends. If target creature is already tapped it stays tapped until you can untap it. If destroyed, target creature is put in its owner's graveyard." The *Unlimited* and *Limited* versions have different wording: "You control target creature until enchantment is discarded or game ends. You can't tap target creature this turn, but if it was already tapped it stays tapped until you can untap it. If destroyed, target creature is put in its owner's graveyard."

Conversion

White / Enchantment / Jesper Myrfors / Uncommon
***Fourth Edition* Text:** All mountains become basic plains. / During your upkeep, pay ✷✷ or destroy Conversion.
Differences: The *Revised* version has different wording: "All mountains are considered basic plains while Conversion is in play. Pay ✷✷ during upkeep or Conversion is discarded." The *Unlimited* and *Limited* versions have different wording: "All mountains are considered plains while Conversion is in play. Pay ✷✷ during upkeep or Conversion is discarded."

Coral Helm

Artifact / Artifact / Amy Weber / Rare
***Fourth Edition* Text:** 3: Discard a card at random from your hand to give target creature +2/+2 until end of turn.
Differences: The *Antiquities* version has different wording: "3: Give target creature +2/+2 until end of turn. Each time you use this ability, you must discard one card at random from your hand. Coral Helm cannot be used if you have no cards in your hand." The *Antiquities* version also has change P.
Rulings Differences: Coral Helm can now be activated if the controller has no cards in hand (although the controller does not benefit from the effect of Coral Helm unless a card is discarded). *The* Antiquities *version did not allow Coral Helm to be activated when the controller had no cards in hand.*

Cosmic Horror

Black / Summon Horror / Jesper Myrfors / Rare
***Fourth Edition* Text:** First strike / During your upkeep, pay 3 ☠☠☠ or destroy Cosmic Horror. If you destroy Cosmic Horror in this way, it deals 7 damage to you.
Differences: The *Legends* version has different wording: "First strike / Pay 3 ☠☠☠ during your upkeep or Cosmic Horror does 7 damage to you and is destroyed." The *Legends* version also has additional flavor text: "Then flashed the living lightning from her eyes, / And".

Counterspell

Blue / Interrupt / Mark Poole / Uncommon
***Fourth Edition* Text:** Counter target spell.
Differences: Previous versions say "Counters" instead of "Counter" and add "as it is being cast" to the end.

Craw Wurm
Green / Summon Wurm / Daniel Gelon /
Common

Creature Bond
Blue / Enchant Creature / Anson Maddocks /
Common
Fourth Edition **Text:** If target creature is put
into the graveyard, Creature Bond deals damage equal to the creature's toughness to that
creature's controller.
Differences: The *Revised* version has different wording: "If target creature is placed in
the graveyard, Creature Bond does an
amount of damage equal to creature's toughness to creature's controller." The *Unlimited*
and *Limited* versions have different wording:
"If target creature is destroyed, Creature
Bond does an amount of damage equal to
creature's toughness to creature's controller."

Crimson Manticore
Red / Summon Manticore / Daniel Gelon /
Rare
Fourth Edition **Text:** Flying / 🔴, 🔄:
Manticore deals 1 damage to target attacking
or blocking creature.
Differences: The *Legends* version has
change B.

Crumble
Green / Instant / Jesper Myrfors /
Uncommon
Fourth Edition **Text:** Bury target artifact.
Artifact's controller gains life equal to the
artifact's casting cost.
Differences: The *Revised* version says
"Buries" instead of "Bury." The *Revised* and
Antiquities versions add "points" after "life"
and say "target" instead of "the." The
Antiquities version says "Destroy" instead of
"Bury" and adds "artifact creatures may not
regenerate" to the end of the first sentence.

Crusade
White / Enchantment / Mark Poole / Rare
Fourth Edition **Text:** All white creatures get
+1/+1.
Differences: Previous versions have change
G.

Crystal Rod
Artifact / Artifact / Amy Weber / Uncommon
Fourth Edition **Text:** ①: Gain 1 life for a successfully cast blue spell. Use this effect
either when the spell is cast or later in the
turn but only once for each blue spell cast.
Differences: The *Revised* version has different wording: "①: Any blue spell cast gives
you 1 life. Can only give 1 life each time a
blue spell is cast." The *Unlimited* and *Limited*
versions have different wording: "①: Any
blue spell cast by any player gives you 1
life." The *Unlimited* and *Limited* versions also
have change P.
Rulings Differences: Crystal Rod now can
be used to gain life later in the same turn
that a blue spell was cast. *Previous versions
implied that Crystal Rod could only be used
immediately after a spell was cast.*

Cursed Land
Black / Enchant Land / Jesper Myrfors /
Uncommon
Fourth Edition **Text:** Cursed Land deals 1
damage to target land's controller during his
or her upkeep.
Differences: Previous versions have change
B. The *Unlimited* and *Limited* versions also
say "each" instead of "his or her."
Rulings Differences: Cursed Land now only
deals damage during target land's controller's
upkeep. Unlimited *and* Limited *versions
allowed damage to be dealt during each player's upkeep.*

Cursed Rack
Artifact / Artifact / Richard Thomas /
Uncommon
Fourth Edition **Text:** Target opponent dis-
cards down to four cards during his or her
discard phase.

Differences: The *Antiquities* version does not have "target" and says "must discard" instead of "discard." The *Antiquities* version also has change C.

Rulings Differences: Cursed Rack now targets an opponent. *The* Antiquities *version stated that Cursed Rack affected "opponent"; thus, in a two-player game, stealing it would change who it affected.*

Cyclopean Mummy
Black / Summon Mummy /
Edward Beard, Jr. / Common
***Fourth Edition* Text:** If Mummy is put into the graveyard from play, remove it from the game.
Differences: The *Legends* version says "placed in" instead of "put into."

Dancing Scimitar
Artifact / Artifact Creature /
Anson Maddocks / Rare
***Fourth Edition* Text:** Flying

Dark Ritual
Black / Interrupt / Sandra Everingham /
Common
***Fourth Edition* Text:** Add 💀💀💀 to your mana pool.
Differences: The *Unlimited* and *Limited* versions say "3 black mana" instead of "💀💀💀."
Rulings Differences: Dark Ritual now has mana symbols instead of a color word on it, thus preventing it from being affected by Sleight of Mind.

Death Ward
White / Instant / Mark Poole / Common
***Fourth Edition* Text:** Regenerate target creature.
Differences: Previous versions say "Regenerates" instead of "Regenerate." The *Limited* (Alpha) version credits the artist as Dan Frazier instead of Mark Poole.

Deathgrip
Black / Enchantment / Anson Maddocks / Uncommon
Fourth Edition Text: 💀💀: Counter target green spell. Play this ability as an interrupt.
Differences: The *Revised* version has different wording: "💀💀: Counter a green spell as it is being cast. This ability is played as an interrupt and does not affect green cards already in play." The *Unlimited* and *Limited* versions have different wording: "💀💀: Destroy a green spell as it is being cast. This action may be played as an interrupt, and does not affect green cards already in play."

Deathlace
Black / Interrupt / Sandra Everingham / Rare
Fourth Edition Text: Change the color of target spell or target permanent to black. Costs to cast, tap, maintain, or use a special ability of target remain unchanged.
Differences: Previous versions say "one card either being played or already in play" instead of "target spell or target permanent."
Rulings Differences: Deathlace can now target any permanent in play, including tokens, but cannot target lands as they are being played. *Previous versions of Deathlace could only target cards; this included targeting lands as they were being played.*

Desert Twister
Green / Sorcery / Susan Van Camp / Uncommon
Fourth Edition Text: Destroy target permanent.
Differences: The *Revised* and *Arabian Nights* versions say "any card in play" instead of "target permanent."
Rulings Differences: Desert Twister can now target any permanent. *The* Arabian Nights *and* Revised *versions stated that Desert Twister could only target cards in play.*

Detonate
Red / Sorcery / Randy Asplund-Faith / Uncommon
Fourth Edition Text: Bury target artifact. Detonate deals X damage to the artifact's controller, where X is the casting cost of the artifact.
Differences: The *Antiquities* version has different wording: "Targets any artifact; X is the casting cost of target artifact. Target artifact is destroyed, and Detonate does X points of damage to artifact's controller. Artifact creatures destroyed in this manner may not be regenerated."

Diabolic Machine
Artifact / Artifact Creature / Anson Maddocks / Uncommon
Fourth Edition Text: ③ : Regenerate
Differences: *The Dark* version has change R.

Dingus Egg
Artifact / Artifact / Dan Frazier / Rare
Fourth Edition Text: Each time a player puts a land into the graveyard from play, Dingus Egg deals 2 damage to that land's controller.
Differences: The *Revised* version has different wording: "Whenever anyone loses a land, Dingus Egg does 2 damage to that player for each land lost." The *Unlimited* and *Limited* versions have different wording: "Whenever anyone loses a land, Egg does 2 damage to that player for each land lost" and have change C.

Disenchant
White / Instant / Amy Weber / Common
Fourth Edition Text: Destroy target enchantment or artifact.
Differences: The *Revised* version has different wording: "Target enchantment or artifact is destroyed." The *Unlimited* and *Limited* versions have different wording: "Target enchantment or artifact must be discarded."

Disintegrate
Red / Sorcery / Anson Maddocks / Common
Fourth Edition Text: Disintegrate deals X damage to target creature or player. The tar-

get cannot regenerate until end of turn. If the target receives lethal damage this turn, remove it from the game entirely.

Differences: The *Revised* version has different wording: "Disintegrate does X damage to one target. If target dies this turn, target is removed from the game entirely." The *Unlimited* and *Limited* versions have different wording: "Disintegrate does X damage to one target. If target dies this turn, it is removed from game entirely and cannot be regenerated. Return target to its owner's deck only when game is over."

Rulings Differences: A creature targeted by Disintegrate now cannot regenerate that turn; however, the creature is now not removed from the game by effects that destroy or bury it. *The* Revised *version implied that the target creature was not prevented from regenerating. Also, previous versions stated that the creature was removed from the game regardless of why it was sent to the graveyard.*

Disrupting Scepter

Artifact / Artifact / Dan Frazier / Rare
Fourth Edition Text: 3, ↻: Target player chooses and discards one card from his or her hand. Use this ability only during your turn.

Differences: The *Revised* version has different wording: " 3 , ⤴: Opponent must discard one card of his or her choice. Can only be used during controller's turn." The *Unlimited* and *Limited* versions have different wording: " 3 : Opponent must discard one card of his or her choice. Can only be used during your turn" and change M.

Rulings Differences: Disrupting Scepter can now target any player. *Previous versions stated that Disrupting Scepter could only affect opponent.*

Divine Transformation

White / Enchant Creature / NéNé Thomas / Uncommon
Fourth Edition Text: Target creature gets +3/+3.
Differences: The *Legends* version has change G.

Dragon Engine

Artifact / Artifact Creature / Anson Maddocks / Rare
Fourth Edition Text: 2 : +1/+0 until end of turn
Differences: The *Revised* version does not say "until end of turn."

Dragon Whelp

Red / Summon Dragon / Amy Weber / Uncommon
Fourth Edition Text: Flying / 🔴 : +1/+0 until end of turn. If you spend more than 🔴🔴🔴 in this way during one turn, destroy Dragon Whelp at end of turn.
Differences: The *Revised* version has different wording: "Flying / 🔴 : +1/+0; if more than 🔴🔴🔴 is spent in this way during one turn, Dragon Whelp is killed at end of turn." The *Unlimited* and *Limited* versions have different wording: "Flying / 🔴 : +1/+0 until end of turn; if more than 🔴🔴🔴 is spent in this way, Dragon Whelp is destroyed at end of turn."

Drain Life

Black / Sorcery / Douglas Shuler / Common
Fourth Edition Text: Drain Life deals 1 damage to a target creature or player for each 🔴 you pay in addition to the casting cost. You then gain 1 life for each 1 damage dealt. You cannot gain more life than the toughness of the creature or the total life of the player Drain Life damages.
Differences: The *Revised* version has different wording: "Drain Life does 1 damage to a single target for each 🔴 spent in addition to the casting cost. Caster gains 1 life for each damage inflicted. If you drain life from a creature, you cannot gain more life than the creature's current toughness." The *Unlimited*

and *Limited* (Beta) versions have different wording: "Drain Life does 1 damage to a single target for each 🍄 spent in addition to the casting cost. Caster gains 1 life for each damage inflicted. If you drain life from a creature, you cannot gain more life than the creature's toughness." The *Limited* (Alpha) version has different wording: "Drain Life does 1 damage to a single target for each 🍄 spent in addition to the casting cost. Caster gains 1 life for each damage inflicted. If you drain life from a creature, you cannot gain more life than the creature's toughness." The *Unlimited* and *Limited* versions have change S.

Rulings Differences: Drain Life no longer allows caster to gain more life than the life of the player Drain Life damages. *Previous versions of Drain Life allowed this.*

➤ Drain Power

Blue / Sorcery / Douglas Shuler / Rare
Fourth Edition Text: Target player must draw all mana from his or her available lands; then, all mana in target player's mana pool drains into your mana pool.
Differences: The *Revised* version has different wording: "Opponent must draw all mana from his or her available lands; this mana and all mana in opponent's mana pool drains into your mana pool. You can't take less than all your opponent's mana." The *Unlimited* and *Limited* versions have different wording: "Tap all opponent's lands, taking all this mana and all mana in opponent's mana pool into your mana pool. You can't tap fewer than all opponent's lands." The *Unlimited* and *Limited* versions have change S.
Rulings Differences: Drain Power can now target any player. *Previous versions stated that Drain Power could only affect opponent. Also, non-mana lands are ignored.*

Drudge Skeletons

Black / Summon Skeletons / Sandra Everingham / Common
Fourth Edition Text: 💀: Regenerate
Differences: Previous versions have change R. (The *Revised* version has "." and the *Unlimited* and *Limited* versions do not.)

Durkwood Boars

Green / Summon Boars / Mike Kimble / Common

Dwarven Warriors

Red / Summon Dwarves / Douglas Shuler / Common
Fourth Edition Text: 🔄: Target creature with power no greater than 2 becomes unblockable until end of turn. Other effects may later be used to increase the creature's power beyond 2.
Differences: The *Revised* version has different wording: "🔄: Make a creature of power no greater than 2 unblockable until end of turn. Other cards may later be used to increase target creature's power beyond 2." The *Unlimited* and *Limited* versions have different wording: "Tap to make a creature of power no greater than 2 unblockable until end of turn. Other cards may be used to increase target creature's power beyond 2 after defense is chosen" and have change S.

Earth Elemental

Red / Summon Elemental / Dan Frazier / Uncommon

Earthquake

Red / Sorcery / Dan Frazier / Rare
Fourth Edition Text: Earthquake deals X damage to each player and each creature without flying.
Differences: Previous versions have different wording: "Does X damage to each player and each non-flying creature in play."

➤ Ebony Horse

Artifact / Artifact / Dameon Willich / Rare
Fourth Edition Text: 2, 🔄: Untap target attacking creature you control. That creature neither receives nor deals damage during combat this turn.
Differences: The *Revised* and *Arabian Nights* versions have different wording: "2, 🔄:

Remove one of your attacking creatures from combat. Treat this as if the creature never attacked, except that defenders assigned to block it cannot choose to block another creature." The *Arabian Nights* version also has change M.

Rulings Differences: Ebony Horse now untaps the target creature; this creature now neither deals nor receives damage in combat. *The* Revised *and* Arabian Nights *versions implied that Ebony Horse did not untap the creature and removed the creature from the combat.*

El-Hajjâj
Black / Summon El-Hajjâj / Dameon Willich / Rare

Fourth Edition Text: Gain 1 life for every 1 damage El-Hajjâj deals. You cannot gain more life in this way than the toughness of the creature or the total life of the player that El-Hajjâj damages.

Differences: The *Revised* and *Arabian Nights* versions have different wording: "You gain 1 life for every point of damage El-Hajjâj inflicts."

Rulings Differences: El-Hajjâj no longer allows controller to gain more life than the toughness of a creature or the total life of a player El-Hajjâj damages. *The* Revised *and* Arabian Nights *versions allowed this.*

Elder Land Wurm
White / Summon Wurm / Quinton Hoover / Rare

Fourth Edition Text: Trample / Cannot attack until assigned as a blocker.

Differences: The *Legends* version adds "Wurm" before "Cannot."

Elven Riders
Green / Summon Riders / Melissa Benson / Uncommon

Fourth Edition Text: Cannot be blocked except by walls and by creatures with flying.

Differences: The *Legends* version has different wording: "Cannot be blocked by any creatures except walls and flying creatures."

Elvish Archers
Green / Summon Elves / Anson Maddocks / Rare

Fourth Edition Text: First strike

Differences: The *Limited* (Alpha) version has a power and toughness of 1/2.

Rulings Differences: Elvish Archers now has a power and toughness of 2/1. *The Alpha version of Elvish Archers had 1/2.*

Energy Flux
Blue / Enchantment / Kaja Foglio / Uncommon

Fourth Edition Text: During each player's upkeep, destroy all artifacts that player controls. The player may pay an additional 2 for each artifact he or she wishes to prevent Energy Flux from destroying.

Differences: The *Revised* and *Antiquities* versions have different wording: "All artifacts in play now require an upkeep cost of 2 in addition to any other upkeep costs they may have. If the upkeep cost for an artifact is not paid, the artifact must be discarded."

Energy Tap
Blue / Sorcery / Daniel Gelon / Common

Fourth Edition Text: Tap target creature you control. Add an amount of colorless mana equal to that creature's casting cost to your mana pool.

Differences: The *Legends* version says "Target creature you control becomes tapped" instead of "Tap target creature you control" and "target untapped" instead of "that."

Rulings Differences: *Fourth Edition* has errata: The first line of Energy Tap should read "Tap target untapped creature..."

Erg Raiders
Black / Summon Raiders / Dameon Willich / Common

Fourth Edition Text: If you do not attack with

Erg Raiders during your turn, it deals 2 damage to you at end of turn. Erg Raiders deals no damage to you the turn it comes into play on your side.

Differences: The *Revised* and *Arabian Nights* versions have different wording: "If you do not attack with Raiders, they do 2 damage to you at end of turn. Raiders do no damage to you during the turn in which they are summoned." The *Arabian Nights* version had two versions of the card with size variations in the uncolored mana symbol.

Rulings Differences: Erg Raiders now does not damage its controller on the first turn it comes into play on that player's side. *The Revised and Arabian Nights versions stated that the only turn Erg Raiders didn't damage its controller was the turn it was summoned.*

Erosion

Blue / Enchant Land / Pete Venters / Common

Fourth Edition Text: During his or her upkeep, target land's controller pays ① or 1 life, or target land is destroyed. Effects that prevent or redirect damage cannot be used to counter this loss of life.

Differences: *The Dark* version has different wording: "Target land is destroyed unless its controller pays ① or pays 1 life during his or her upkeep. Effects that prevent or redirect damage may not be used to counter this loss of life."

Eternal Warrior

Red / Enchant Creature / Anson Maddocks / Common

Fourth Edition Text: Attacking does not cause target creature to tap.

Differences: The *Legends* version says "tap target creature" instead of "cause target creature to tap."

Evil Presence

Black / Enchant Land / Sandra Everingham / Uncommon

Fourth Edition Text: Target land becomes a basic swamp.

Differences: Previous versions say "is now" instead of "becomes." The *Unlimited* and *Limited* versions do not say "basic."

➤Eye for an Eye

White / Instant / Mark Poole / Rare

Fourth Edition Text: You may cast Eye for an Eye only when a creature, spell, or effect deals damage to you. Eye for an Eye deals an equal amount of damage to the controller of that creature, spell, or effect. If another spell or effect reduces the amount of damage you receive, it does not reduce the damage dealt by Eye for an Eye.

Differences: The *Revised* version has different wording: "Can be cast only when a creature, spell, or effect does damage to you. Eye for an Eye does an equal amount of damage to the controller of that creature, spell, or effect. If some spell or effect reduces the amount of damage you receive, it does not reduce the damage dealt by Eye for an Eye." The *Arabian Nights* version has different wording: "Can be cast only when a creature or spell does damage to you. Eye for an Eye does an equal amount of damage to the controller of that creature or spell. If some spell or effect reduces the amount of damage you receive, it does not reduce the damage dealt by Eye for an Eye."

Rulings Differences: Eye for an Eye can now be cast when any creature, spell, or effect damages you. *The Arabian Nights version only allowed for damage from creatures or spells, not effects.*

Fear

Black / Enchant Creature / Mark Poole / Common

Fourth Edition Text: Target creature cannot be blocked except by black creatures and artifact creatures.

Differences: The *Revised* version says "by any creatures except" instead of "except by." The *Unlimited* and *Limited* versions say "by any creatures other than artifact creatures and black creatures" instead of "except by black creatures and artifact creatures."

✒Feedback
Blue / Enchant Enchantment / Quinton Hoover / Uncommon
***Fourth Edition* Text:** Feedback deals 1 damage to controller of target enchantment during that player's upkeep.
Differences: Previous versions have change B. The *Revised* version says "its controller's" instead of "that player's." The *Unlimited* and *Limited* versions say "each" instead of "that player's."
Rulings Differences: Feedback now only deals damage during the target enchantment's controller's upkeep. *The* Unlimited *and* Limited *versions stated that Feedback dealt damage during each player's upkeep.*

✒Fellwar Stone
Artifact / Artifact / Quinton Hoover / Uncommon
***Fourth Edition* Text:** ⊙: Add one mana to your mana pool. This mana may be of any type that any land opponent controls can produce. Play this ability as an interrupt.
Differences: *The Dark* version has different wording: "⬧: Add 1 mana to your mana pool. This mana may be of any color that any of opponent's lands can produce. This ability is played as an interrupt."
Rulings Differences: Fellwar Stone can now produce colorless mana if opponent controls a land that produces colorless mana. The Dark *version stated that Fellwar Stone could only produce colored mana.*

Fire Elemental
Red / Summon Elemental / Melissa Benson / Uncommon

Fireball
Red / Sorcery / Mark Tedin / Common
***Fourth Edition* Text:** Fireball deals X damage, divided evenly (round down) among any number of target creatures and/or players. Pay an additional ① for each target beyond the first.
Differences: Previous versions add "total" after "damage," say "1 extra mana" instead of "an additional ① " and have changes B and T.

Firebreathing
Red / Enchant Creature / Dan Frazier / Common
***Fourth Edition* Text:** ➋: Target creature Firebreathing enchants gets +1/+0 until end of turn.
Differences: Previous versions have different wording: " ➋: +1/+0."

Fissure
Red / Instant / Douglas Shuler / Common
***Fourth Edition* Text:** Bury target land or creature.
Differences: *The Dark* version has different wording: "Target land or creature is buried."

Flashfires
Red / Sorcery / Dameon Willich / Uncommon
***Fourth Edition* Text:** Destroy all plains.
Differences: Previous versions have different wording: "All plains in play are destroyed."

Flight
Blue / Enchant Creature / Anson Maddocks / Common
***Fourth Edition* Text:** Target creature gains flying.
Differences: Previous versions say "is now a flying creature" instead of "gains flying."

Flood
Blue / Enchantment / Dennis Detwiller / Common
***Fourth Edition* Text:** ⬢ ⬢: Tap target creature without flying.
Differences: *The Dark* version has different wording: " ⬢ ⬢: Target non-flying creature

becomes tapped." *The Dark* version also has change D.

Flying Carpet
Artifact / Artifact / Mark Tedin / Rare
Fourth Edition Text: ②, ♦: Target creature gains flying until end of turn. If that creature is put into the graveyard before end of turn, destroy Flying Carpet.
Differences: The *Revised* and *Arabian Nights* versions have different wording: "②, ⋟: Gives one creature flying ability until end of turn. If that creature is destroyed before end of turn, so is Flying Carpet." The *Arabian Nights* version has change M.

⋟ Fog
Green / Instant / Jesper Myrfors / Common
Fourth Edition Text: No creatures deal damage in combat this turn.
Differences: The *Revised* version has different wording: "Creatures attack and block as normal, but none deal any damage or otherwise affect any creature as a result of an attack or block. All attacking creatures are still tapped. Play any time before attack damage is dealt." The *Unlimited* and *Limited* versions have different wording: "Creatures attack and block as normal, but none deal any damage. All attacking creatures are still tapped. Play any time before attack damage is dealt."
Rulings Differences: Fog now only prevents creatures from dealing damage in combat. Also, Fog may be played at any time. *The* Revised *version stated that Fog also prevented blocking effects, such as the Basilisk's power, from occuring. Also, previous versions stated that Fog could only be played before damage dealing.*

⋟ Force of Nature
Green / Summon Force / Douglas Shuler / Rare
Fourth Edition Text: Trample / During your upkeep, pay 🌲🌲🌲🌲 or Force of Nature deals 8 damage to you.
Differences: The *Revised* version has different wording: "You must pay 🌲🌲🌲🌲 during your upkeep or Force of Nature does 8 damage to you. You may still attack with Force of Nature even if you failed to pay the upkeep." The *Unlimited* and *Limited* (Beta) versions have different wording: "You must pay 🌲🌲🌲🌲 during upkeep or Force of Nature does 8 damage to you. You may still attack with Force of Nature even if you failed to pay the upkeep." The *Limited* (Alpha) version has different wording: "You must pay GGGG during upkeep or Force of Nature does 8 damage to you. You may still attack with Force of Nature even if you failed to pay the upkeep." The *Unlimited* and *Limited* versions have change S.
Rulings Differences: The controller of Force of Nature only has to pay Force of Nature's upkeep during the controller's upkeep. *Previous versions required Force of Nature's upkeep to be paid during each player's upkeep.*

Forest (variation 1)
Land / Land / Christopher Rush / Common
Fourth Edition Text: ♦: Add 🌲 to your mana pool.
Differences: The *Unlimited* and *Limited* versions have change A.

Forest (variation 2)
Land / Land / Christopher Rush / Common
Fourth Edition Text: ♦: Add 🌲 to your mana pool.
Differences: The *Unlimited* and *Limited* versions have change A.

Forest (variation 3)
Land / Land / Christopher Rush / Common
Fourth Edition Text: ♦: Add 🌲 to your mana pool.
Differences: The *Unlimited* and *Limited* (Beta) versions have change A. This version of Forest did not appear in the *Limited* (Alpha) version.

Fortified Area

White / Enchantment / Randy Asplund-Faith / Common

Fourth Edition Text: All walls you control gain banding and get +1/+0.

Differences: The *Legends* version has different wording: "All your walls gain +1/+0 and banding."

Frozen Shade

Black / Summon Shade / Douglas Shuler / Common

Fourth Edition Text: ☻: +1/+1 until end of turn

Differences: Previous versions do not contain "until end of turn." The *Unlimited* and *Limited* versions have change S.

Fungusaur

Green / Summon Fungusaur / Daniel Gelon / Rare

Fourth Edition Text: At the end of any turn in which Fungusaur receives damage but does not leave play, put a +1/+1 counter on it.

Differences: The *Revised* version has different wording: "At the end of any turn during which Fungusaur was damaged but not destroyed, put a +1/+1 counter on it." The *Unlimited* and *Limited* versions have different wording: "Each time Fungusaur is damaged but not destroyed, put a +1/+1 counter on it."

Rulings Differences: *In the* Unlimited *and* Limited *versions the Fungusaur received the counter before the end of the turn and could receive multiple counters each turn.*

Gaea's Liege

Green / Summon Gaea's Liege / Dameon Willich / Rare

Fourth Edition Text: Gaea's Liege has power and toughness each equal to the number of forests you control; when Gaea's Leige attacks, these are instead equal to the number of forests defending player controls. / ⟳: Target land becomes a basic forest until Gaea's Liege leaves play.

Differences: The *Revised* version has different wording: "⟳: Turn any one land into a basic forest. Mark changed lands with counters, removing the counters when Gaea's Liege leaves play. Gaea's Liege has power and toughness equal to the number of forests controller has in play; when it's attacking, they are equal to the number of forests defending player has in play." The *Unlimited* and *Limited* versions have different wording: "When defending, Gaea's Liege has power and toughness equal to the number of forests you have in play; when it's attacking, they are equal to the number of forests opponent has in play. Tap to turn any one land into a forest until Gaea's Liege leaves play. Mark changed lands with counters, removing counters when Gaea's Liege leaves play."

Gaseous Form

Blue / Enchant Creature / Phil Foglio / Common

Fourth Edition Text: Target creature neither deals nor receives damage during combat.

Differences: The *Legends* version has a different wording: "Damage done to target creature by creatures it blocks, or that block it, is reduced to 0. Creature deals no damage during combat." The *Legends* version's flavor text contains a "/" and is formatted differently.

Rulings Differences: The creature Gaseous Form enchants now cannot have damage assigned to it during combat. *The* Legends *version did allow damage to be assigned to the creature during combat, but that damage was reduced to 0.*

Ghost Ship

Blue / Summon Ship / Tom Wänerstrand / Uncommon

Fourth Edition Text: Flying / 🔵🔵🔵: Regenerate

Differences: *The Dark* version has both abilities on the same line separated by a comma.

Giant Growth
Green / Instant / Sandra Everingham /
Common
Fourth Edition Text: Target creature gets
+3/+3 until end of turn.
Differences: Previous versions have change
G.

Giant Spider
Green / Summon Spider /
Sandra Everingham / Common
Fourth Edition Text: Can block creatures with
flying.
Differences: Previous versions have different
wording: "Does not fly, but can block flying
creatures."

Giant Strength
Red / Enchant Creature / Justin Hampton /
Common
Fourth Edition Text: Target creature gets
+2/+2.
Differences: The *Legends* version has
change G and has no period at the end.

Giant Tortoise
Blue / Summon Tortoise / Kaja Foglio /
Common
Fourth Edition Text: Giant Tortoise gets
+0/+3 while untapped.
Differences: The *Arabian Nights* version has
change G and had two versions of the card
with shading variations in the uncolored
mana symbol.

↗ Glasses of Urza
Artifact / Artifact / Douglas Shuler /
Uncommon
Fourth Edition Text: 👁: Look at target player's hand.
Differences: Previous versions have different
wording: "👁: You may look at opponent's
hand." The *Unlimited* and *Limited* versions
have changes M and S.
Rulings Differences: Glasses of Urza may now target controller of Glasses of Urza. Previous versions
stated that Glasses of Urza affected "opponent."

↗ Gloom
Black / Enchantment / Dan Frazier /
Uncommon
Fourth Edition Text: White spells cost an
additional 3 to cast. White enchantments

with activation costs require an additional 3
to use.
Differences: Previous versions use "3 more
mana" instead of "an additional 3 ." The
Unlimited and *Limited* versions have "Circles
of Protection cost" instead of "White
enchantments with activation costs require."
Rulings Differences: Gloom now affects all
white enchantments with activation costs.
The Unlimited *and* Limited *versions of Gloom
did not affect white enchantments other than
Circles of Protection.*

↗ Goblin Balloon Brigade
Red / Summon Goblins / Andi Rusu /
Uncommon
Fourth Edition Text: 🔴: Flying until end of
turn
Differences: The *Revised* version has different
wording: "🔴: Gains flying ability until end of
turn." The *Unlimited* and *Limited* versions have
different wording: "🔴: Goblins gain flying ability
until end of turn. Controller may not choose to
make Goblins fly after they have been blocked."
Previous versions do not contain a line break
separating the two quotes in the flavor text.
Rulings Differences: Only Goblin Balloon
Brigade gains the ability to fly and can use
ability after defense has been been declared.
The Unlimited *and* Limited *versions of Goblin
Balloon Brigade implied that all Goblins
gained flying until end of turn, and Goblin
Balloon Brigade's ability could not be used
after defense was chosen.*

Goblin King
Red / Summon Lord / Jesper Myrfors / Rare
Fourth Edition Text: All Goblins gain moun-
tainwalk and get +1/+1.
Differences: Previous versions have differ-
ent wording: "All Goblins in play gain moun-

tainwalk and +1/+1 while this card remains in play." The *Unlimited* and *Limited* versions do not contain the word "All" in the above wording.

Goblin Rock Sled

Red / Summon Rock Sled / Dennis Detwiller / Common

***Fourth Edition* Text:** Trample / Cannot attack if defending player controls no mountains. Rock Sled does not untap during your untap phase if it attacked during your last turn.

Differences: *The Dark* version has different wording: "Trample / Rock Sled may not attack unless opponent controls at least one mountain. Rock Sled does not untap as normal during your untap phase if it attacked during your last turn." *The Dark* version has change D.

Grapeshot Catapult

Artifact / Artifact Creature / Dan Frazier / Common

***Fourth Edition* Text:** ☉: Grapeshot Catapult deals 1 damage to target creature with flying.

Differences: The *Antiquities* version has different wording: "Tap to deal 1 damage to target flying creature." The *Antiquities* version has the flavor text "For years scholars debated whether these were Urza's or Mishra's creations. Recent research suggests they were invented by the brothers' original master, Tocasia, and that both used these devices." instead of "Recent research suggests these creatures were invented by Urza's and Mishra's original master, Tocasia, and that both brothers used them."

Gray Ogre

Red / Summon Ogre / Dan Frazier / Common
Differences: *Revised, Unlimited,* and *Limited*

(Alpha) versions contain "and preferred" instead of "preferring" in the flavor text.

⚔ Greed

Black / Enchantment / Phil Foglio / Rare

***Fourth Edition* Text:** 💀: Pay 2 life to draw a card. Effects that prevent or redirect damage cannot be used to counter this loss of life.

Differences: The *Legends* version has different wording: "💀: Draw an extra card and lose 2 life. Effects that prevent or redirect damage may not be used to prevent this loss of life." The *Legends* version's flavor text contains the line, "There is no greater guilt than discontentment" instead of the elipses.

Rulings Differences: Greed now has a cost of 2 life to use its effect. *The* Legends *version states that the controller loses 2 life when the effect resolves.*

Green Mana Battery

Artifact / Artifact / Christopher Rush / Rare

***Fourth Edition* Text:** 2 , ☉: Put one charge counter on Green Mana Battery. / ☉: Add 🌰 to your mana pool and remove as many charge counters as you wish. For each charge counter removed from Green Mana Battery, add 🌰 to your mana pool. Play this ability as an interrupt.

Differences: The *Legends* version has different wording: "2 , ☉: Put one counter on Green Mana Battery. ☉: Add 🌰 to your mana pool. Remove as many counters as you wish. For each counter removed add 🌰 to your mana pool. This ability is played as an interrupt."

⚔ Green Ward

White / Enchant Creature / Dan Frazier / Uncommon

***Fourth Edition* Text:** Target creature gains protection from green. The protection granted by Green Ward does not destroy Green Ward.

Differences: Previous versions do not have "The protection granted by Green Ward does not destroy Green Ward."

Rulings Differences: The protection granted by Green Ward now cannot destroy Green Ward. *Previous versions of Green Ward would destroy themselves under the right circumstances.*

Grizzly Bears
Green / Summon Bears / Jeff A. Menges / Common

Healing Salve
White / Instant / Dan Frazier / Common
Fourth Edition **Text:** Give target player 3 life, or prevent up to 3 damage to any creature or player.
Differences: Previous versions have different wording: "Gain 3 life, or prevent up to 3 damage from being dealt to a single target."
Rulings Differences: Healing Salve may target another player to give that player 3 life. Healing Salve no longer targets the creature or player being damaged. *Previous versions implied that Healing Salve could not give another player 3 life. Also, these versions stated that Healing Salve targeted the creature or player receiving damage, not the damage being dealt.*

Helm of Chatzuk
Artifact / Artifact / Mark Tedin / Rare
Fourth Edition **Text:** 1, ⊖: Target creature gains banding until end of turn.
Differences: Previous versions have different wording: "1, ⊘: You may give one creature banding ability until end of turn." The *Unlimited* and *Limited* versions contain "the ability to band" instead of "banding ability" in the above, and have change M.

Hill Giant
Red / Summon Giant / Dan Frazier / Common

The Hive
Artifact / Artifact / Sandra Everingham / Rare
Fourth Edition **Text:** 5, ⊖: Put a Wasp token into play. Treat this token as a 1/1 artifact creature with flying.
Differences: Previous versions have different wording: "5, ⊘: Creates one Giant Wasp, a 1/1 flying creature. Represent Wasps with tokens, making sure to indicate when each Wasp is tapped. Wasps can't attack during the turn created. Treat Wasps like artifact creatures in every way, except that they are removed from the game entirely if they ever leave play. If the Hive is destroyed, the Wasps must still be killed individually." The *Unlimited* and *Limited* versions have change M.

Holy Armor
White / Enchant Creature / Melissa Benson / Common
Fourth Edition **Text:** Target creature gets +0/+2. / ✹: Target creature Holy Armor enchants gets +0/+1 until end of turn.
Differences: The *Revised* version has different wording: "Target creature gains +0/+2. / ✹: +0/+1." The *Unlimited* and *Limited* versions have different wording: "Target creature gains +0/+2. / ✹: Target creature gets extra +0/+1 until end of turn."

Holy Strength
White / Enchant Creature / Anson Maddocks / Common
Fourth Edition **Text:** Target creature gets +1/+2.
Differences: Previous versions have change G.

Howl from Beyond
Black / Instant / Mark Poole / Common
Fourth Edition **Text:** Target creature gets +X/+0 until end of turn.
Differences: Previous versions have change G.

Howling Mine
Artifact / Artifact / Mark Poole / Rare
Fourth Edition **Text:** Each player draws one extra card during his or her draw phase.
Differences: The *Revised* version has different wording: "Each player must draw one extra card during the draw phase of each of his or her turns." The *Unlimited* and *Limited* versions have different wording: "Each player draws one extra card each turn during his or her draw phase" and have change C.

Hurkyl's Recall

Blue / Instant / NéNé Thomas / Rare
***Fourth Edition* Text:** All artifacts in play owned by target player are returned to that player's hand.
Differences: The *Revised* and *Antiquities* versions have different wording: "All artifacts in play owned by target player are returned to target player's hand. Any enchantments on those artifacts are discarded." The *Antiquities* version also includes the additional sentence "Cannot be played during the damage-dealing phase of an attack." The *Revised* and *Antiquities* versions' flavor text use "wife" instead of "wife and former student." The *Antiquities* version's flavor text does not contain the phrase "like many."

Hurloon Minotaur

Red / Summon Minotaur / Anson Maddocks / Common

Hurr Jackal

Red / Summon Jackal / Drew Tucker / Rare
***Fourth Edition* Text:** ↻: Target creature cannot regenerate this turn.
Differences: The *Arabian Nights* version has different wording: "Tap to prevent a target creature from regenerating for the remainder of the turn."

Hurricane

Green / Sorcery / Dameon Willich / Uncommon
***Fourth Edition* Text:** Hurricane deals X damage to each player and each creature with flying.
Differences: Previous versions have different wording: "All players and flying creatures suffer X damage."

Hypnotic Specter

Black / Summon Specter / Douglas Shuler / Uncommon
***Fourth Edition* Text:** Flying / An opponent damaged by Specter discards a card at random from his or her hand. Ignore this effect if opponent has no cards in hand.
Differences: Previous versions have "must discard" instead of "discards" and "left in hand" instead of "in hand." The *Revised* version does not contain a line break for the attribution in the flavor text. Previous ver-

sions do not contain a line break between the two verses in the flavor text. The *Unlimited* and *Limited* versions have change S.

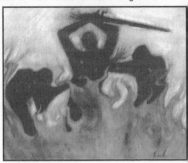

Immolation

Red / Enchant Creature / Scott Kirschner / Common
***Fourth Edition* Text:** Target creature gets +2/-2.
Differences: The *Legends* version has change G.

Inferno

Red / Instant / Randy Asplund-Faith / Rare
***Fourth Edition* Text:** Inferno deals 6 damage to all players and all creatures.
Differences: *The Dark* version has change B.

⚔ Instill Energy

Green / Enchant Creature / Dameon Willich / Uncommon
***Fourth Edition* Text:** Target creature can attack the turn it comes into play on your side. / 0 : During your turn, untap target creature Instill Energy enchants. Use this ability only once each turn.
Differences: The *Revised* version has different wording: "You may untap target creature one additional time during your turn. Target creature may also attack the turn it comes into play." The *Unlimited* and *Limited* versions have different wording: "You may untap target creature both during your untap phase and one additional time during your turn. Target creature may attack the turn it comes into play."
Rulings Differences: Instill Energy now has an activation cost to untap the creature Instill Energy enchants. The creature Instill Energy enchants may attack the turn it comes into

play on a player's side, not simply the turn it comes into play. *Previous versions did not include an activation cost. Previous versions implied that the creature Instill Energy enchanted could not attack that turn if the player took control of the creature from an opponent.*

➤ Iron Star
Artifact / Artifact / Dan Frazier / Uncommon
Fourth Edition **Text:** 1 : Gain 1 life for a successfully cast red spell. Use this effect either when the spell is cast or later in the turn but only once for each red spell cast.
Differences: The *Revised* version has different wording: " 1 : Any red spell cast gives you 1 life. Can only give 1 life each time a red spell is cast." The *Unlimited* and *Limited* versions have different wording: " 1 : Any red spell cast by any player gives you 1 life." The *Unlimited* and *Limited* versions also have change P.
Rulings Differences: Iron Star now can be used to gain life later in the same turn that a red spell was cast. *Previous versions implied that Iron Star could only be used immediately after a spell was cast.*

Ironclaw Orcs
Red / Summon Orcs / Anson Maddocks / Common
Fourth Edition **Text:** Cannot be assigned to block any creature with power greater than 1.
Differences: The *Unlimited* and *Limited* versions have different wording: "Cannot be used to block any creature of power more than 1."

Ironroot Treefolk
Green / Summon Treefolk / Jesper Myrfors / Common

Island (variation 1)
Land / Land / Mark Poole / Common
Fourth Edition **Text:** ⚲: Add 💧 to your mana pool.
Differences: The *Unlimited* and *Limited* versions have change A.

Island (variation 2)
Land / Land / Mark Poole / Common
Fourth Edition **Text:** ⚲: Add 💧 to your mana pool.

Differences: The *Unlimited* and *Limited* versions have change A.

Island (variation 3)
Land / Land / Mark Poole / Common
Fourth Edition **Text:** ⚲: Add 💧 to your mana pool.
Differences: The *Unlimited* and *Limited* (Beta) versions have change A. This version of Island did not appear in the *Limited* (Alpha) version.

➤ Island Fish Jasconius
Blue / Summon Island Fish / Jesper Myrfors / Rare
Fourth Edition **Text:** Does not untap during your untap phase. / Cannot attack if defending player controls no islands. If at any time you control no islands, bury Island Fish Jasconius. / 💧 💧 💧: Untap Island Fish. Use this ability only during your upkeep.
Differences: The *Revised* version has different wording: "You must pay 💧 💧 💧 during your upkeep phase to untap Island Fish. Island Fish cannot attack unless opponent has islands in play. Island Fish is destroyed immediately if at any time you have no islands in play." The *Arabian Nights* version says "during your untap phase" instead of "during your upkeep phase."
Rulings Differences: Island Fish Jasconius now has an activiation cost to untap; also, Island Fish Jasconius is buried if at any time its controller controls no islands. *Previous versions did not include an activation cost to untap; also, Island Fish Jasconius was destroyed if at any time its controller controlled no islands.*

⚔ Island Sanctuary

White / Enchantment / Mark Poole / Rare
Fourth Edition **Text:** During your draw phase, you may draw one less card from your library. If you do so, until start of your next turn the only creatures that can attack you are those with flying or islandwalk.
Differences: Previous versions have different wording: "You may decline to draw a card from your library during draw phase. In exchange, until start of your next turn the only creatures that may attack you are those that fly or have islandwalk." The *Limited* (Alpha) version uses "damage" instead of "attack" in the above.
Rulings Differences: Island Sanctuary prevents non-flying, non-islandwalking creatures from attacking. *The* Limited *"Alpha" version of Island Sanctuary prevented creatures from damaging opponent in any way.*

⚔ Ivory Cup

Artifact / Artifact / Anson Maddocks / Uncommon

Fourth Edition **Text:** ①: Gain 1 life for a successfully cast white spell. Use this effect either when the spell is cast or later in the turn but only once for each white spell cast.
Differences: The *Revised* version has different wording: "①: Any white spell cast gives you 1 life. Can only give 1 life each time a white spell is cast." The *Unlimited* and *Limited* versions have different wording: "① Any white spell cast by any player gives you 1 life." The *Unlimited* and *Limited* versions also have change P.
Rulings Differences: Ivory Cup now can be used to gain life later in the same turn that a white spell was cast. *Previous versions implied that Ivory Cup could only be used immediately after a spell was cast.*

⚔ Ivory Tower

Artifact / Artifact / Margaret Organ-Kean / Rare
Fourth Edition **Text:** At the beginning of your upkeep, gain 1 life for each card in your hand

in excess of four.

Differences: The *Revised* and *Antiquities* versions have different wording: "During your upkeep phase, gain 1 life for each card in your hand above four." The *Antiquities* version also has change C.

Rulings Differences: The controller of Ivory Tower now gains life at the beginning of his or her upkeep. *Previous versions stated that Ivory Tower affected its controller "during" upkeep instead of at "beginning of" upkeep.*

Jade Monolith
Artifact / Artifact / Anson Maddocks / Rare
Fourth Edition **Text:** 1 : Redirect to yourself all damage done to any creature. The source of the damage does not change.

Differences: Previous versions have different wording: " 1 : You may take damage done to any creature on yourself instead, but you must take all of it. Source of damage is unchanged." The *Unlimited* and *Limited* versions also have change P.

Jandor's Saddlebags
Artifact / Artifact / Dameon Willich / Rare
Fourth Edition **Text:** 3 , ↻: Untap target creature.

Differences: The *Revised* and *Arabian Nights* versions use "a" instead of "target." The *Arabian Nights* version also has change M.

Jayemdae Tome
Artifact / Artifact / Mark Tedin / Rare
Fourth Edition **Text:** 4 , ↻: Draw one card.

Differences: Previous versions have "one extra" instead of "one." The *Unlimited* and *Limited* versions also have "You may draw" instead of "Draw" and have change M.

Jump
Blue / Instant / Mark Poole / Common
Fourth Edition **Text:** Target creature gains flying until end of turn.

Differences: Previous versions have different wording: "Target creature is a flying creature until end of turn."

Junún Efreet
Black / Summon Efreet / Christopher Rush / Uncommon
Fourth Edition **Text:** Flying / During your upkeep, pay 💀💀 or bury Junún Efreet.

Differences: The *Arabian Nights* version has different wording: "Flying / You must pay 💀💀 during your upkeep or Junún Efreet is destroyed and may not regenerate."

⚔Karma
White / Enchantment / Richard Thomas / Uncommon
Fourth Edition **Text:** During each player's upkeep, Karma deals 1 damage to that player for each swamp he or she controls.

Differences: The *Revised* version has different wording: "During a player's upkeep, Karma does 1 point of damage to that player for each swamp he or she has in play." The *Unlimited* and *Limited* versions have different wording: "For each swamp in play, Karma does 1 damage to the swamp owner during the swamp owner's upkeep." The *Limited* (Alpha) version has different wording: "Karma does 1 damage to player for each swamp player has in play. Damage occurs during player's upkeep. Affects both players."

Rulings Differences: Karma now deals damage to the controller of a swamp. *The* Unlimited *version dealt damage to the owner, regardless of who controlled the swamp.*

Keldon Warlord
Red / Summon Lord / Kev Brockschmidt / Uncommon
Fourth Edition **Text:** Keldon Warlord has power and toughness each equal to the number of non-wall creatures you control, including Warlord. For example, if you control two other non-wall creatures, Warlord is 3/3. If one of those creatures leaves play, Warlord immediately becomes 2/2.

Differences: Previous versions have different wording: "The *'s below are the number of non-wall creatures on your side, including

Warlord. Thus if you have two other non-wall creatures, Warlord is 3/3. If one of those creatures is killed during the turn, Warlord immediately becomes 2/2." The *Unlimited* and *Limited* versions use "X" instead of "*" (this is also true in the lower right hand corner) and "2 other" instead of "two other."

Killer Bees

Green / Summon Bees / Phil Foglio / Uncommon

Fourth Edition Text: Flying / 🜨: +1/+1 until end of turn

Differences: The *Legends* version contains a period after the word "turn."

Kismet

White / Enchantment / Kaja Foglio / Uncommon

Fourth Edition Text: All of target player's creatures, lands, and artifacts come into play tapped.

Differences: The *Legends* version has different wording: "All creatures, lands, and artifacts played by opponent come into play tapped."

Rulings Differences: Kismet now targets one player. (Thus, Kismet can now target its caster.) *The* Legends *version stated that Kismet affected "opponent"; thus, in a two-player game, stealing it would change who it affected.*

Kormus Bell

Artifact / Artifact / Christopher Rush / Rare

Fourth Edition Text: All swamps become 1/1 black creatures. The swamps still count as lands but cannot be tapped for mana the turn they come into play.

Differences: Previous versions have different wording: "Treat all swamps in play as 1/1 creatures. Now they can be enchanted,

killed, and so forth, and they can be tapped either for mana or to attack." The *Unlimited* and *Limited* versions contain the additional sentence "Swamps have no color; they are not considered black cards" and have change C.

Rulings Differences: *Fourth Edition* has errata: The swamps affected by Kormus Bell are not made black.

Land Leeches

Green / Summon Leeches / Quinton Hoover / Common

Fourth Edition Text: First strike

Land Tax

White / Enchantment / Brian Snōddy / Rare

Fourth Edition Text: During your upkeep, if an opponent controls more land than you, you may search your library and remove up to three basic land cards and put them into your hand. Reshuffle your library afterwards.

Leviathan

Blue / Summon Leviathan / Mark Tedin / Rare

Fourth Edition Text: Trample / Comes into play tapped and does not untap during your untap phase. / During your upkeep, you may sacrifice two islands to untap Leviathan. / Leviathan cannot attack unless you sacrifice two islands during your attack.

Differences: *The Dark* version has different wording: "Trample / Leviathan comes into play tapped, and does not untap as normal during your untap phase. / Sacrifice two islands during your upkeep phase to untap Leviathan. / Leviathan may not attack unless you sacrifice two islands during your attack."

Ley Druid

Green / Summon Cleric / Sandra Everingham / Uncommon

Fourth Edition Text: 🜨: Untap target land. Play this ability as an interrupt.

Differences: The *Revised* version has different wording: "🜨: Untap a land of your choice. This ability is played as an interrupt." The *Unlimited* and *Limited* versions have different wording: "Tap Druid to untap a land of your choice. This action can be played as an interrupt."

⋏ Library of Leng

Artifact / Artifact / Daniel Gelon / Uncommon

Fourth Edition Text: Skip the discard phase of your turn. If a spell or effect forces you to discard, you may discard to the top of your library rather than to your graveyard. If the discard is random, you may look at the card before choosing where to discard it.

Differences: Previous versions have different wording: "You must skip the discard phase of your turn. If a card forces you to discard, you may choose to discard to top of your library rather than to graveyard. If discard is random, you may look at card before deciding where to discard it." The *Unlimited* and *Limited* versions have a different first sentence from the above: "There is no limit to size of your hand" and have change C.

Rulings Differences: Library of Leng now causes a player to skip the discard phase entirely, rather than eliminating the need (or ability) to discard down to seven cards.

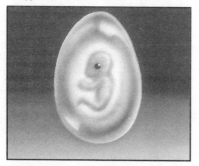

Lifeforce

Green / Enchantment / Dameon Willich / Uncommon

Fourth Edition Text: 🌑🌑: Counter target black spell. Play this ability as an interrupt.

Differences: Previous versions have different wording: "🌑🌑: Counter a black spell as it is being cast. This use is played as an interrupt and does not affect black cards already in play." The *Unlimited* and *Limited* versions use "Destroy" instead of "Counter" in the above; "use may be" instead of "use is"; and "interrupt, and" instead of "interrupt and."

⋏ Lifelace

Green / Interrupt / Amy Weber / Rare

Fourth Edition Text: Change the color of target spell or target permanent to green. Costs

to cast, tap, maintain or use a special ability of target remain unchanged.

Differences: Previous versions have different wording: "Changes the color of one card either being played or already in play to green. Cost to cast, tap, maintain, or use a special ability of target card remains entirely unchanged."

Rulings Differences: Lifelace can now target any permanent in play, including tokens, but cannot target lands as they are being played. *Previous versions of Lifelace could only target cards; this included targeting lands as they were being played.*

Lifetap

Blue / Enchantment / Anson Maddocks / Uncommon

Fourth Edition Text: Gain 1 life each time a forest controlled by target opponent becomes tapped.

Differences: Previous versions have different wording: "You gain 1 life each time any forest of opponent's becomes tapped."

Lightning Bolt

Red / Instant / Christopher Rush / Common

Fourth Edition Text: Lightning Bolt deals 3 damage to target creature or player.

Differences: Previous versions have different wording: "Lightning Bolt does 3 damage to one target."

⋏ Living Artifact

Green / Enchant Artifact / Anson Maddocks / Rare

Fourth Edition Text: Put a vitality counter on Living Artifact for each damage dealt to you. 0 : During your upkeep, remove a vitality counter to gain 1 life. Remove only one vitality counter during each of your upkeeps.

Differences: Previous versions have different wording: "Put a counter on target artifact for each life you lose. During your upkeep you may trade one counter for one life, but you can only trade in one counter during each of your upkeeps." The *Unlimited* and *Limited* versions have "During upkeep" instead of "During your upkeep" and "counter each turn" instead of "counter during each of your upkeeps." in the above.

Rulings Differences: Removing counters from Living Artifact now has an activation cost. The counters generated by Living Artifact are now placed on Living Artifact. Counters are generated by damage, not by loss of life effects such as Greed. *Previous versions of Living Artifact did not have an activation cost to remove counters. Previous versions stated that the counters generated by Living Artifact were placed on the artifact Living Artifact enchanted. Also, previous versions received counters for loss-of-life effects as well as for damage.*

Living Lands

Green / Enchantment / Jesper Myrfors / Rare
Fourth Edition Text: All forests become 1/1 creatures. The forests still count as lands but cannot be tapped for mana the turn they come into play.
Differences: Previous versions have different wording: "Treat all forests in play as 1/1 creatures. Now they can be enchanted, killed, and so forth, and they can be tapped either for mana or to attack." The *Unlimited* and *Limited* versions also contain the additional sentence "The living lands have no color; they are not considered green cards."

⋏ Llanowar Elves

Green / Summon Elves / Anson Maddocks / Common
Fourth Edition Text: ⏁: Add 🌲 to your mana pool. Play this ability as an interrupt.
Differences: The *Revised* version has "This ability is played" instead of "Play this ability." The *Unlimited* and *Limited* versions added "green mana" instead of 🌲, have "This tap can be played" instead of "Play this ability" and change A. Previous versions have different flavor text: "Whenever the Llanowar Elves gather the fruits of their forest, they leave one plant of each type untouched, considering that nature's portion."
Rulings Differences: Llanowar Elves now has a mana symbol instead of a color word on it, thus preventing it from being affected by Sleight of Mind.

Lord of Atlantis

Blue / Summon Lord / Melissa Benson / Rare
Fourth Edition Text: All Merfolk gain islandwalk and get +1/+1.
Differences: Previous versions have different wording: "All Merfolk in play gain islandwalk and +1/+1 while this card is in play."

The *Unlimited* and *Limited* versions have "Summon Lord of Atlantis" instead of "Summon Lord."

⋏ Lord of the Pit

Black / Summon Demon / Mark Tedin / Rare
Fourth Edition Text: Flying, trample / During your upkeep, sacrifice a creature. If you cannot sacrifice a creature, Lord of the Pit deals 7 damage to you. You cannot sacrifice Lord of the Pit to itself.
Differences: Previous versions have different wording: "Flying, trample / You must sacrifice one of your own creatures during your upkeep or Lord of the Pit does 7 damage to you. You may still attack with Lord of the Pit even if you failed to sacrifice a creature. Lord of the Pit may not be sacrificed to itself." The *Unlimited* and *Limited* versions have "during upkeep" instead of "during your upkeep" in the above and do not contain the last sentence.
Rulings Differences: Lord of the Pit can now not be sarificed to itself. *The Unlimited and* Limited *versions allowed the Lord of the Pit to be sacrificed to itself. These versions also required a sacrifice during every upkeep.*

Lost Soul

Black / Summon Lost Soul / Randy Asplund-Faith / Common
Fourth Edition Text: Swampwalk
Differences: The *Legends* version contains the additional beginning verses in the flavor text: "She walks in the twilight, her steps make no sound,/ Her feet leave no tracks on the dew-covered ground./"

Lure

Green / Enchant Creature / Anson Maddocks / Uncommon
Fourth Edition Text: All creatures able to

block target creature must do so. Lure does not prevent a creature from blocking more than one creature if blocker has that ability. If blocker is forced to block more creatures than it is allowed to, defender chooses which of these creatures to block, but must block as many creatures as allowed.

Differences: Previous versions have different wording: "All creatures able to block target creature must do so. If a creature has the ability to block more than one creature, Lure does not prevent this. If there is more than one attacking creature with Lure, defender may choose which of them each defending creature blocks."

↗ Magical Hack

Blue / Interrupt / Julie Baroh / Rare
***Fourth Edition* Text:** Change the text of target spell or target permanent by replacing all occurrences of one basic land type with another. For example, you may change "swampwalk" to "plainswalk."

Differences: Previous versions have a different first sentence: "Change the text of any card being played or already in play by replacing one basic land type with another."

Rulings Differences: Magical Hack can now target any permanent in play, including tokens, but cannot target lands as they are being played. *Previous versions of Magical Hack could only target cards; this included targeting lands as they were being played.*

Magnetic Mountain

Red / Enchantment / Susan Van Camp / Rare
***Fourth Edition* Text:** Blue creatures do not untap during their controllers' untap phase. During his or her upkeep, a player may pay an additional 4 to untap a blue creature he or she controls.

Differences: The *Revised* and *Arabian Nights* versions have different wording: "Blue creatures do not untap as normal. During their upkeep phases, players must spend 4 for each blue creature they wish to untap. This cost must be paid in addition to any other untap cost a given blue creature may already require."

Mahamoti Djinn

Blue / Summon Djinn / Dan Frazier / Rare
***Fourth Edition* Text:** Flying

↗ Mana Clash

Red / Sorcery / Mark Tedin / Rare
***Fourth Edition* Text:** You and target opponent each flip a coin. Mana Clash deals 1 damage to any player whose coin comes up tails. Repeat this process until both players' coins come up heads at the same time.

Differences: *The Dark* version says "target player" instead of "target opponent" and "does" instead of "deals."

Rulings Differences: Mana Clash now cannot target the caster of Mana Clash. The Dark *version stated that Mana Clash affected target player and thus could affect the caster.*

Mana Flare

Red / Enchantment / Christopher Rush / Rare
***Fourth Edition* Text:** Whenever a player taps a land for mana, it produces one additional mana of the same type.

Differences: Previous versions have a different wording: "Whenever either player taps a land for mana, it produces 1 extra mana of the appropriate type." The *Unlimited* and *Limited* versions have "land" instead of "a land" and "each land" instead of "it" in the above.

Mana Short

Blue / Instant / Dameon Willich / Rare
***Fourth Edition* Text:** Mana Short empties target player's mana pool and taps that player's lands.

Differences: Previous versions have different wording: "All opponent's lands are tapped, and opponent's mana pool is emptied. Opponent takes no damage from unspent mana." The *Limited* (Alpha) version does not have the last sentence in the above.

Mana Vault

Artifact / Artifact / Mark Tedin / Rare

Fourth Edition Text: Mana Vault does not untap during your untap phase. If it remains tapped during your upkeep, Mana Vault deals 1 damage to you. / 4 : Untap Mana Vault. Use this ability only during your upkeep.

: Add three colorless mana to your mana pool. Play this ability as an interrupt.

Differences: Previous versions have different wording: " : Add 3 colorless mana to your mana pool. Mana Vault doesn't untap normally during untap phase; to untap it, you must pay 4 mana during your upkeep. If Mana Vault remains tapped during upkeep it does 1 damage to you. Drawing mana from this artifact is played as an interrupt." The *Unlimited* and *Limited* versions do not contain "during your upkeep" in the above; have change M; and have a different last sentence: "Tapping this artifact can be played as an interrupt."

Rulings Differences: Controller can now pay to untap Mana Vault during his or her upkeep; also, Mana Vault has an activation cost to untap. *Previous versions allowed controller of Mana Vault to untap it at any time.*

Manabarbs

Red / Enchantment / Christopher Rush / Rare

Fourth Edition Text: Each time any land is tapped for mana, Manabarbs deals 1 damage to that land's controller.

Differences: Previous versions have different wording: "Whenever mana is drawn from a land, Manabarbs does 1 damage to the land's controller." The *Unlimited* and *Limited* versions have "any land is tapped" instead of "mana is drawn from a land."

Rulings Differences: Manabarbs now only damages a player when a land is tapped for mana. *The Unlimited and Limited versions stated that Manabarbs damaged a player whenever a land was tapped.*

Marsh Gas

Black / Instant / Douglas Shuler / Common

Fourth Edition Text: All creatures get -2/-0 until end of turn.

Marsh Viper

Green / Summon Viper / Ron Spencer / Common

Fourth Edition Text: If Marsh Viper damages a player, he or she gets two poison counters. If a player has ten or more poison counters, he or she loses the game.

Differences: *The Dark* version has different wording: "If Marsh Viper damages opponent, opponent gets two poison counters. If opponent ever has ten or more poison counters, opponent loses the game."

Rulings Differences: Marsh Viper now gives poison counters to any player damaged by Marsh Viper. (Thus, if the damage is redirected back to the controller, the controller gets poison counters.) *The Dark version stated that Marsh Viper gave poison counters to an opponent.*

Meekstone

Artifact / Artifact / Quinton Hoover / Rare

Fourth Edition Text: No creatures with power greater than 2 untap during their controllers' untap phase.

Differences: Previous versions have a different wording: "Any creature with power greater than 2 may not be untapped as normal during the untap phase." The *Unlimited* and *Limited* versions have change C.

Merfolk of the Pearl Trident

Blue / Summon Merfolk / Jeff A. Menges / Common

Mesa Pegasus

White / Summon Pegasus / Melissa Benson / Common

Fourth Edition Text: Flying, banding

Differences: Previous versions have "bands" instead of "banding."

Millstone

Artifact / Artifact / Kaja Foglio / Rare
***Fourth Edition* Text:** ②, ⊙: Take the top two cards from target player's library and put them into that player's graveyard.
Differences: The *Revised* and *Antiquities* versions have "in target" instead of "into that." The *Antiquities* version has change M.

Mind Bomb

Blue / Sorcery / Mark Tedin / Uncommon
***Fourth Edition* Text:** Mind Bomb deals 3 damage to each player. All players may discard up to three cards of their choice from their hands. Each card a player discards in this manner prevents 1 damage to that player from Mind Bomb.
Differences: The *Legends* version has change B.

⚒ Mind Twist

Black / Sorcery / Julie Baroh / Rare
***Fourth Edition* Text:** Target player discards X cards at random from his or her hand. If that player does not have enough cards, his or her entire hand is discarded.
Differences: Previous versions have different wording: "Opponent must discard X cards at random from hand. If opponent doesn't have enough cards in hand, entire hand is discarded."
Rulings Differences: Mind Twist may now target any player, including the caster. *Previous versions stated that Mind Twist could only target an opponent.*

Mishra's Factory

Land / Land / Kaja & Phil Foglio / Uncommon
***Fourth Edition* Text:** ⊙: Add one colorless mana to your mana pool. / ①: Mishra's Factory becomes an Assembly Worker, a 2/2 artifact creature, until end of turn. Assembly Worker still counts as a land but cannot be tapped for mana the turn it comes into play. / ⊙: Target Assembly Worker gets +1/+1 until end of turn.
Differences: The *Antiquities* version has different wording: "Tap to add 1 colorless mana to your mana pool *or* give any Assembly Worker +1/+1 until end of turn. / ①: Mishra's Factory becomes an Assembly

Worker, a 2/2 artifact creature, until end of turn. Assembly Worker is still considered a land as well." The *Antiquities* version also contains 3 additional Mishra's Factory cards with different art.

Mishra's War Machine

Artifact / Artifact Creature / Amy Weber / Rare
***Fourth Edition* Text:** Banding / During your upkeep, choose and discard one card from your hand, or Mishra's War Machine deals 3 damage to you. If Mishra's War Machine deals damage to you in this way, tap it.
Differences: *Revised* and *Antiquities* have different wording: "Bands / During your upkeep, discard one card of your choice from your hand, or Mishra's War Machine becomes tapped and does 3 points of damage to you."

Mons's Goblin Raiders

Red / Summon Goblins / Jeff A. Menges / Common

Morale

White / Instant / Mark Poole / Common
***Fourth Edition* Text:** All attacking creatures get +1/+1 until end of turn.
Differences: *The Dark* version has change G.

Mountain (variation 1)

Land / Land / Douglas Shuler / Common
***Fourth Edition* Text:** ⊙: Add 🔴 to your mana pool.
Differences: The *Unlimited* and *Limited* versions have changes S and A.

Mountain (variation 2)

Land / Land / Douglas Shuler / Common
***Fourth Edition* Text:** ⊕: Add ◆ to your mana pool.
Differences: The *Unlimited* and *Limited* versions have changes S and A.

Mountain (variation 3)

Land / Land / Douglas Shuler / Common
***Fourth Edition* Text:** ⊕: Add ◆ to your mana pool.
Differences: The *Unlimited* and *Limited* (Beta) versions have changes S and A. This version of Mountain did not appear in the *Limited* (Alpha) version.

Murk Dwellers

Black / Summon Murk Dwellers / Drew Tucker / Common
***Fourth Edition* Text:** When attacking and not blocked, Murk Dwellers gets +2/+0 until end of turn.
Differences: *The Dark* version has different wording: "When attacking, Murk Dwellers gain +2/+0 if not blocked."

⋏Nafs Asp

Green / Summon Asp / Christopher Rush / Common
***Fourth Edition* Text:** If Nafs Asp damages a player, it also deals 1 damage to that player during his or her next draw phase. Before then, the player may pay ① to prevent this damage.
Differences: The *Arabian Nights* version has different wording: "If Asp inflicts any damage on your opponent, your opponent must spend ① before the draw phase of his or her next turn or lose an additional 1 life." The *Arabian Nights* version had two versions of

the card with size and shading variations in the uncolored mana symbol.
Rulings Differences: Nafs Asp can now deal damage during the draw phase to any player it damages, including its controller. *Previous versions stated that Nafs Asp gave poison counters to an opponent.*

⋏Nether Shadow

Black / Summon Shadow / Christopher Rush / Rare
***Fourth Edition* Text:** At the end of your upkeep, if Shadow is in your graveyard with at least three creature cards above it, you may return it to play. Shadow can attack the turn it comes into play.
Differences: Previous versions have different wording: "If Shadow is in graveyard with any combination of cards above it that includes at least three creatures, it can be returned to play during your upkeep. Shadow can attack on same turn summoned or returned to play." The *Unlimited* and *Limited* versions have "upkeep for its normal casting cost" instead of "your upkeep" in the above.
Rulings Differences: Nether Shadow now requires no cost to return and returns to play only at the end of its controller's upkeep. *Previous versions allowed Shadow to return at any time during its controller's upkeep. The* Unlimited *and* Limited *versions required the controller to pay the Nether Shadow's casting cost to return it to play.*

⋏Nevinyrral's Disk

Artifact / Artifact / Mark Tedin / Rare
***Fourth Edition* Text:** Comes into play tapped. ①, ⊕: Destroy all creatures, enchantments, and artifacts, including Nevinyrral's Disk itself.
Differences: The *Revised* version has different wording: " ①: Destroys all creatures, enchantments, and artifacts in play, including Disk itself. Disk begins play tapped but can be untapped as usual." The *Unlimited* and *Limited* versions have change M and different wording: " ①: Destroys all creatures, enchantments, and artifacts in play. Disk begins tapped but can be untapped as usual. Disk destroys itself when used."
Rulings Differences: Nevinyrral's Disk now taps when used; this is written as an activation cost. *The* Revised *version did not require controller to tap the Disk.*

Nightmare

Black / Summon Nightmare /
Melissa Benson / Rare
Fourth Edition Text: Flying / Nightmare has power and toughness each equal to the number of swamps its controller controls.
Differences: Previous versions have different wording: "Flying / Nightmare's power and toughness both equal the number of swamps its controller has in play."

➹ Northern Paladin

White / Summon Paladin /
Douglas Shuler / Rare
Fourth Edition Text: ✹✹, ⟲: Destroy target black permanent.
Differences: Previous versions have different wording: "✹✹, ➷: Destroys a black card in play. Cannot be used to cancel a black spell as it is being cast." The *Unlimited* and *Limited* versions have "and tap:" instead of ", ⟲:". Previous versions have change S.
Rulings Differences: *In previous versions, Northern Paladin could only destroy black cards in play. Northern Paladin can now target any black permanent in play, including tokens.*

Oasis

Land / Land / Brian Snõddy / Uncommon
Fourth Edition Text: ⟲: Prevent 1 damage to any creature.
Differences: The *Arabian Nights* version has different wording: "Tap to prevent 1 damage to any creature."

Obsianus Golem

Artifact / Artifact Creature / Jesper Myrfors / Uncommon

Onulet
Artifact / Artifact Creature / Anson Maddocks / Rare
Fourth Edition Text: If Onulet is put into the graveyard from play, you gain 2 life.
Differences: The *Revised* and *Antiquities* versions have different wording: "If Onulet is placed in the graveyard, its controller gains 2 life." The *Antiquities* version has "goes to" instead of "is placed in" in the above.
Rulings Differences: Onulet now only gives controller life if placed in the graveyard from play. *Previous versions implied that Onulet gave controller life if it was placed in the graveyard from controller's hand or library.*

Orcish Artillery
Red / Summon Orcs / Anson Maddocks / Uncommon
Fourth Edition Text: ✧: Orcish Artillery deals 2 damage to target creature or player and 3 damage to you.
Differences: The *Revised* version has different wording: "⟑: Orcish Artillery does 2 damage to any target, but it also does 3 damage to you." The *Unlimited* and *Limited* versions have different wording: "Tap to do 2 damage to any target, but you suffer 3 damage as well." The *Limited* (Alpha) version has a casting cost of ① ②; other versions have a casting cost of ① ② ②.
Rulings Differences: Orcish Artillery's casting cost is ① ② ②. *The Limited (Alpha) version had a casting cost of ① ②.*

Orcish Oriflamme
Red / Enchantment / Dan Frazier / Uncommon
Fourth Edition Text: All attacking creatures you control get +1/+0.
Differences: Previous versions have different wording: "During your attack, all of your attacking creatures gain +1/+0." The *Unlimited* and *Limited* versions have "When attacking" instead of "During your attack" in the above. The *Limited* (Alpha) version has a casting cost of ① ②; other versions have a casting cost of ③ ②.
Rulings Differences: Orcish Oriflamme's casting cost is ③ ②. *The Limited (Alpha) had a casting cost of ① ②.*

Ornithopter
Artifact / Artifact Creature / Amy Weber / Uncommon
Fourth Edition Text: Flying

Osai Vultures
White / Summon Vultures / Dan Frazier / Uncommon
Fourth Edition Text: Flying / At the end of any turn in which a creature is put into the graveyard from play, put a carrion counter on Vultures. / ⓪: Remove two carrion counters to give Vultures +1/+1 until end of turn.
Differences: The *Legends* version has different wording: "Flying / At the end of any turn in which a creature is placed in the graveyard from play, put a counter on the Vultures. Remove two counters to give Vultures +1/+1 until end of turn." The *Legends* version contains the additional flavor text "A sign of battle, the Vultures circle and wait for the victorious to depart."
Rulings Differences: Osai Vultures now has an activation cost to remove counters. *The Legends version did not include an activation cost.*

Paralyze
Black / Enchant Creature / Anson Maddocks / Common
Fourth Edition Text: Target creature does not untap during its controller's untap phase. That player may pay an additional ④ during his or her upkeep to untap it. Tap target creature when Paralyze comes into play.
Differences: The *Revised* version has different wording: "Target creature is not untappped as normal during untap phase. Creature's controller may spend ④ during his or her upkeep to untap it. Tap target creature when Paralyze is cast." The *Unlimited* and *Limited* versions have different wording:

"Target creature is not untapped as normal during untap phase unless 4 mana are spent. Tap target creature when Paralyze is cast."
Rulings Differences: The controller of target creature Paralyze enchants may pay ④ during his or her upkeep to untap the target creature. This must be paid in addition to any other untap costs. *Previous versions did not specify that cost to untap was cumulative; also, the* Unlimited *and* Limited *versions required target creature's controller to pay during the untap phase, and target creature's controller could not pay more than once.*

Pearled Unicorn

White / Summon Unicorn / Cornelius Brudi / Common
Differences: Previous versions have the word "have" in italics in the flavor text. The *Revised* version does not have the attribution on a separate line in the flavor text.

Personal Incarnation

White / Summon Avatar / Kev Brockschmidt / Rare
Fourth Edition **Text:** Owner may redirect any or all damage done to Personal Incarnation to self instead. If Personal Incarnation is put into the graveyard from play, owner loses half his or her remaining life, rounding up the loss. Effects that redirect or prevent damage cannot be used to counter this loss of life.
Differences: Previous versions have different wording: "Caster can redirect any or all damage done to Personal Incarnation to self instead. The source of the damage is unchanged. If Personal Incarnation goes to the graveyard, caster loses half his or her remaining life points, rounding up the loss." The *Unlimited* and *Limited* versions have "is

destroyed" instead of "goes to the graveyard" in the above.

Pestilence

Black / Enchantment / Jesper Myrfors / Common
Fourth Edition **Text:** At the end of any turn, if there are no creatures in play, bury Pestilence. / 💀: Pestilence deals 1 damage to all creatures and players.
Differences: The *Revised* version has different wording: "💀: Do 1 damage to each creature and to both players. If there are no creatures in play at the end of any turn, Pestilence must be discarded." The *Unlimited* and *Limited* versions have different wording: "💀: Do 1 damage to each creature and to both players. Pestilence must be discarded at end of any turn in which there are no creatures in play at end of turn."

Phantasmal Forces

Blue / Summon Phantasm / Mark Poole / Uncommon
Fourth Edition **Text:** Flying / During your upkeep, pay 💧 or destroy Phantasmal Forces.
Differences: Previous versions have different wording: "Flying / Controller must spend 💧 during upkeep to maintain or Phantasmal Forces are destroyed." The *Limited* (Alpha) version has "U" instead of "💧".

Phantasmal Terrain

Blue / Enchant Land / Dameon Willich / Common
Fourth Edition **Text:** Target land becomes any basic land type of your choice.
Differences: Previous versions have different wording: "Target land changes to any basic land type of caster's choice. Land type is set when cast and may not be further altered by this card." The *Unlimited* and *Limited* versions have "enchantment" instead of "card" in the above.

Phantom Monster

Blue / Summon Phantom / Jesper Myrfors / Uncommon
Fourth Edition **Text:** Flying

Piety

White / Instant / Mark Poole / Common
Fourth Edition Text: All blocking creatures get +0/+3 until end of turn.
Differences: The *Arabian Nights* version says "defending" instead of "blocking" and has change G. The *Arabian Nights* version also had two versions of the card with size and shading variations in the uncolored mana symbol.

Pikemen

White / Summon Pikemen / Dennis Detwiller / Common
Fourth Edition Text: Banding, first strike
Differences: *The Dark* version has change D.

Pirate Ship

Blue / Summon Ship / Tom Wänerstrand / Rare
Fourth Edition Text: Cannot attack if defending player controls no islands. If at any time you control no islands, bury Pirate Ship. ⟨tap⟩: Pirate Ship deals 1 damage to target creature or player.
Differences: Previous versions have different wording: "⟨tap⟩: Do 1 damage to any target. Cannot attack unless opponent has islands in play, though controller may still use special ability. Pirate Ship is destroyed immediately if at any time controller has no islands in play." The *Unlimited* version has change A and has "tap" instead of "use special ability" in the above.
Rulings Differences: Pirate Ship is now buried if controller does not control any islands. *Previous versions of Pirate Ship were destroyed if at any time controller controlled no islands.*

Pit Scorpion

Black / Summon Scorpion / Scott Kirschner / Common
Fourth Edition Text: If Pit Scorpion damages a player, he or she gets a poison counter. If a player has ten or more poison counters, he or she loses the game.
Differences: The *Legends* version has different wording: "If Scorpion damages opponent, opponent gets a poison counter. If opponent ever has ten or more poison counters, opponent loses game."

Rulings Differences: Pit Scorpion now gives poison counters to any player damaged by Pit Scorpion. (Thus, if the damage is redirected back to the controller, the controller gets a poison counter.) *The* Legends *version stated that Pit Scorpion gave poison counters to an opponent.*

Plague Rats

Black / Summon Rats / Anson Maddocks / Common
Fourth Edition Text: Plague Rats has power and toughness each equal to the number of Plague Rats in play, no matter who controls them. For example, if there are two Plague Rats in play, each has power and toughness 2/2.
Differences: Previous versions have different wording: "The *'s below are the number of Plague Rats in play, counting both sides. Thus if there are two Plague Rats in play, each has power and toughness 2/2." The *Unlimited* and *Limited* versions used "X" instead of "*" (this is also true in the lower right hand corner) in the above.

Plains (variation 1)

Land / Land / Jesper Myrfors / Common
Fourth Edition Text: ⟨tap⟩: Add ✴ to your mana pool.
Differences: The *Unlimited* and *Limited* versions have change A.

Plains (variation 2)

Land / Land / Jesper Myrfors / Common
Fourth Edition Text: ⟨tap⟩: Add ✴ to your mana pool.
Differences: The *Unlimited* and *Limited* versions have change A.

Plains (variation 3)
Land / Land / Jesper Myrfors / Common
Fourth Edition Text: ⊙: Add ✳ to your
mana pool.
Differences: The *Unlimited* and *Limited* (Beta)
versions have change A. This version of Plains
did not appear in the *Limited* (Alpha) version.

Power Leak
Blue / Enchant Enchantment / Drew Tucker /
Common
Fourth Edition Text: During the upkeep of
target enchantment's controller, Power Leak
deals 2 damage to him or her. That player
may pay ① for each damage he or she wishes to prevent from Power Leak.
Differences: Previous versions have different
wording: "Target enchantment costs 2 extra
mana during the upkeep phase of each of its
controller's turns. If target enchantment's
controller cannot or will not pay this extra
mana, Power Leak does 1 damage to him or
her for each unpaid mana." The *Unlimited*
and *Limited* versions have "upkeep" instead
of "the upkeep phase of each of its controller's turns" in the above.

Power Sink
Blue / Interrupt / Richard Thomas / Common
Fourth Edition Text: Counter a target spell if
its caster does not pay Ⓧ. Target spell's
caster must draw and pay all available mana
from lands and mana pool until Ⓧ is paid;
he or she may also pay mana from other
sources if desired.
Differences: The *Revised* version has different wording: "Target spell is countered
unless its caster spends X more mana.
Caster of target spell must draw and spend
all available mana from lands and mana pool
until X is spent; he or she may also spend

mana from other sources if desired. If this is
not enough mana, target spell will still be
countered." The *Unlimited* and *Limited* versions have different wording: "Target spell is
countered unless its caster spends X more
mana; caster of target spell can't choose to
let it be countered. If caster of target spell
doesn't have enough mana, all available
mana from lands and mana pool must be
paid but target spell will still be countered."

↗ Power Surge
Red / Enchantment / Douglas Shuler / Rare
Fourth Edition Text: During each player's
upkeep, Power Surge deals that player 1
damage for each land he or she controls that
was untapped at the beginning of the turn,
before the untap phase.
Differences: The *Revised* version has different wording: "At the beginning of a player's
turn, before the untap phase, the player must
take a counter for each of his or her lands
that is not tapped. / During the player's
upkeep, Power Surge does 1 damage to that
player for each counter; counters are then
discarded." The *Limited* and *Unlimited* versions have change S, and have different
wording: "Before untapping lands at the start
of a turn, each player takes 1 damage for
each land he or she controls but did not tap
during the previous turn."
Rulings Differences: Power Surge now deals
damage during upkeep and simply counts
untapped lands to determine damage. *The
Limited and Unlimited versions dealt damage
at the start of the turn, and did not simply
count untapped lands.*

Pradesh Gypsies
Green / Summon Gypsies / Quinton Hoover /
Common
Fourth Edition Text: ① ♣, ⊙: Target crea-
ture gets -2/-0 until end of turn.

↗ Primal Clay
Artifact / Artifact Creature / Kaja Foglio / Rare
Fourth Edition Text: When Primal Clay
comes into play, choose whether to make it a
1/6 wall, a 2/2 creature with flying, or a 3/3
creature.
Differences: The *Antiquities* and *Revised* versions have different wording: "When you
cast Primal Clay, you must choose whether

to make it a 1/6 wall, a 3/3 creature, or a 2/2 flying creature. Primal Clay then remains in this form until altered by another card or removed from play."

Rulings Differences: The form for Primal Clay is now chosen each time it enters play rather than when it is cast. (Thus, an opponent must counter the spell before knowning which form of the Clay the caster will choose.) *Previous versions stated that the caster chose the form of Primal Clay when it was first played.*

Prodigal Sorcerer
Blue / Summon Wizard / Douglas Shuler / Common
***Fourth Edition* Text:** ⊕: Prodigal Sorcerer deals 1 damage to target creature or player.
Differences: Previous versions have changes B and T and are missing "Prodigal Sorcerer." The *Unlimited* and *Limited* versions also have changes A and S.

Psionic Entity
Blue / Summon Entity / Justin Hampton / Rare
***Fourth Edition* Text:** ⊕: Psionic Entity deals 2 damage to target creature or player and 3 damage to itself.
Differences: The *Legends* version has changes B and T and says "but" instead of "and." The *Legends* version credits the artist as Susan Van Camp instead of Justin Hampton.

Psychic Venom
Blue / Enchant Land / Brian Snöddy / Common
***Fourth Edition* Text:** Whenever target land becomes tapped, Psychic Venom deals 2

damage to that land's controller.
Differences: Previous versions have change B and say "target land's" instead of "that land's." The *Unlimited* and *Limited* versions also say "is" instead of "becomes."

⊁ Purelace
White / Interrupt / Sandra Everingham / Rare
***Fourth Edition* Text:** Change the color of target spell or target permanent to white. Costs to cast, tap, maintain, or use a special ability of target remain unchanged.
Differences: Previous versions say "card" before "remain" and their first sentence says "Changes the color of one card either being played or already in play to white."
Rulings Differences: Purelace can now target any permanent in play, including tokens, but cannot target lands as they are being played. *Previous versions of Purelace could only target cards; this included targeting lands as they were being played.*

Pyrotechnics
Red / Sorcery / Anson Maddocks / Uncommon
***Fourth Edition* Text:** Pyrotechnics deals 4 damage divided any way you choose among any number of target creatures and/or players.
Differences: The *Legends* version has changes B and T.

⊁ The Rack
Artifact / Artifact / Richard Thomas / Uncommon
***Fourth Edition* Text:** At the end of target opponent's upkeep, The Rack deals that player 1 damage for each card in his or her hand fewer than three.
Differences: The *Antiquities* and *Revised* versions have different wording: "If opponent has fewer than three cards in hand during his or her upkeep, the Rack does 1 damage to opponent for each card fewer than three." The *Antiquities* version also has change C.
Rulings Differences: The Rack now targets an opponent and deals damage at end of that player's upkeep. *Previous versions stated that The Rack affected "opponent"; thus, in a two-player game, stealing The Rack would change who it affected. Also, The Rack affected opponent "during" upkeep instead of at "end of" upkeep.*

Radjan Spirit
Green / Summon Spirit / Christopher Rush / Uncommon
Fourth Edition **Text:** ✪: Target creature loses flying until end of turn.
Differences: The *Legends* version says "flying ability" instead of "flying."

Rag Man
Black / Summon Rag Man / Daniel Gelon / Rare
Fourth Edition **Text:** ☠☠☠, ✪: Look at target opponent's hand. If that player has any creature cards in hand, he or she discards one of them at random. Use this ability only during your turn.
Differences: *The Dark* version does not say "target," says "opponent" instead of "that player," and has "This ability can only be used during controller's turn" as the last sentence.

⚔ Raise Dead
Black / Sorcery / Jeff A. Menges / Common
Fourth Edition **Text:** Take target creature from your graveyard and put it into your hand.
Differences: Previous versions have different wording: "Bring one creature from your graveyard to your hand." The *Unlimited* and *Limited* versions say "Return" instead of "Bring one."
Rulings Differences: Raise Dead now targets the card in the graveyard.

Rebirth
Green / Sorcery / Mark Tedin / Rare
Fourth Edition **Text:** Each player may be healed to 20 life. Any player choosing to be healed antes an additional card from the top of his or her library. Remove Rebirth from your

deck before playing if not playing for ante.
Differences: The *Legends* version says "may choose" instead of "may" and has "Remove this card from your deck before playing if you are not playing for ante" as the last sentence.

⚔ Red Elemental Blast
Red / Interrupt / Richard Thomas / Common
Fourth Edition **Text:** Counter target blue spell or destroy target blue permanent.
Differences: Previous versions have different wording: "Counters a blue spell being cast or destroys a blue card in play." The *Limited* (Alpha) version also says "Instant" instead of "Interrupt."
Rulings Differences: Red Elemental Blast can now target any blue permanent in play, including tokens. *Previous versions stated that Red Elemental Blast could only target blue spells being cast or blue cards in play.*

Red Mana Battery
Artifact / Artifact / Mark Tedin / Rare
Fourth Edition **Text:** ②, ✪: Put one charge counter on Red Mana Battery. / ✪: Add 🔴 to your mana pool and remove as many charge counters as you wish. For each charge counter removed from Red Mana Battery, add 🔴 to your mana pool. Play this ability as an interrupt.
Differences: The *Legends* version has different wording: "②, ⟋: Put one counter on Red Mana Battery. / ⟋: Add 🔴 to your mana pool. Remove as many counters as you wish. For each counter removed add 🔴 to your mana pool. This ability is played as an interrupt."

⚔ Red Ward
White / Enchant Creature / Dan Frazier / Uncommon
Fourth Edition **Text:** Target creature gains protection from red. The protection granted by Red Ward does not destroy Red Ward.
Differences: Previous versions do not have the second sentence.
Rulings Differences: The protection granted by Red Ward now cannot destroy Red Ward. *Previous versions of Red Ward would destroy themselves under the right circumstances.*

Regeneration

Green / Enchant Creature / Quinton Hoover / Common

Fourth Edition Text: 🌲: Regenerate target creature Regeneration enchants.

Differences: Previous versions have different wording: "🌲: Target creature regenerates."

🔨 Relic Bind

Blue / Enchant Artifact / Christopher Rush / Uncommon

Fourth Edition Text: When target artifact opponent controls becomes tapped, you may give 1 life or have Relic Bind deal 1 damage to target player.

Differences: The *Legends* version has a different wording: "When target artifact is tapped, the controller of Relic Bind can choose to do 1 damage to any player or give 1 life to any player."

Rulings Differences: Relic Bind now has no effect while on an artifact controlled by the caster of Relic Bind. Relic Bind cannot be placed on an artifact caster controls. *The Legends version implied that Relic Bind worked regardless of which player controlled the artifact.*

Reverse Damage

White / Instant / Dameon Willich / Rare

Fourth Edition Text: All damage dealt to you so far this turn by one source is retroactively added to your life total instead of subtracted. Further damage this turn is treated normally.

Differences: Previous versions have different wording: "All damage you have taken from any one source this turn is added to your life total instead of subtracted from it."

Righteousness

White / Instant / Douglas Shuler / Rare

Fourth Edition Text: Target blocking creature gets +7/+7 until end of turn.

Differences: Previous versions have change G and say "defending" instead of "blocking." The *Unlimited* and *Limited* versions also have change S.

Rod of Ruin

Artifact / Artifact / Christopher Rush / Uncommon

Fourth Edition Text: ③ , ⚙: Rod of Ruin deals 1 damage to target creature or player.

Differences: The *Revised* version has changes B and T. The *Unlimited* and *Limited* versions also have change M.

Royal Assassin

Black / Summon Assassin / Tom Wänerstrand / Rare

Fourth Edition Text: ⚙: Destroy target tapped creature.

Differences: The *Revised* version says "any" instead of "target." The *Unlimited* and *Limited* versions also have change A. Previous versions of the flavor text have "Royal Assassins" in lowercase.

🔨 Samite Healer

Common / Summon Cleric / Tom Wänerstrand / Common

Fourth Edition Text: ⚙: Prevent 1 damage to any creature or player.

Differences: The *Revised* version says "target" instead of "creature or player." The *Unlimited* and *Limited* versions also have change A.

Rulings Differences: Samite Healer now targets just the damage, not the creature or player to which damage is being dealt. *Previous versions stated that Samite Healer targeted the creature or player receiving damage, not the damage being dealt.*

Sandstorm

Green / Instant / Brian Snõddy / Common

Fourth Edition Text: Sandstorm deals 1 damage to all attacking creatures.

Differences: The *Arabian Nights* version has different wording: "All attacking creatures suffer 1 damage."

Savannah Lions
White / Summon Lions / Daniel Gelon / Rare
Differences: The *Unlimited* and *Limited* versions of the flavor text have a comma between "endless" and "flat."

Scathe Zombies
Black / Summon Zombies / Jesper Myrfors / Common
Differences: Previous versions of the flavor text have slashes in place of line breaks.

Scavenging Ghoul
Black / Summon Ghoul / Jeff A. Menges / Uncommon
Fourth Edition **Text:** At the end of each turn, put a corpse counter on Scavenging Ghoul for each creature put into the graveyard during that turn. / 0: Remove a corpse counter from Scavenging Ghoul to regenerate it.
Differences: The *Revised* version has different wording: "At the end of each turn, put one counter on Ghoul for each other creature that was placed in the graveyard during the turn. If Ghoul takes lethal damage, you may use a counter to regenerate it; counters remain until used." The *Unlimited* and *Limited* versions have different wording: "At the end of each turn, put one counter on the Ghoul for each other creature that was destroyed without regenerating during the turn. If Ghoul dies you may use a counter to regenerate it; counters remain until used."
Rulings Differences: Scavenging Ghoul can now regenerate whenever appropriate. *The Revised version stated that Scavenging Ghoul could only regenerate from lethal damage.*

Scryb Sprites
Green / Summon Faeries / Amy Weber / Common
Fourth Edition **Text:** Flying

Sea Serpent
Blue / Summon Serpent / Jeff A. Menges / Common
Fourth Edition **Text:** Cannot attack if defending player controls no islands. If at any time you control no islands, bury Sea Serpent.
Differences: Previous versions have different wording: "Serpent cannot attack unless opponent has islands in play. Serpent is buried immediately if at any time controller has no islands in play." The *Unlimited* and *Limited* versions also say "destroyed" instead of "buried."
Rulings Differences: Sea Serpent is buried if at any time its controller controls no islands. *The Unlimited and Limited versions stated that Sea Serpent was destroyed if its controller controlled no islands.*

Seeker
White / Enchant Creature / Mark Poole / Common
Fourth Edition **Text:** Target creature cannot be blocked except by white creatures and artifact creatures.
Differences: The *Legends* version says "blocked by any creatures" instead of "blocked."

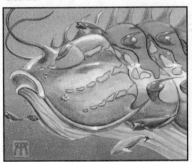

Segovian Leviathan
Blue / Summon Leviathan / Melissa Benson / Uncommon
Fourth Edition **Text:** Islandwalk
Differences: The *Legends* version has a slash after "fish-hook" in the flavor text.

Sengir Vampire
Black / Summon Vampire / Anson Maddocks / Uncommon
Fourth Edition **Text:** Flying / Put a +1/+1 counter on Sengir Vampire each time a creature is put into the graveyard the same turn Sengir Vampire damaged it.
Differences: Previous versions have different wording: "Flying / Vampire gets a +1/+1 counter each time a creature dies during a turn in which Vampire damaged it." The *Unlimited* and *Limited* versions added "unless the dead creature is regenerated."

Serra Angel
White / Summon Angel / Douglas Shuler / Uncommon
Fourth Edition Text: Flying / Attacking does not cause Serra Angel to tap.
Differences: The *Unlimited* and *Limited* versions have change S and different wording: "Flying / Does not tap when attacking."

Shanodin Dryads
Green / Summon Nymphs / Anson Maddocks / Common
Fourth Edition Text: Forestwalk

Shapeshifter
Artifact / Artifact Creature / Dan Frazier / Uncommon
Fourth Edition Text: Shapeshifter has power and toughness that add up to seven, but neither may be more than seven. Set them when Shapeshifter comes into play; you may change them during your upkeep.
Differences: The *Antiquities* version has different wording: "The *s below represent any number from 0 to 6. You set * when Shapeshifter is cast, and you may change it during your upkeep." The *Antiquities* version also has the flavor text *Born like a Phoenix from the Flame,/ But neither Bulk nor Shape the same./ —Jonathan Swift, "Vanbrug's House"*
Rulings Differences: The toughness of Shapeshifter can now be set to 0. *The* Antiquities *version stated that the toughness of Shapeshifter could not be set below 1.*

Shatter
Red / Instant / Amy Weber / Common
Fourth Edition Text: Destroy target artifact.
Differences: Previous versions have different wording: "Shatter destroys target artifact."

Shivan Dragon
Red / Summon Dragon / Melissa Benson / Rare
Fourth Edition Text: Flying / 🔴: +1/+0 until end of turn
Differences: Previous versions have a semi-colon in place of the line break. The *Revised* version also is missing the "until end of turn."

Simulacrum
Black / Instant / Mark Poole / Uncommon
Fourth Edition Text: All damage done to you so far this turn is instead retroactively applied to a target creature you control. Further damage this turn is treated normally.
Differences: Previous versions have different wording: "All damage done to you so far this turn is instead retroactively applied to one of your creatures in play. Even if there's more than enough damage to kill the creature, you don't suffer any of it. Further damage this turn is treated normally." The *Unlimited* and *Limited* versions also start the second sentence with "If this damage kills the creature it can be regenerated;".

Sindbad
Blue / Summon Sindbad / Julie Baroh / Uncommon
Fourth Edition Text: ⟳: Draw a card. If it is not a land, discard it.
Differences: The *Arabian Nights* version has different wording: "Tap to draw a card from your library, but discard that card if it is not a land."

Siren's Call
Blue / Instant / Anson Maddocks / Uncommon
Fourth Edition Text: All of target opponent's creatures that can attack must do so. At end of turn, destroy any non-wall creatures that did not attack. Play only during opponent's turn, before opponent's attack. Siren's Call does not affect creatures brought under opponent's control this turn.
Differences: Previous versions have different wording: "All of opponent's creatures that can attack must do so. Any non-wall creatures that cannot attack are killed at end of turn. Can be played only during opponent's turn, before opponent's attack. Creatures

summoned this turn are unaffected by Siren's Call." The *Unlimited* and *Limited* versions also say "destroyed" instead of "killed" and say "Play" instead of "Can be played only."

Rulings Differences: Siren's Call now targets the affected opponent; also, Siren's Call now does not affect any creature brought under an opponent's control this turn. *Previous versions implied that Siren's Call destroyed non-wall creatures that had not been summoned this turn but that could not attack due to summoning sickness (such as a creature stolen earlier in the turn).*

Sisters of the Flame

Red / Summon Sisters / Jesper Myrfors / Common

Fourth Edition Text: ☉: Add ● to your mana pool. Play this ability as an interrupt.

Differences: *The Dark* version has "This ability is played as an interrupt" as the second sentence.

➤ Sleight of Mind

Blue / Interrupt / Mark Poole / Rare

Fourth Edition Text: Change the text of target spell or target permanent by replacing all occurrences of one color word with another. For example, you may change "Counters black spells" to "Counters blue spells." Sleight of Mind cannot change mana symbols.

Differences: Previous versions say "any card being played or already in play" instead of "target spell or target permanent." The *Unlimited* and *Limited* versions are missing "Sleight of Mind" in the last sentence.

Rulings Differences: Sleight of Mind can now target any permanent in play, including tokens, but cannot target lands as they are being played. *Previous versions of Sleight of Mind could only target cards; this included targeting lands as they were being played.*

Smoke

Red / Enchantment / Jesper Myrfors / Rare

Fourth Edition Text: No player may untap more than one creature during his or her untap phase.

Differences: Previous versions have different wording: "Each player can only untap one creature during his or her untap phase."

Sorceress Queen

Black / Summon Sorceress / Kaja Foglio / Rare

Fourth Edition Text: ☉: Target creature other than Sorceress Queen becomes 0/2 until end of turn.

Differences: The *Revised* and *Arabian Nights* versions have different wording: "↗: Make another creature 0/2 until end of turn. Treat this exactly as if the numbers in the lower right of the target card were 0/2. All special characteristics and enchantments on the creature are unaffected." The *Arabian Nights* version also has change A.

➤ Soul Net

Artifact / Artifact / Dameon Willich / Uncommon

Fourth Edition Text: ①: Gain 1 life when a creature is put into the graveyard from play. Use this effect only once each time a creature is put into the graveyard.

Differences: The *Revised* version has different wording: "①: You gain 1 life every time a creature is placed in the graveyard. Can only give 1 life each time a creature is placed in the graveyard." The *Unlimited* and *Limited* versions have change P and different wording: "①: You gain 1 life every time a creature is destroyed, unless it is then regenerated."

Rulings Differences: Soul Net now only allows 1 life to be gained per creature put into the graveyard. *The Unlimited and Limited versions of Soul Net allowed multiple life to be gained per creature put into the graveyard.*

➤ Spell Blast

Blue / Interrupt / Brian Snöddy / Common

Fourth Edition Text: Counter target spell. X is

the casting cost of the target spell.

Differences: Previous versions have different wording: "Target spell is countered; X is casting cost of target spell." The *Unlimited* and *Limited* versions also say "cost" instead of "casting cost."

Rulings Differences: Spell Blast does not require caster to pay for additional mana paid for the spell to be countered. For example, it only costs 2 🔴 to Spell Blast a Drain Life; Spell Blast's caster no longer has to pay to counter the black mana used to deal damage. *Previous versions required additional payment to counter these types of spells.*

Spirit Link
White / Enchant Creature / Kaja Foglio / Uncommon

Fourth Edition **Text:** Gain 1 life for every 1 damage target creature deals. You may gain more life than the toughness or the total life of the creature or player damaged by the creature Spirit Link enchants.

Differences: The *Legends* version has different wording: "For every point of damage target creature does, you gain 1 life."

Spirit Shackle
Black / Enchant Creature / Edward Beard, Jr. / Uncommon

Fourth Edition **Text:** Put a -0/-2 counter on target creature every time it becomes tapped. These counters remain even if Spirit Shackle is removed.

Differences: The *Legends* version doesn't say "These" and says "enchantment" instead of "Spirit Shackle."

Stasis
Blue / Enchantment / Fay Jones / Uncommon

Fourth Edition **Text:** Players do not get an untap phase. During your upkeep, pay 🔵 or destroy Stasis.

Differences: Previous versions replace the second sentence with "Pay 🔵 during your upkeep or Stasis is destroyed; cards still do not untap until the next untap phase." The *Unlimited* and *Limited* versions also were missing "cards still do not untap until the next untap phase."

Steal Artifact
Blue / Enchant Artifact / Amy Weber / Uncommon

Fourth Edition **Text:** Gain control of target artifact.

Differences: Previous versions have different wording: "You control target artifact until enchantment is discarded or game ends. If target artifact was tapped when stolen it stays tapped until you can untap it. If destroyed, target artifact is put in its owner's graveyard."

Stone Giant
Red / Summon Giant / Dameon Willich / Uncommon

Fourth Edition **Text:** 🔄: Target creature you control, which must have toughness less than Stone Giant's power, gains flying until end of turn. Destroy that creature at end of turn. Other effects may later be used to increase the creature's toughness beyond Stone Giant's power.

Differences: Previous versions have different wording: "↗: Make one of your own creatures a flying creature until end of turn. Target creature, which must have toughness less than Stone Giant's power at the time it gains flying ability, is killed at end of turn." The *Unlimited* and *Limited* versions also have change A and say "destroyed" instead of "killed." Previous versions also have the flavor text "What goes up, must come down."

Stone Rain
Red / Sorcery / Daniel Gelon / Common

Fourth Edition **Text:** Destroy target land.

Differences: Previous versions have different wording: "Destroys any one land."

Stream of Life
Green / Sorcery / Mark Poole / Common

Fourth Edition **Text:** Target player gains X life.

⚔ Strip Mine

Land / Land / Daniel Gelon / Uncommon
***Fourth Edition* Text:** ⚙: Add one colorless mana to your mana pool. / ⚙: Sacrifice Strip Mine to destroy target land.
Differences: The *Antiquities* version has different wording: "Tap to add 1 colorless mana to your mana pool *or* place Strip Mine in your graveyard and destroy one land of your choice." The *Antiquities* version also contains 3 additional Strip Mine cards with different art.
Rulings Differences: Strip Mine is now sacrificed when used to destroy a land; also, Strip Mine abilities now have an activation cost. *The* Antiquities *version stated that Strip Mine wasn't placed in the graveyard until the effect resolved.*

Sunglasses of Urza

Artifact / Artifact / Dan Frazier / Rare
***Fourth Edition* Text:** You may use white mana in your mana pool as either white or red mana.
Differences: Previous versions have different wording: "White mana in your mana pool can be used as either white or red mana." The *Unlimited* and *Limited* versions also have change C.

Sunken City

Blue / Enchantment / Jesper Myrfors / Common
***Fourth Edition* Text:** All blue creatures get +1/+1. / During your upkeep, pay ⬤⬤ or destroy Sunken City.
Differences: *The Dark* version has change G and has "If you do not pay ⬤⬤ during your upkeep, Sunken City is destroyed."

Swamp (variation 1)

Land / Land / Dan Frazier / Common
***Fourth Edition* Text:** ⚙: Add ☠ to your mana pool.
Differences: The *Unlimited* and *Limited* versions have change A.

Swamp (variation 2)

Land / Land / Dan Frazier / Common
***Fourth Edition* Text:** ⚙: Add ☠ to your mana pool.
Differences: The *Unlimited* and *Limited* versions have change A.

Swamp (variation 3)

Land / Land / Dan Frazier / Common
***Fourth Edition* Text:** ⚙: Add ☠ to your mana pool.
Differences: The *Unlimited* and *Limited* (Beta) versions have change A. This version of Swamp did not appear in the *Limited* (Alpha) version.

Swords to Plowshares

White / Instant / Jeff A. Menges / Uncommon
***Fourth Edition* Text:** Remove target creature from the game. The creature's controller gains life equal to its power.
Differences: Previous versions have different wording: "Target creature is removed from the game entirely. Creature's controller gains life points equal to creature's power." The *Unlimited* and *Limited* versions add "; return to owner's deck only when the game is over" to the first sentence.

Sylvan Library

Green / Enchantment / Harold McNeill / Uncommon
***Fourth Edition* Text:** You may draw two extra cards during your draw phase. If you do so, put two of the cards drawn this turn back on top of your library (in any order) or pay 4 life per card not replaced. Effects that prevent or redirect damage cannot be used to counter this loss of life.
Differences: The *Legends* version says ", then either" instead of ". If you do so," and says ", or lose" instead of " or pay."

⚔ Tawnos's Wand

Artifact / Artifact / Douglas Shuler / Uncommon
***Fourth Edition* Text:** ②, ⚙: Target creature with power no greater than 2 becomes

unblockable until end of turn. Other effects may later be used to increase the creature's power beyond 2.

Differences: The *Antiquities* version has change M and different wording: " 2 : Make a creature of power no greater than 2 unblockable by all creatures except artifact creatures until end of turn. Other cards may be used to increase target creature's power beyond 2 after defense is chosen."

Rulings Differences: Artifact creatures are no longer allowed to block a creature made unblockable by Tawnos's Wand. *The Antiquities version allowed artifact creatures to block the affected creature.*

Tawnos's Weaponry
Artifact / Artifact / Dan Frazier / Uncommon

Fourth Edition **Text:** 2 , ↻: Target creature gets +1/+1 as long as Tawnos's Weaponry remains tapped. / You may choose not to untap Tawnos's Weaponry during your untap phase.

Differences: The *Antiquities* version has change M and different wording: " 2 : Target creature gains +1/+1 as long as Tawnos's Weaponry remains tapped. You may choose not to untap Tawnos's Weaponry during untap phase."

Tempest Efreet
Red / Summon Efreet / NéNé Thomas / Rare

Fourth Edition **Text:** ↻: Choose a card at random from target opponent's hand and put it in yours. Bury Tempest Efreet in opponent's graveyard. The change in ownership is permanent. Play this ability as an interrupt. Before you choose the card to be switched, the opponent may prevent effect by paying 10 life or conceding game; if this is done, bury Tempest Efreet. Effects that prevent or

redirect damage cannot be used to counter this loss of life. Remove Tempest Efreet from your deck before playing if not playing for ante.

Differences: The Legends version had different wording: "↻: Pick a card at random from opponent's hand and place it in yours. Bury Tempest Efreet in opponent's graveyard. The change in ownership is permanent. Play as an interrupt, but opponent can prevent effect by paying 10 life points or conceding game before the card to be switched is chosen—if this is done, Tempest Efreet is buried. Effects that prevent or redirect damage may not be used to counter this loss of life. Remove this card from deck if not playing for ante."

Terror
Black / Instant / Ron Spencer / Common

Fourth Edition **Text:** Bury target non-black, non-artifact creature.

Differences: The *Revised* version has different wording: "Buries target creature. Cannot target black creatures or artifact creatures." The *Unlimited* and *Limited* versions have different wording: "Destroys target creature without possibility of regeneration. Does not affect black creatures and artifact creatures."

Tetravus
Artifact / Artifact Creature / Mark Tedin / Rare

Fourth Edition **Text:** Flying / When Tetravus comes into play, put three +1/+1 counters on it. During your upkeep, you may move each of these counters on or off of Tetravus, regardless of who controls them. Counters that are removed become Tetravite tokens. Treat these tokens as 1/1 artifact creatures with flying. These creatures cannot have enchantments played on them and do not share any enchantments on Tetravus.

Differences: The *Antiquities* version has different wording: "Flying / Tetravus gets three +1/+1 counters when cast. During your upkeep, you may move each of these counters on or off of Tetravus. Counters moved off of Tetravus become independent 1/1 flying artifact creatures. If such a creature dies, the counter is removed from play. Such creatures may not have enchantments cast on them, and they do not share any enchantments on Tetravus."

Thicket Basilisk

Green / Summon Basilisk / Dan Frazier / Uncommon

Fourth Edition Text: At the end of combat, destroy all non-wall creatures blocking or blocked by Basilisk.

Differences: Previous versions have different wording: "Any non-wall creature blocking Basilisk is destroyed, as is any creature blocked by Basilisk. Creatures destroyed in this way deal their damage before dying."

Rulings Differences: Creatures blocking or blocked by Thicket Basilisk are now destroyed at the end of combat. Also, Thicket Basilisk now cannot destroy attacking walls that it blocks. *Previous versions stated that creatures blocking or blocked by Thicket Basilisk were destroyed during damage dealing. Also, previous versions destroyed attacking walls.*

Thoughtlace

Blue / Interrupt / Mark Poole / Rare

Fourth Edition Text: Change the color of target spell or target permanent to blue. Costs to cast, tap, maintain, or use a special ability of target permanent remain unchanged.

Differences: The *Revised* version says "card" before "remain" and its first sentence says "Changes the color of one card either being played or already in play to blue."

Rulings Differences: Thoughtlace can now target any permanent in play, including tokens, but cannot target lands as they are being played. *Previous versions of Thoughtlace could only target cards; this included targeting lands as they were being played.*

Throne of Bone

Artifact / Artifact / Anson Maddocks / Uncommon

Fourth Edition Text: 1 : Gain 1 life for a successfully cast black spell. Use this effect either when the spell is cast or later in the turn but only once for each black spell cast.

Differences: The *Revised* version has different wording: " 1 : Any black spell cast gives you 1 life. Can only give 1 life each time a black spell is cast." The *Unlimited* and *Limited* versions have change P and different wording: " 1 : Any black spell cast by any player gives you 1 life."

Rulings Differences: Throne of Bone can now be used to gain life later in the same turn that a black spell was cast. *Previous versions implied that Throne of Bone could only be used immediately after a spell was cast.*

Timber Wolves

Green / Summon Wolves / Melissa Benson / Rare

Fourth Edition Text: Banding

Differences: Previous versions say "Bands" instead of "Banding."

Time Elemental

Blue / Summon Elemental / Amy Weber / Rare

Fourth Edition Text: 2 6 6 , ⚅ : Return target permanent to owner's hand. You cannot use this ability on permanents with enchantment cards played on them. If Time Elemental blocks or attacks, destroy it at end of combat. In this case, Time Elemental deals 5 damage to its controller.

Differences: The *Legends* version says "Cannot target" instead of "You cannot use this ability on" and has "If Time Elemental blocks or attacks it is destroyed and does 5 damage to controller" instead of the last two sentences.

Rulings Differences: Time Elemental is now destroyed at end of combat. Also, the 5 damage is dealt at end of combat, regardless of whether the Time Elemental is still in play at that time. *The* Legends *version stated that Time Elemental was destroyed and dealt 5 damage to its controller at the time it was declared to attack or block.*

Titania's Song

Green / Enchantment / Kerstin Kaman / Rare

Fourth Edition Text: All non-creature artifacts

lose all their usual abilities and become artifact creatures with toughness and power each equal to their casting costs. If Titania's Song leaves play, artifacts return to normal just before the untap phase of the next turn.
Differences: The *Antiquities* and *Revised* versions say "artifacts in play" in the first sentence and say "both" instead of "each."

Tranquility
Green / Sorcery / Douglas Shuler / Common
***Fourth Edition* Text:** Destroy all enchantments.
Differences: Previous versions have different wording: "All enchantments in play must be discarded." The *Unlimited* and *Limited* versions have change S.

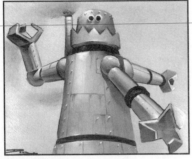

↗ Triskelion
Artifact / Artifact Creature / Douglas Shuler / Uncommon
***Fourth Edition* Text:** When Triskelion comes into play, put three +1/+1 counters on it. / 0 : Remove one of these counters from Triskelion to have Triskelion deal 1 damage to target creature or player.
Differences: The *Antiquities* version has different wording: "Triskelion gets three +1/+1 counters when cast. Controller may discard a +1/+1 counter at any time to do 1 damage to any target." The *Antiquities* version also has different flavor text: "A brainchild of Tawnos, the Triskelion proved its versatility and usefulness in many of the later battles between the brothers."
Rulings Differences: Triskelion now has an activation cost to remove a counter. (Thus, Triskelion can now deal multiple damage to a single target as one activation.) *The Antiquities version did not have an activation cost and implied that Triskelion could only remove one counter at a time.*

Tsunami
Green / Sorcery / Richard Thomas / Uncommon
***Fourth Edition* Text:** Destroy all islands.
Differences: Previous versions have different wording: "All islands in play are destroyed."

Tundra Wolves
White / Summon Wolves / Quinton Hoover / Common
***Fourth Edition* Text:** First strike

Tunnel
Red / Instant / Dan Frazier / Uncommon
***Fourth Edition* Text:** Bury target wall.
Differences: The *Revised* version has different wording: "Buries one wall." The *Unlimited* and *Limited* versions have different wording: "Destroys 1 wall. Target wall cannot be regenerated."

Twiddle
Blue / Instant / Rob Alexander / Common
***Fourth Edition* Text:** Tap or untap target land, artifact, or creature.
Differences: The *Unlimited* and *Limited* versions have different wording: "Caster may tap or untap any one land, creature, or artifact in play. No effects are generated by the target card." The *Limited* (Alpha) version does not have the second sentence.

Uncle Istvan
Black / Summon Uncle Istvan / Daniel Gelon / Uncommon
***Fourth Edition* Text:** All damage done to Uncle Istvan by creatures is reduced to 0.

Unholy Strength
Black / Enchant Creature / Douglas Shuler / Common
***Fourth Edition* Text:** Target creature gets +2/+1.
Differences: Previous versions have change G and a pentagram appears in the background of the art. The *Unlimited* and *Limited* versions also have change S.

Unstable Mutation
Blue / Enchant Creature / Douglas Shuler / Common
***Fourth Edition* Text:** Target creature gets +3/+3. During each of its controller's

upkeeps, put a -1/-1 counter on the creature. These counters remain even if Unstable Mutation is removed.

Differences: The *Arabian Nights* and *Revised* versions have different wording: "Target creature gains +3/+3. During the upkeep phase of each of its controller's turns, put a -1/-1 counter on the creature. These counters remain even if this enchantment is removed before the creature dies." The *Arabian Nights* version replaces the second sentence with "Each round, put a -1/-1 counter on the creature during its controller's upkeep."

Unsummon

Blue / Instant / Douglas Shuler / Common
Fourth Edition **Text:** Return target creature to owner's hand.

Differences: The *Revised* version adds "; enchantments on target creature are discarded." The *Unlimited* and *Limited* versions have change S, are missing both cases of "target," and add the sentence "Unsummon cannot be played during the damage-dealing phase of an attack." The *Limited* (Alpha) version also says "CARD ed" instead of "discarded."

Untamed Wilds

Green / Sorcery / NéNé Thomas / Uncommon
Fourth Edition **Text:** Search your library for any one basic land and put it directly into play. This does not count towards your one land per turn limit. Reshuffle your library afterwards.

Urza's Avenger

Artifact / Artifact Creature / Amy Weber / Rare
Fourth Edition **Text:** 0 : Urza's Avenger gets -1/-1 until end of turn and your choice of flying, banding, first strike, or trample until

end of turn.

Differences: The *Antiquities* version has different wording: " 0 : Avenger loses -1/-1 and gains one of your choice of flying, banding, first strike, or trample until end of turn. Attribute losses and ability gains are cumulative."

Uthden Troll

Red / Summon Troll / Douglas Shuler / Uncommon
Fourth Edition **Text:** ● : Regenerate
Differences: Previous versions have change R and say "Traditional" instead of "Troll chant" in the flavor text. The *Unlimited* and *Limited* versions also have change S.

Vampire Bats

Black / Summon Bats / Anson Maddocks / Common
Fourth Edition **Text:** Flying / ● : +1/+0 until end of turn. You cannot spend more than ●● in this way each turn.

Differences: The *Legends* version has a semicolon instead of line break after "Flying," and says "No" instead of "You cannot spend." Also, the flavor text had a slash instead of a line break after "place," and no line break before the attribution.

Venom

Green / Enchant Creature / Tom Wänerstrand / Common
Fourth Edition **Text:** At the end of combat, destroy all non-wall creatures blocking or blocked by target creature.

Differences: *The Dark* version has different wording: "All non-wall creatures target creature blocks or is blocked by are destroyed at end of combat." Also, the flavor text says "a wee scratch," before "but the next time."

⚔ Verduran Enchantress

Green / Summon Enchantress / Kev Brockschmidt / Rare
Fourth Edition **Text:** 0 : Draw a card when you successfully cast an enchantment. Use this effect only once for each enchantment cast.

Differences: Previous versions have different wording: "While Enchantress is in play, you may immediately draw a card from your library each time you cast an enchantment."

Rulings Differences: Verduran Enchantress now has an activation cost to draw a card. *Previous versions did not include an activation cost.*

Visions

White / Sorcery / NéNé Thomas / Uncommon
Fourth Edition **Text:** Look at the top five cards of any library. You may then shuffle that library.
Differences: The *Legends* version has different wording: "You may look at the top five cards of any library. You may then choose to shuffle that library." The *Legends* version has a slash instead of a line break after "sight," and no line break before the attribution in the flavor text.

↗**Volcanic Eruption**
Blue / Sorcery / Douglas Shuler / Rare
Fourth Edition **Text:** Destroy X target mountains. Volcanic Eruption deals 1 damage to each creature and player for each mountain put into the graveyard in this way.
Differences: The *Revised* version has different wording: "Destroys X mountains of your choice, and does 1 damage to each player and each creature in play for each mountain destroyed." The *Unlimited* and *Limited* versions have change S and different wording: "Destroys X mountains of your choice, and does X damage to each player and each creature in play."
Rulings Differences: Volcanic Eruption deals an amount of damage equal to the number of mountains put into the graveyard by the effect. *Previous versions dealt damage equal to the number of mountains targeted.*

Wall of Air

Blue / Summon Wall / Richard Thomas / Uncommon
Fourth Edition **Text:** Flying

Wall of Bone

Black / Summon Wall / Anson Maddocks / Uncommon
Fourth Edition **Text:** ☠: Regenerate
Differences: Previous versions have change R.

Wall of Brambles

Green / Summon Wall / Anson Maddocks / Uncommon
Fourth Edition **Text:** ♣: Regenerate
Differences: Previous versions have change R.

Wall of Dust

Red / Summon Wall / Richard Thomas / Uncommon
Fourth Edition **Text:** No creature blocked by Wall of Dust may attack during its controller's next turn.
Differences: The *Legends* version has different wording: "Creatures blocked by Wall of Dust cannot attack during your opponent's next turn. Use counters to mark these creatures."

Wall of Fire

Red / Summon Wall / Richard Thomas / Uncommon
Fourth Edition **Text:** ⚫: +1/+0 until end of turn
Differences: The *Revised* version is missing "until end of turn"; the *Unlimited* and *Limited* versions restore "until end of turn" but add a period. Previous versions of the flavor text did not have a line break before "the fiery wall."

Wall of Ice

Green / Summon Wall / Richard Thomas / Uncommon
Differences: Previous versions of the flavor text had slashes instead of line breaks between the lines of the poem.

Wall of Spears
Artifact / Artifact Creature / Sandra Everingham / Common
Fourth Edition Text: First strike, counts as a wall
Differences: The *Antiquities* version has a period at the end.

Wall of Stone
Red / Summon Wall / Dan Frazier / Uncommon
Differences: The *Unlimited* and *Limited* versions of the flavor text did not have a line break after "her strength."

Wall of Swords
White / Summon Wall / Mark Tedin / Uncommon
Fourth Edition Text: Flying

Wall of Water
Blue / Summon Wall / Richard Thomas / Uncommon
Fourth Edition Text: 🌢 : +1/+0 until end of turn
Differences: The *Revised* version is missing "until end of turn." The *Unlimited* and *Limited* versions restore "until end of turn" but add a period.

Wall of Wood
Green / Summon Wall / Mark Tedin / Common

➤ Wanderlust
Green / Enchant Creature / Cornelius Brudi / Uncommon
Fourth Edition Text: Wanderlust deals 1 damage to target creature's controller during that player's upkeep.
Differences: The *Revised* version has change

B and says "his or her" instead of "that creature." The *Unlimited* and *Limited* versions have different wording: "Wanderlust does 1 damage to target creature's controller during upkeep."
Rulings Differences: Wanderlust now only deals damage during the upkeep of the target creature's controller. Unlimited *and* Limited *versions dealt damage during each upkeep.*

War Mammoth
Green / Summon Mammoth / Jeff A. Menges / Common
Fourth Edition Text: Trample

➤ Warp Artifact
Black / Enchant Artifact / Amy Weber / Rare
Fourth Edition Text: Warp Artifact deals 1 damage to target artifact's controller during his or her upkeep.
Differences: The *Revised* version has change B and says "his or her" instead of "target artifact's." The *Unlimited* and *Limited* versions have different wording: "Warp Artifact does 1 damage to target artifact's controller at start of each turn."
Rulings Differences: Warp Artifact now only deals damage during the upkeep of the artifact's controller. *Previous versions dealt damage at the start of each turn.*

Water Elemental
Blue / Summon Elemental / Jeff A. Menges / Uncommon

Weakness
Black / Enchant Creature / Douglas Shuler / Common
Fourth Edition Text: Target creature gets -2/-1.
Differences: The *Revised* version says "loses" instead of "gets." The *Unlimited* and *Limited* versions have change S and different wording: "Target creature loses -2/-1; if this drops the creature's toughness below 1, it is dead."

Web
Green / Enchant Creature / Rob Alexander / Rare
Fourth Edition Text: Target creature gets +0/+2 and can block creatures with flying.
Differences: Previous versions have different

wording: "Target creature gains +0/+2 and can now block flying creatures, though it does not gain flying ability." The *Unlimited* and *Limited* versions also say "the ability to fly" instead of "flying ability."

Whirling Dervish

Green / Summon Dervish /
Susan Van Camp / Uncommon
Fourth Edition Text: Protection from black /
Put a +1/+1 counter on Whirling Dervish at the end of each turn in which it damages opponent.
Differences: The *Legends* version has different wording: "Protection from black / Gains +1/+1 (use counters) at the end of each turn in which it does damage to opponent."

White Knight

White / Summon Knight / Daniel Gelon /
Uncommon
Fourth Edition Text: Protection from black, first strike
Differences: Previous versions have the word "Knight" in lowercase in the flavor text.

White Mana Battery

Artifact / Artifact / Anthony Waters / Rare
Fourth Edition Text: 2, ⊙: Put one charge counter on White Mana Battery.
⊙: Add ✴ to your mana pool and remove as many charge counters as you wish. For each charge counter removed from White Mana Battery, add ✴ to your mana pool. Play this ability as an interrupt.
Differences: The *Legends* version has different wording: " 2, ⟁: Put one counter on White Mana Battery. / ⟁: Add ✴ to your mana pool. Remove as many counters as you wish. For each counter removed add ✴ to your mana pool. This ability is played as an interrupt.

⚔White Ward

White / Enchant Creature / Dan Frazier /
Uncommon
Fourth Edition Text: Target creature gains protection from white. The protection granted by White Ward does not destroy White Ward.
Differences: Previous versions do not have the second sentence.
Rulings Differences: The protection granted

by White Ward now cannot destroy White Ward, though its protection will destroy other wards normally. *Previous versions of White Ward implied that White Ward destroyed itself.*

Wild Growth

Green / Enchant Land / Mark Poole /
Common
Fourth Edition Text: Wild Growth adds 🍎 to your mana pool each time target land is tapped for mana.
Differences: The *Revised* version has different wording: "Whenever the usual mana is drawn from target land, Wild Growth provides an extra 🍎." The *Unlimited* and *Limited* versions have different wording: "When tapped target land provides 1 green mana in addition to the mana it normally provides."
Rulings Differences: Wild Growth cannot have the color of mana it produces changed by spells like Sleight of Mind. Wild Growth now provides mana to enchanted land's controller only if land enchanted is tapped for mana. *Previous versions could be altered by spells like Sleight of Mind to provide a different color of mana and provided one green mana whenever the land became tapped (even if it was not tapped for mana).*

Will-O'-The-Wisp

Black / Summon Will-O'-The-Wisp / Jesper Myrfors / Rare
Fourth Edition Text: Flying / ☠: Regenerate
Differences: Previous versions have different wording: "Flying; ☠: Regenerates." The *Unlimited* and *Limited* versions do not have the period at the end.

Winds of Change
Red / Sorcery / Justin Hampton / Rare
Fourth Edition Text: All players shuffle their hands into their libraries and then draw the same number of cards they originally held.
Differences: The *Legends* version has a comma after "libraries" and has a slash instead of a line break after "gales" in the flavor text.

Winter Blast
Green / Sorcery / Kaja Foglio / Uncommon
Fourth Edition Text: Tap X target creatures. Winter Blast deals 2 damage to each of these target creatures with flying.
Differences: The *Legends* version has different wording: "X target creatures become tapped. Winter Blast does 2 damage to each target creature that has flying."

Winter Orb
Artifact / Artifact / Mark Tedin / Rare
Fourth Edition Text: No player may untap more than one land during his or her untap phase.
Differences: The *Revised* version says "A player" instead of "No player" and adds "of each of his or her turns" to the end. The *Unlimited* and *Limited* versions have change C and different wording: "Players can untap only one land each during untap phase. Creatures and artifacts are untapped as normal."

Wooden Sphere
Artifact / Artifact / Mark Tedin / Uncommon
Fourth Edition Text: 1 : Gain 1 life for a successfully cast green spell. Use this effect either when the spell is cast or later in the turn but only once for each green spell cast.
Differences: The *Revised* version has different wording: " 1 : Any green spell cast gives you 1 life. Can only give 1 life each time a green spell is cast." The *Unlimited* and *Limited* versions have change P and different wording: " 1 : Any green spell cast by any player gives you 1 life."
Rulings Differences: Wooden Sphere now can be used to gain life later in the same turn that a green spell was cast. *Previous versions implied that Wooden Sphere could only be used immediately after a spell was cast.*

Word of Binding
Black / Sorcery / Ron Spencer / Common
Fourth Edition Text: Tap X target creatures.
Differences: *The Dark* version has different wording: "X target creatures become tapped."

Wrath of God
White / Sorcery / Quinton Hoover / Rare
Fourth Edition Text: Bury all creatures.
Differences: Previous versions have different wording: "All creatures in play are buried." The *Unlimited* and *Limited* versions also say "destroyed and cannot regenerate" instead of "buried."

Xenic Poltergeist
Black / Summon Poltergeist / Dan Frazier / Rare
Fourth Edition Text: ☼: Target non-creature artifact becomes an artifact creature with power and toughness each equal to its casting cost. Target retains all original abilities. This change lasts until your next upkeep.
Differences: The *Antiquities* version has different wording: "Tap to turn target non-creature artifact into an artifact creature with both power and toughness equal to its casting cost. This transformation lasts until your next upkeep; target retains all of its original abilities as well."

Yotian Soldier
Artifact / Artifact Creature / Christopher Rush / Common
Fourth Edition Text: Attacking does not cause Yotian Soldier to tap.

Zephyr Falcon
Blue / Summon Falcon / Heather Hudson / Common
Fourth Edition Text: Flying / Attacking does not cause Zephyr Falcon to tap.

Zombie Master
Black / Summon Lord / Jeff A. Menges / Rare
Fourth Edition Text: All zombies gain swampwalk and "💀: Regenerate."
Differences: Previous versions have different wording: "All zombies in play gain swampwalk and '💀: Regenerates' for as long as this card remains in play."

Discontinued Cards

⚔Atog

Revised Text: ⓪ : +2/+2. Each time you use this ability, you must sacrifice one of your artifacts in play.

Differences: The *Antiquities* version has different wording: " ⓪ : +2/+2 until end of turn. Each time you use this ability, you must choose one of your artifacts in play and place it in the graveyard. This artifact cannot be one that is already on its way to the graveyard, and artifact creatures killed this way may not be regenerated."

Rulings Differences: Atog now requires the sacrifice of an artifact. *The* Antiquities *version required that an artifact be placed in the graveyard without being regenerated.*

⚔Badlands

Revised Text: ⌖: Add either 🔴 or 💀 to your mana pool. Counts as both mountains and swamp and is affected by spells that affect either. If a spell destroys one of these land types, this card is destroyed; if a spell alters one of these land types, the other land type is unaffected.

Differences: The *Unlimited* and *Limited* versions have different wording: "Counts as both mountains and swamp and is affected by spells that affect either. Tap to add either 🔴 or 💀 to your mana pool."

Rulings Differences: If one of the land types of Badlands is changed, the other type is not. *Previous versions of Badlands did not make this distinction.*

Basalt Monolith

Revised Text: ⌖: Add 3 colorless mana to your mana pool. Does not untap as normal during untap phase; you may spend 3 at any other time to untap. Drawing mana from this artifact is played as an interrupt.

Differences: The *Unlimited* and *Limited* versions have change M. The *Unlimited* and *Limited* (Beta) versions have different wording: "Tap to add 3 colorless mana to your mana pool. Does not untap as normal during untap phase; spend ③ to untap. Tapping this artifact can be played as an interrupt." The *Limited* (Alpha) version has different wording: "Tap to add 3 colorless mana to your mana pool. Does not untap as normal during

untap phase, but can be untapped at any time for 3 mana. Tapping this artifact can be played as an interrupt."

⚔Bayou

Revised Text: ⌖: Add either 💀 or 🌳 to your mana pool. Counts as both swamp and forest and is affected by spells that affect either. If a spell destroys one of these land types, this card is destroyed; if a spell alters one of these land types, the other land type is unaffected.

Differences: The *Unlimited* and *Limited* versions have different wording: "Counts as both swamp and forest and is affected by spells that affect either. Tap to add either 💀 or 🌳 to your mana pool."

Rulings Differences: If one of the land types of Bayou is changed, the other type is not. *Previous versions of Bayou did not make this distinction.*

Black Lotus

Unlimited Text: Adds 3 mana of any single color of your choice to your mana pool, then is discarded. Tapping this artifact can be played as an interrupt.

Rulings Differences: *Unlimited* and *Limited* have errata: The first sentence of Black Lotus should read "Sacrifice Black Lotus to add three mana of any color to your mana pool."

Braingeyser

Revised Text: Target player must draw X cards.

Differences: The *Unlimited* and *Limited* versions have different wording: "Draw X cards or force opponent to draw X cards."

Chaos Orb

Unlimited Text: ① : Flip Chaos Orb onto the playing area from a height of at least one foot. Chaos Orb must turn completely over at least once or it is discarded with no effect. When Chaos Orb lands, any cards in play that it touches are destroyed, as is Chaos Orb.

Clone

Revised Text: Upon summoning, Clone acquires all characteristics, including color, of any one creature in play on either side; any creature enchantments on original creature are not copied. Clone retains these characteristics even after original creature is destroyed. Clone cannot be summoned if there are no creatures in play.

Differences: The *Unlimited* and *Limited* versions do not have "creature" before "enchantments" and say "played" instead of "summoned."

Contract from Below

Revised Text: Discard your current hand and draw eight new cards, adding the first drawn to your ante. Remove this card from your deck before playing if you are not playing for ante.

Differences: The *Unlimited* and *Limited* versions have change S.

Copy Artifact

Revised Text: Select any artifact in play. This enchantment acts as a duplicate of that artifact; it is affected by cards that affect either enchantments or artifacts. The copy remains even if the original artifact is destroyed. Enchantments on the original artifact are not copied.

Differences: The *Unlimited* and *Limited* versions say "enchantment copy" instead of "it" and do not have "Enchantments on the original are not copied."

Cyclopean Tomb

Unlimited Text: 2 : Turn any one non-swamp land into swamp during upkeep. Mark the changed lands with tokens. If Cyclopean Tomb is destroyed, remove one token of your choice each upkeep, returning that land to its original nature.

Differences: The *Limited* (Alpha) version does not have a casting cost.

Darkpact

Revised Text: Swap top card of your library with either card of the ante; this swap is permanent. You must have a card in your library to cast this spell. Remove this card from your deck before playing if you are not playing for ante.

Differences: The *Unlimited* and *Limited* versions say "Without looking at it first," before "swap."

Demonic Hordes

Revised Text: 🪓: Destroy 1 land. / Pay 💀 💀 💀 during your upkeep or the Hordes become tapped and you lose a land of opponent's choice.

Differences: The *Unlimited* and *Limited* versions do not say "your" before "upkeep" and have change A. The *Limited* (Alpha) version says "BBB" instead of "💀 💀 💀."

Rulings Differences: Demonic Hordes now requires its upkeep cost to be paid only during your upkeep. *Previous versions of Demonic Hordes required that its upkeep cost be paid during each player's upkeep.*

Demonic Tutor

Revised Text: Search your library for one card and take it into your hand. Reshuffle your library afterwards.

Differences: The *Unlimited* and *Limited* versions add "you may" before "Search" and have change S.

Dwarven Weaponsmith

Revised Text: 🪓: During your upkeep, add a permanent +1/+1 counter to any creature. Each time you use this ability, you must sacrifice one of your artifacts in play.

Differences: The *Antiquities* version has different wording: "Tap during your upkeep to add a permanent +1/+1 counter to any creature. Each time you use this ability, you must choose one of your artifacts in play and place it in the graveyard. This artifact cannot be one that is already on its way to the graveyard, and artifact creatures killed this way may not be regenerated."

Rulings Differences: Dwarven Weaponsmith now requires the sacrifice of an artifact. *The* Antiquities *version required that an artifact be placed in the graveyard without being regenerated.*

Earthbind

Revised Text: If cast on a flying creature, Earthbind removes flying ability and does 2 damage to target creature; this damage only occurs once, at the time Earthbind is cast. If another spell or effect later gives target creature flying ability, Earthbind does not affect this. Earthbind has no effect on non-flying creatures.

Differences: The *Unlimited* and *Limited* versions say "Enchant Non-Flying Creature" instead of "Enchant Creature" and had different wording: "Earthbind does 2 damage to target flying creature, which also loses flying ability."

Rulings Differences: Earthbind can now be cast on a creature without flying. *Previous versions of Earthbind did not allow this.*

Farmstead

Revised **Text:** Target land's controller gains 1 life if ✹✹ is spent during controller's upkeep. You cannot gain more than 1 life each turn through this enchantment.

Differences: The *Unlimited* and *Limited* versions have different wording: "Target land's controller gains 1 life each upkeep if ✹✹ is spent. Target land still generates mana as usual."

Rulings Differences: Farmstead now gives life only during target land's controller's upkeep. *Previous versions of Farmstead allowed it to give life during each player's upkeep.*

Forcefield

Unlimited **Text:** ①: Lose only 1 life to an unblocked creature.

Rulings Differences: *Unlimited* and *Limited* have errata: Forcefield should read "①: Prevent all but 1 damage to you from an unblocked attacking creature."

Granite Gargoyle

Revised **Text:** Flying / ②: +0/+1

Differences: The *Unlimited* and *Limited* versions have "+0/+1 until end of turn." instead of "+0/+1."

Icy Manipulator

Unlimited **Text:** ①: You may tap any land, creature, or artifact in play on either side. No effects are generated by the target card.

Differences: The *Limited* (Alpha) version has change D and does not contain the second sentence.

Rulings Differences: *Unlimited* and *Limited* versions have errata: Icy Manipulator should read "Artifact" instead of "Mono Artifact" and

"①, ✎: Tap target artifact, creature, or land." *The* Unlimited *version contains the second sentence merely as a reminder.*

Jandor's Ring

Revised **Text:** ②, ✎: Discard a card you just drew from your library, and draw another card to replace it."

Differences: The *Arabian Nights* version has change M.

Kird Ape

Revised **Text:** While controller has forests in play, Kird Ape gains +1/+2.

Differences: The *Arabian Nights* version has different wording: "Kird Ape gains +1/+2 if you have any forests in play."

Lich

Unlimited **Text:** You lose all life. If you gain life later in the game, instead draw one card from your library for each life. For each point of damage you suffer, you must destroy one of your cards in play. Creatures destroyed in this way cannot be regenerated. You lose if this enchantment is destroyed or if you suffer a point of damage without sending a card to the graveyard.

Rulings Differences: *Unlimited* and *Limited* versions have errata: Lich should read "leaves play" instead of "is destroyed"; also, "you must destroy" should be interpreted as "sacrifice."

Nettling Imp

Revised **Text:** ✎: Force a particular one of opponent's non-wall creatures to attack. If target creature cannot attack, it is killed at end of turn. This ability can only be used during opponent's turn, before the attack. May not be used on creatures summoned this turn.

Differences: The *Unlimited* and *Limited* (Alpha) versions have change A; "destroyed" instead of "killed"; and "This tap should be played" instead of "This ability can only be used."

Rulings Differences: Previous versions have errata: Nettling Imp's last sentence should read "May not target a creature brought under opponent's control this turn."

⚔Plateau

Revised Text: ⟨⟩: Add either 🔴 or ⚪ to your mana pool. Counts as both mountains and plains and is affected by spells that affect either. If a spell destroys one of these land types, this card is destroyed; if a spell alters one of these land types, the other land type is unaffected.

Differences: The *Unlimited* and *Limited* (Alpha) versions have different wording: "Counts as both mountains and plains and is affected by spells that affect either. Tap to add either 🔴 or ⚪ to your mana pool." The *Unlimited* and *Limited* versions have a different piece of art by Drew Tucker. The *Revised* version credits the artist as Drew Tucker instead of Cornelius Brudi.

Rulings Differences: If one of the land types of Plateau is changed, the other type is not. *Previous versions of Plateau did not make this distinction.*

Reconstruction

Revised Text: Bring one artifact from your graveyard to your hand.

Differences: The *Antiquities* version was missing the expansion symbol.

Regrowth

Revised Text: Bring any card from your graveyard to your hand.

Differences: The *Unlimited* and *Limited* versions say "Return" instead of "Bring."

Resurrection

Revised Text: Take a creature from your graveyard and put it directly into play. Treat this creature as though it were just summoned.

Differences: The *Unlimited* and *Limited* versions replace the second sentence with "You can't tap it until your next turn."

Reverse Polarity

Revised Text: All damage done to you by artifacts so far this turn is retroactively added to your life total instead of subtracted. Further damage this turn is treated normally.

Differences: The *Antiquities* version says "so far this turn by artifacts" instead of "by artifacts so far this turn."

Rock Hydra

Revised Text: Put X +1/+1 counters (heads) on Hydra. Each point of damage Hydra suffers kills one head unless controller spends 🔴 per head. During controller's upkeep, new heads may be grown for 🔴🔴🔴 apiece.

Differences: The *Unlimited* version says "🔴 is spent" instead of "controller spends 🔴 per head" and does not say "controller's." The *Limited* (Alpha) version also has "R" in place of each "🔴".

Rocket Launcher

Revised Text: ②: Do 1 damage to any target. Rocket Launcher may not be used until it begins a turn in play on your side. If it is used, Rocket Launcher is destroyed at end of turn.

Differences: The *Antiquities* version has change P.

⚔Sacrifice

Revised Text: Sacrifice one of your creatures to add to your mana pool a number of black mana equal to that creature's casting cost.

Differences: The *Unlimited* and *Limited* versions have different wording: "Destroy one of your creatures without regenerating it, and add to your mana pool a number of black mana equal to creature's casting cost."

Rulings Differences: As soon as Sacrifice is played, the creature to be sacrificed is placed in the graveyard. *In previous versions, the creature was not sent to the graveyard until Sacrifice resolved.*

⚔Savannah

Revised Text: ⟨⟩: Add either ⚪ or 🟢 to your mana pool. Counts as both plains and forest and is affected by spells that affect either. If a spell destroys one of these land types, the card is destroyed; if a spell alters one of these land types, the other land type is unaffected.

Differences: The *Unlimited* and *Limited* versions have different wording: "Counts as both plains and forest and is affected by spells that affect either. Tap to add either ⚪ or 🟢 to your mana pool."

Rulings Differences: If one of the land types of Savannah is changed, the other type is not. *Previous versions of Savannah did not make this distinction.*

↗Scrubland

Revised Text: ⚒: Add either ✳ or ☠ to your mana pool. Counts as both plains and swamp and is affected by spells that affect either. If a spell destroys one of these land types, the card is destroyed; if a spell alters one of these land types, the other land type is unaffected.

Differences: The *Unlimited* and *Limited* versions have different wording: "Counts as both plains and swamp and is affected by spells that affect either. Tap to add either ✳ or ☠ to your mana pool."

Rulings Differences: If one of the land types of Scrubland is changed, the other type is not. *Previous versions of Scrubland did not make this distinction.*

Sedge Troll

Revised Text: ☠: Regenerates. / While controller has swamps in play, Sedge Troll gains +1/+1.

Differences: The *Unlimited* and *Limited* versions have different wording: "☠: Regenerates. Troll gains +1/+1 if controller has swamps in play." The *Limited* (Alpha) version has these sentences reversed.

Serendib Efreet

Revised Text: Flying / Serendib Efreet does 1 damage to you during your upkeep.

Differences: The *Arabian Nights* version has the same text. The *Revised* version is a misprint: its border is green, it has the art for Ifh-Biff Efreet instead, and it credits the artist as Jesper Myrfors, who did the art for Ifh-Biff Efreet.

Shatterstorm

Revised Text: All artifacts in play are buried.

Differences: The *Antiquities* version has different wording: "All artifacts in play are discarded. Artifact creatures cannot be regenerated."

Sol Ring

Revised Text: ⚒: Add 2 colorless mana to your mana pool. This ability is played as an interrupt.

Differences: The *Unlimited* and *Limited* versions have change M and replace the second sentence with "Tapping this artifact can be played as an interrupt."

↗Taiga

Revised Text: ⚒: Add either ♣ or ⚄ to your mana pool. Counts as both forest and mountains and is affected by spells that affect either. If a spell destroys one of these land types, the card is destroyed; if a spell alters one of these land types, the other land type is unaffected.

Differences: The *Unlimited* and *Limited* versions have different wording: "Counts as both forest and mountains and is affected by spells that affect either. Tap to add either ♣ or ⚄ to your mana pool."

Rulings Differences: If one of the land types of Taiga is changed, the other is not. *Previous versions of Taiga did not make this distinction.*

Timetwister

Unlimited Text: Set Timetwister aside in a new graveyard pile. Shuffle your hand, library, and graveyard together into a new library and draw a new hand of seven cards, leaving all cards in play where they are; opponent must do the same.

↗Tropical Island

Revised Text: ⚒: Add either ♣ or 💧 to your mana pool. Counts as both forest and islands and is affected by spells that affect either. If a spell destroys one of these land types, the card is destroyed; if a spell alters one of these land types, the other land type is unaffected.

Differences: The *Unlimited* and *Limited* versions have different wording: "Counts as both forest and islands and is affected by spells that affect either. Tap to add either ♣ or 💧 to your mana pool."

Rulings Differences: If one of the land types of Tropical Island is changed, the other is not. *Previous versions of Tropical Island did not make this distinction.*

↗Tundra

Revised Text: ⚒: Add either 💧 or ✳ to your mana pool. Counts as both islands and plains and is affected by spells that affect either. If a spell destroys one of these land types, the card is destroyed; if a spell alters one of these land types, the other land type is unaffected.

Differences: The *Unlimited* and *Limited* versions have different wording: "Counts as both islands and plains and is affected by spells that affect either. Tap to add either ◉ or ❋ to your mana pool."

Rulings Differences: If one of the land types of Tundra is changed, the other is not. *Previous versions of Tundra did not make this distinction.*

➹ Vesuvan Doppelganger

***Revised* Text:** Upon summoning, Doppelganger acquires all characteristics except color of any one creature in play on either side; any creature enchantments on the original creature are not copied. During controller's upkeep, Doppelganger may take on the characteristics of a different creature in play instead. Doppelganger may continue to copy a creature even after that creature leaves play, but if it switches it won't be able to switch back.

Differences: The *Unlimited* and *Limited* versions have parentheses around "except color."

Rulings Differences: Previous versions have errata: "During upkeep" should be read as "during your upkeep." *Previous versions permitted the Vesuvan Doppelganger to switch form during each upkeep.*

➹ Veteran Bodyguard

***Revised* Text:** Unless Bodyguard is tapped, any damage done to you by unblocked crea-

tures is done instead to Bodyguard. You may not take this damage yourself, though you can prevent it if possible. No more than one Bodyguard of your choice can take damage for you in this manner each turn.

Differences: The *Unlimited* and *Limited* versions have change S and are missing the last sentence.

Rulings Differences: Only one of your Bodyguards can now take damage for you each turn. *Previous versions forced each Veteran Bodyguard to take the full brunt of any appropriate damage dealt to their controller.*

➹ Volcanic Island

***Revised* Text:** ➷: Add either ◉ or ⬢ to your mana pool. Counts as both islands and mountains and is affected by spells that affect either. If a spell destroys one of these land types, the card is destroyed; if a spell alters one of these land types, the other land type is unaffected.

Differences: The *Unlimited* and *Limited* versions have different wording: "Counts as both islands and mountains and is affected by spells that affect either. Tap to add either ◉ or ⬢ to your mana pool."

Rulings Differences: If one of the land types of Volcanic Island is changed, the other type is not. *Previous versions of Volcanic Island did not make this distinction.*

Arabian Nights

Army of Allah
***Arabian Nights* Text:** All attacking creatures gain +2/+0 until end of turn.
Differences: The *Arabian Nights* version had two versions of the card with size and shading variations in the uncolored mana symbol.

➹ Cyclone
***Arabian Nights* Text:** Put one chip on Cyclone each round during your upkeep, then pay ⬢ for each chip or discard Cyclone. If not discarded, Cyclone immediately does 1 damage per chip to each player and each creature in play.

Rulings Differences: *Arabian Nights* has errata: The word "discard" in Cyclone's text should be read as "destroy."

➹ Desert
***Arabian Nights* Text:** Tap to add 1 colorless mana to your mana pool *or* do 1 damage to an attacking creature after it deals its damage.
Rulings Differences: *Arabian Nights* has errata: Desert should read "...at end of combat, deal 1 damage to target attacking creature."

Fishliver Oil
Arabian Nights Text: Target creature gains islandwalk ability.
Differences: The *Arabian Nights* version had two versions of the card with size and shading variations in the uncolored mana symbol.

Hasran Ogress
Arabian Nights Text: Unless you pay ② each time Hasran Ogress attacks, Hasran Ogress does 3 damage to you.
Differences: The *Arabian Nights* version had two versions of the card with size and shading variations in the uncolored mana symbol and the mana symbol.

Moorish Cavalry
Arabian Nights Text: Trample
Differences: The *Arabian Nights* version had two versions of the card with size and shading variation in the uncolored mana symbol.

Oubliette
Arabian Nights Text: Select a creature in play when Oubliette is cast. That creature is considered out of play as long as Oubliette is in play. Hence the creature cannot be the target of spells and cannot receive damage, use special powers, attack, or defend. All counters and enchantments on the creature remain but are also out of play. If Oubliette is removed, creature returns to play tapped.
Differences: The *Arabian Nights* version had two versions of the card with size and shading variation in the uncolored mana symbol.

Rukh Egg
Arabian Nights Text: If Rukh Egg goes to the graveyard, a Rukh—a 4/4 red flying creature—comes into play on your side at the end of that turn. Use a counter to represent Rukh. Rukh is treated exactly like a normal creature except that if it leaves play it is removed from the game entirely.
Rulings Differences: *Arabian Nights* has errata: Rukh Egg should be read as "goes to the graveyard from play." (So a Rukh Egg can only become a Rukh if it goes to the graveyard from play.) *In the* Arabian Nights *version, a Rukh was brought into play any time the Egg went to the graveyard, including as a result of discarding the Egg.*

Stone-Throwing Devils
Arabian Nights Text: First strike
Differences: The *Arabian Nights* version had two versions of the card with size and shading variations in the uncolored mana symbols.

War Elephant
Arabian Nights Text: Trample, bands
Differences: The *Arabian Nights* version had two versions of the card with size and shading variations in the uncolored mana symbols.

Wyluli Wolf
Arabian Nights Text: Tap to give any creature in play +1/+1 until end of turn.
Differences: The *Arabian Nights* version had two versions of the card with size and shading variation in the uncolored mana symbol.

Antiquities

Argivian Blacksmith
Antiquities Text: Tap to prevent up to 2 damage to target artifact creature.
Rulings Differences: *Antiquities* has errata: Argivian Blacksmith should not target the artifact creature.

Ashnod's Transmogrant
Antiquities Text: Target non-artifact creature gains +1/+1 and is now considered an artifact creature, though it retains its original color.

Discard Ashnod's Transmogrant after it is used.
Rulings Differences: *Antiquities* has errata: The +1/+1 and artifact status should be represented by a counter.

Citanul Druid
Antiquities Text: Druid gains a +1/+1 counter each time opponent casts an artifact.
Rulings Differences: *Antiquities* has errata: Citanul Druid should read "target opponent"

Antiquities

not "opponent"; thus, in a two-player game, taking control of Citanul Druid would not change its counters or how it acquires them.

Goblin Artisans

Antiquities Text: You may tap Goblin Artisans as you cast an artifact. Then flip a coin; opponent calls heads or tails while coin is in the air. If the flip ends up in opponent's favor, your artifact is countered. Otherwise, draw another card from your library. You can only use this ability once for each time you cast an artifact.
Rulings Differences: *Antiquities* has errata: Goblin Artisans should additionally read "Play this ability as an interrupt."

Orcish Mechanics

Antiquities Text: Tap to do 2 points of damage to any target. Each time you use this ability, you must choose one of your artifacts in play and place it in the graveyard. This artifact cannot be one already on its way to the graveyard, and artifact creatures killed this way may not be regenerated.
Rulings Differences: *Antiquities* has errata: Orcish Mechanics should read "sacrifice an artifact." instead of "you must choose...may not be regenerated."

Priest of Yawgmoth

Antiquities Text: Tap to add an amount of black mana equal to target artifact's casting cost to your mana pool. This effect is played as an interrupt. Target artifact, which must belong to you, is discarded. This artifact cannot be one that is already on its way to the graveyard, and artifact creatures killed this way may not be regenerated.
Rulings Differences: *Antiquities* has errata: Priest of Yawgmoth should be read as sacrificing the artifact chosen. *The* Antiquities *version did not put the artifact into the graveyard until the effect resolved, and methods other than regeneration could be used to save it.*

Rakalite

Antiquities Text: ② : Prevent 1 damage to any target. If Rakalite is used, it returns to its owner's hand at end of turn; all enchantments on Rakalite are then discarded.
Rulings Differences: *Antiquities* has errata: "Any target" should be read as "any creature or player." *The* Antiquities *version stated that Rakalite targeted the creature or player receiving damage, not the damage being dealt.*

Sage of Lat-Nam

Antiquities Text: Tap to draw a card from your library. Each time you use this ability, you must choose one of your artifacts in play and place it in the graveyard. This artifact cannot be one that is already on its way to the graveyard, and artifact creatures killed this way may not be regenerated.
Rulings Differences: *Antiquities* has errata: Sage of Lat-Nam should be read as sacrificing the artifact chosen. *The* Antiquities *version did not put the artifact into the graveyard until the effect resolved, and methods other than regeneration could be used to save it.*

Su-Chi

Antiquities Text: If Su-Chi goes to the graveyard, its controller gains 4 colorless mana.
Rulings Differences: *Antiquities* has errata: Su-Chi should be read as "goes to the graveyard from play." *The* Antiquities *version allowed a player to gain mana any time Su-Chi went to the graveyard, including as a result of discarding Su-Chi.*

Transmute Artifact

Antiquities Text: Search through your library for one artifact and immediately place it into play; also, choose any artifact in play that you control and place it in its owner's graveyard. If the new artifact has a casting cost greater than that of the discarded one, you must pay the difference or Transmute Artifact fails and both artifacts are discarded. Shuffle your library after playing this card.

Rulings Differences: *Antiquities* has errata: Transmute Artifact should be read as sacrificing the artifact in play. *The* Antiquities *version did not put the chosen artifact into the graveyard until the spell resolved.*

➤Urza's Miter

Antiquities Text: ③ : Draw one card from your library every time an artifact of yours goes to the graveyard. Can only let you draw one card per artifact destruction. May not be used when you destroy an artifact to gain benefits from another card.

Rulings Differences: *Antiquities* has errata: The last sentence should be interpreted as "May not be used when an artifact was placed in the graveyard due to being sacrificed."

Legends

Active Volcano

Legends Text: Destroy target blue permanent or return target island to owner's hand. Enchantments on target land are destroyed.

Differences: The *Legends* version credits the artist as Brian Snōddy instead of Justin Hampton.

➤Akron Legionnaire

Legends Text: None of your non-artifact creatures may attack except Akron Legionnaire.

Rulings Differences: *Legends* has errata: Akron Legionnaire should read "...except Akron Legionnaires" not "...except Akron Legionnaire."

➤All Hallow's Eve

Legends Text: Put two counters on this card. Remove a counter during your upkeep. When you remove the last counter from All Hallow's Eve, all players take all creatures from their graveyards and put them directly into play. Treat these creatures as though they were just summoned. You choose what order they come into play.

Rulings Differences: *Legends* has errata: All Hallow's Eve should read "Enchantment" not "Sorcery."

➤Yawgmoth Demon

Antiquities Text: Flying, first strike During your upkeep, choose one of your artifacts in play and place it in the graveyard, or Yawgmoth Demon becomes tapped and deals 2 points of damage to you. Artifact creatures destroyed this way may not be regenerated.

Rulings Differences: *Antiquities* has errata: Yawgmoth Demon should be read as "sacrifice an artifact or Yawgmoth Demon...to you" instead of "choose one of your arti- facts...not be regenerated." *The* Antiquities *version did not put the chosen artifact into the graveyard until the upkeep effect resolved, and means other than regeneration could be used to save an artifact creature.*

➤Cocoon

Legends Text: Tap target creature you con- trol and put three counters on it. Target crea- ture does not untap as normal while it has one or more of these counters on it. Remove one counter during your upkeep. During the upkeep phase after the one in which the last counter was removed, Cocoon is destroyed and target creature gains a +1/+1 counter and flying ability.

Rulings Differences: *Legends* has errata: Cocoon should read "Put three counters on Cocoon" not "Put three counters on it."

Disharmony

Legends Text: Target attacking creature comes under your control untapped. Return to current controller at end of turn. This crea- ture is no longer considered to have attacked. Play before defense is chosen.

Differences: The *Legends* version credits the artist as Phil Foglio instead of Bryon Wackwitz.

➤Firestorm Phoenix

Legends Text: Flying / If Phoenix is placed in the graveyard from play, return it to owner's hand instead. It may not be summoned again until owner's next turn.

Rulings Differences: *Legends* has errata: Firestorm Phoenix should not read "instead"; ignore the word "instead."

Knowledge Vault

Legends Text: 2 ⟋: Take a card from your library without looking at it and place it face down under Knowledge Vault. Sacrifice Knowledge Vault to discard entire hand and take the cards under the vault into your hand. If Knowledge Vault leaves play, put all cards under it in your graveyard.

Rulings Differences: *Legends* has errata: Knowledge Vault should read "leaves play or you lose control of Knowledge Vault" instead of "leaves play."

Recall

Legends Text: Sacrifice X cards from your hand and then bring X cards from your graveyard to your hand. Then remove Recall from the game.

Rulings Differences: *Legends* has errata: Recall should be read as "discard," instead of "sacrifice." (So, the cards are not lost until the effect resolves, though they are chosen when Recall is played.) *The* Legends *version sacrificed the cards as soon as Recall was played.*

Spectral Cloak

Legends Text: Target creature cannot be the target of instants, sorceries, fast effects, or enchantments unless creature is tapped.

Rulings Differences: *Legends* has errata: Spectral Cloak should addtionally read "Spectral Cloak does not cause any enchantments on target creature to be destroyed." *The* Legends *version would cause Spectral Cloak to destroy itself since it made the creature an invalid target for the Spectral Cloak.*

Spiritual Sanctuary

Legends Text: Any player with plains under his or her control gains 1 life point during upkeep.

Rulings Differences: *Legends* has errata: "During upkeep" should read "during his or her upkeep." *The* Legends *version allowed a player to gain life during each upkeep.*

Venarian Gold

Legends Text: Put X counters on target creature. Target creature becomes tapped when Venarian Gold is cast. Creature does not untap as normal if it has any of these counters on it. Remove one counter during creature's controller's upkeep phase.

Rulings Differences: *Legends* has errata: Venarian Gold should be read "Put X counters on Venarian Gold." (So, the counters will move with the enchantment if the enchantment is moved by other spells or effects like Enchantment Alteration.) *The* Legends *version stated that counters were placed on the creature instead of on Venarian Gold.*

Voodoo Doll

Legends Text: Put one counter on Voodoo Doll during your upkeep. If Voodoo Doll is not tapped at end of your turn, it does X damage to you and is destroyed. X equals the number of counters on Voodoo Doll. X X ⟋: Voodoo Doll does X damage to any one target.

Rulings Differences: *Legends* has errata: Voodoo Doll should read "Voodoo Doll gets a counter at start of upkeep." *The* Legends *version of the Voodoo Doll could be used every turn before it got a counter, preventing it from ever getting any bigger.*

The Dark

Eater of the Dead

The Dark Text: 0 : Take one creature from any graveyard and remove it from the game. Untap Eater of the Dead.

Rulings Differences: *The Dark* has errata: Eater of the Dead should read " 0 : Untap Eater of the Dead to remove target creature in the graveyard from the game."

Merfolk Assasin

The Dark Text: ⟋: Destroy target creature that has islandwalk.

Differences: *The Dark* version had change D.

Scavenger Folk
***The Dark* Text:** ♣, ↗: Sacrifice Scavenger Folk to destroy target artifact.
Differences: *The Dark* version has change D.

Squire
Differences: *The Dark* version has change D.

Tivadar's Crusade
***The Dark* Text:** All Goblins are destroyed.
Differences: *The Dark* version has change D.

Fallen Empires

Raiding Party
***Fallen Empires* Text:** Raiding Party may not be the target of white spells or effects.
O: Sacrifice an Orc to destroy all plains. A player may tap a white creature to prevent up to two plains from being destroyed. Any number of creatures may be tapped in this manner.
Rulings Differences: *Fallen Empires* has errata: Raiding Party should be read as "tap target untapped white creature he or she controls" instead of "Tap a white creature." *The* Fallen Empires *version allows a player to tap any one player's white creatures to prevent plains from being destroyed.*

Tourach's Gate
***Fallen Empires* Text:** Can only be played on a target land you control. Sacrifice a Thrull to put three time counters on Tourach's Gate. During your upkeep, remove a time counter from Tourach's Gate. If there are no time counters on Tourach's Gate, bury it. / O: Tap land Tourach's Gate enchants. All attacking creatures you control get +2/-1 until end of turn.
Rulings Differences: *Fallen Empires* has errata: Tourach's Gate's activated effect should be read as " O: Tap land Tourach's Gate enchants to give all attacking creatures you control +2/-1 until end of turn." (So, the effect may only be used once per turn unless you can untap the enchanted land.) *The* Fallen Empires *version was written assuming old rules. The land could be tapped by the effect as many times as desired in a turn.*

game support

Rich Redman and Eric Doohan

So you have a question for Wizards of the Coast? Or maybe a hundred questions? Fear not—there are many ways to contact us. The most common means of reaching us is to call, write, or fax one of three offices:

If you live in the United States, Canada, Australia, or New Zealand, please contact our main office:

Wizards of the Coast
P.O. Box 707
Renton, WA, U.S. 98057-0707

Our Customer Service Phone Line for our players is (206) 624-0933, and this line is open from 8:00 a.m. to 6:00 p.m., Pacific Time, Monday through Friday. If you are a retailer in the United States, we now have a Merchant Customer Service team dedicated to helping our retailers. You can contact this service at (800) 821-8028 during our normal business hours, or via fax at (206) 226-3182.

If you live in the United Kingdom, please contact:
Wizards of the Coast UK Ltd.
Customer Service
P.O. Box No. 1562
Glasgow
G2 8BW
Scotland
Tel: 0345-125599 (within the United Kingdom only)
+44 141 226 5205 (from Ireland)
Internet: uk@wizards.com

In Germany, please contact:

Amigo Spiel + Freizeit GmbH
Messenhäuser Straße 65
63322 Rödermark
Tel: +49 (0) 60 74/ 61 313
Compuserve: 100635,3631 Hirsch,Magicinfo

In Italy, please contact:

Stratelibri
Via Paisiello 4
20131 Milano
Tel: +39-2-295-103-17
Fax: +39-2-295-105-78
Internet: thx1138@io.com or thx1138@galactica.it

In Spain, please contact:

Ediciones Marínez Roca, S.A.
Enric Granados, 84, bajos.
08008 Barcelona

In Brazil, please contact:

Devir Livraria Ltda.
Rua Augusto de Toledo, 83
Cambuci São Paulo

In Belgium and the rest of continental Europe, please contact:

Wizards of the Coast, Belgium
Customer Service Department
P.O. Box 16
2140 Borgerhout 2
Belgium
Tel: +32 (03)-272-0511
Internet: custserv@wizards.be

If you're wired to the Internet, there are numerous ways to reach us. The Customer Service Team can be reached for rules questions in the United States at questions@wizards.com, in the United Kingdom at uk@wizards.com, and in other European countries at custserv@wizards.be. We're here to answer your questions about:

- specific "official" rulings for Wizards of the Coast games (please keep in mind that our rulings are meant to keep the games similar all over the world and to provide official tournament rulings. You are not obliged to actually *play* the way we rule. Feel free to develop your own variations)

- release dates for Wizards of the Coast products

- requests for information on all kinds of Wizards of the Coast-related subjects
- Frequently Asked Questions (FAQs) (if at all possible, we will respond to questions with a document called an FAQ, which contains answers to these frequently asked questions about card sets)

We receive from 60 to 120 messages a day at `questions@wizards.com`; if our replies seem brief, this is only because we are trying to handle messages in the most efficient and timely manner possible. Feel free to respond with a more specific question and include the original correspondence in your message. If you have damaged product or other comments or concerns about our products, you can direct these over the Internet to `custserv@wizards.com`.

Please keep in mind that no one person can possibly know everything—some messages have to be forwarded to the experts. If you have questions related to sales, marketing, or legal issues, it's actually faster to call one of our offices during local normal business hours and contact the department in question.

We also have NetReps on America OnLine, CompuServe, Prodigy, and the Imagination Network. On America OnLine, contact WotC for all the places where **Deckmaster** games are discussed. Collectible card games have become quite popular on CompuServe; check out the CARDGAMES forum (Section 15: Magic Talk, Section 16: Magic Games, Section 17: Other Cards Talk, Section 18: Other Card Games, and Section 19: Game Card Trading) and the CARDS forum (Section 4: Game Cards, Section 18: Game Card News, and Section 19: Game Card Auctions). On Prodigy, you can contact gfvh50a for all the places where **Deckmaster** games are discussed. On the Imagination Network, NetReps also monitor most of our mailing lists (see below).

The best source for answers to **Deckmaster** questions are the "gg" mailing lists. To find out what lists are available, send a message to `listserv@wizards.com`, with no title and a body of only "list." To subscribe, send an electronic mail message to `listserv@oracle.wizards.com`. The body of the message should contain the following line:

```
subscribe <The name of the list> <Your real name>
```

For example, "subscribe gg-trading-1 Bob Johnson". To unsubscribe, send an electronic mail message to `listserv@wizards.com` with a body containing

```
unsubscribe <The name of the list> <Your real name>
```

Note that sending the subscription request (or unsubscription request) to questions@wizards.com or custserv@wizards.com won't accomplish what you're hoping it will; the above procedures will get you to the answers you're looking for.

Electronic Mailing Lists

General discussion of Magic products
mtg-l@oracle.wizards.com

Advanced strategy for **Magic**
mtg-strategy-l@oracle.wizards.com

List of auctions for **Magic** cards
mtg-auction-l@oracle.wizards.com

Trading and collecting **Deckmaster** cards
mtg-trading-l@oracle.wizards.com

List of trade auctions
mtg-trade-auc-l@oracle.wizards.com

Wizards of the Coast announcement list
wizinfo-l@oracle.wizards.com

To subscribe to any of these lists, send an email request to listserv@oracle.wizards.com.

FTP

For even more information, you can get a lot of interesting files from our archive site at ftp.itis.com by using anonymous FTP to retrieve files from that site's /pub/deckmaster directory. World Wide Web (WWW) access is available from http://www.wizards.com. Please remember that these sites are archives, and some of the files there are merely of historical interest. Check with custserv@wizards.com or questions@wizards.com to make sure that the file you access is still accurate. At the time this book was written, we were in the process of building a World Wide Web homepage at wizards.com, so please ask custserv@wizards.com about it, or look for it at the above address!

Other Fun E-mail Addresses at WotC

dci@wizards.com   The Duelists' Convocation

You can still get sanctioning policies and tournament rules from questions@wizards.com, but other questions should go here.

duelist@wizards.com   *The Duelist* magazine

Contact point for magazine subscriptions.

lawman@wizards.com   our attorney

Contact if you have legal questions about using Wizards of the Coast intellectual property. He's a nice guy. Really.

One Final Note

Please do not send in product ideas electronically. If you wish to submit a product idea, ask questions@wizards.com for a submissions packet to be mailed to you. Our research and development team has asked us not to accept any card ideas (individual cards, expansions, or entire games) for the time being. Feel free to ask if that has changed, but we will make an announcement when it does.

Acquiring Original Artwork

If you would like to purchase original artwork (or prints of original artwork) used in the **Magic: The Gathering** game (or any other game produced by Wizards of the Coast, Inc.), you may request an Original Artwork Availability List and Artist Contact Sheet from us. Simply send us a self-addressed stamped envelope and write on the outside of the envelope "Attn: Artwork Listing." Please don't include any rules questions or any other requests so that we may return the information to you as quickly as possible.

Wizards of the Coast provides this information as a service to both its customers and the artists it employs. The listing is merely an offer by the artist or the artist's representative to negotiate. Wizards of the Coast makes no guarantees as to availability, pricing, or current accuracy of any information contained within.

Please be aware that as of this printing, the prices of original artwork range between $90 to $2,000, with an average price around $550. Prints range between $5 to $80 with an average price around $25.

The Duelist Magazine

The Duelist is Wizards of the Coast's official **Deckmaster** magazine. This full-color bimonthly publication offers you the lastest information on **Magic: The Gathering** and other **Deckmaster** games. In *The Duelist,* you'll find the latest rules clarifications, game variants, and deck-building strategies, as well as official card lists, collecting information, and tournament news. Learn about the future of trading card games from **Magic**'s creator Richard Garfield, or pit your wits against challenging **Magic** puzzles by Mark Rosewater. The magazine also offers an inside look at the evolution of trading card games with previews of the latest releases and interviews with your favorite **Deckmaster** designers and artists. Whether you are a beginning player or a **Magic** veteran, *The Duelist* will you help keep you on top of the game.

To subscribe to *The Duelist,* complete the subscription form at the back of this book.

index

The following is a subject-matter index to the *Pocket Players' Guide*. For information on a specific card, see page F-5.

UVWY

We'd love to hear your opinions.

❒ I would love to receive product information.
❒ Please include me in future WotC phone & postal surveys.

Wizards OF THE COAST

❒ Ms.
❒ Mr. _____
   First Name   Last Name

Address: _____ Number _____ Street _____ Apt. #

_____ City _____ State/Province _____ ZIP/Postal Code _____ Country

(___) _____ Date: _____
Area Code   Telephone #   Month / Year

Internet Address

AGE:
❒ under 13
❒ 13–17
❒ 18–24
❒ 25–34
❒ 35–44
❒ 45–54
❒ over 55

I've purchased these WotC products:

❒ **Magic: The Gathering**™ cards
❒ **Vampire: The Eternal Struggle**™ or **Jyhad**™ cards
❒ *The Duelist*™ magazine
❒ **RoboRally**™ board game
❒ **The Great Dalmuti**™ card game
❒ **Ars Magica**™, **Everway**™, **SLA Industries**™, or **The Primal Order**™ roleplaying books
❒ **Deckmaster**™ fiction books (*Arena, Whispering Woods,* etc.)
❒ T-shirts, posters, calendars, etc.

How long have you been playing **Magic***?*

_____ / _____
  Months   **Years**

How many members of your family play **Magic***?*

_____

The activities I enjoy most (top 5):

❒ collecting cards
❒ playing board games
❒ playing cards
❒ playing computer games
❒ playing roleplaying games
❒ playing TV/video games
❒ playing wargames
❒ playing **Magic**
❒ playing **Vampire:TheEternal Struggle**™
❒ reading fiction
❒ reading non-fiction
❒ other: _____

I first played **Magic** *at:*

❒ my local game retailer
❒ my home or a friends home
❒ a club / activity center
❒ a convention
❒ my school (or) ❒ my work place

Concerning the *Fourth Edition Pocket Players Guide*™ Gift Box:

I liked _____

I disliked _____

PPG-

Please Retain this card for your information.

ou have questions or comments, please contact **Wizards of the Coast**® by:

il: Attn: Customer Services; P.O. Box 707; Renton, WA 98057-0707

ne: (206) 624-0933   Rules Questions
ernet: **fppg@wizards.com**   Comments on Forth Edition PPG
         questions@wizards.com   Rules Questions
         custserv@wizards.com   Customer Service Questions

to the address shown below.

Thank you for your time.
Your responses will be used to improve our future products.

Please address your reply to:

Attn.: Customer Services
Wizards of the Coast
P.O. Box 707
Renton, WA 98057-0707

Duelists' Convocation

WOTC's Official Deckmaster Games Organization
P.O. Box 707 Renton WA 98057-0707

Membership Application

First Name: _____ Last Name: _____

Birthdate: _____

Address: _____

City: _____ State: _____ Zip Code: _____

Country: _____

Home Phone: _____

Work Phone: _____

Email: _____

_____

Your Signature

_____

Parent/Guardian Signature
(If applicant is under 18 years of age)

Annual $18.00 Membership Fee (U.S. Funds)

Make check or money order payable to Wizards of the Coast
Please allow 3-4 weeks for handling
The Duelists' Convocation reserves the right to change membership fees without prior notice

WIZARDS OF THE COAST, INC.

P.O. Box 707, Renton, WA 98057-0707
tel: 206-226-6500 *fax:* 206-226-9683

SEATTLE, USA   ANTWERP, BELGIUM   GLASGOW, SCOTLAN